To Defy the Monster

To Defy the Monster

Albert Arthur Allison

iUniverse, Inc.
New York Lincoln Shanghai

To Defy the Monster

iUniverse books may be ordered through booksellers or by contacting:

iUniverse
2021 Pine Lake Road, Suite 100
Lincoln, NE 68512
www.iuniverse.com
1-800-Authors (1-800-288-4677)

ISBN-13: 978-0-595-33298-4 (pbk)
ISBN-13: 978-0-595-78192-8 (cloth)
ISBN-13: 978-0-595-78089-1 (ebk)
ISBN-10: 0-595-33298-6 (pbk)
ISBN-10: 0-595-78192-6 (cloth)
ISBN-10: 0-595-78089-X (ebk)

Printed in the United States of America

To the late Jim Nunnelley,
Who introduced me to Sandy,
Who made this book possible

Contents

Foreword

"You know I was in the car the night that black man shot your Uncle Albert."

We did not know. My brother Wick and I had been aware that we had had an uncle who had died young, probably under mysterious circumstances, but we never knew the details. So when our late father's first cousin, Robert Cobb, casually dropped this bombshell in the midst of a family reunion cocktail conversation, we were taken aback.

That evening, under Wick's persistent grilling, cousin Robert gave us a few details. The incident had occurred in 1932 in Austin, Texas. Robert assumed that the killer had either been lynched or sent to the electric chair. He was unable to explain why our father, Lod Allison, had never discussed the matter.

A few years later, my wife and I moved to Austin, and, out of curiosity, I looked into the incident. After researching old newspapers and copies of court records, I began to form a mental narrative of this tragedy and its aftermath. At first, I thought I owed my grandchildren an account of their family legacy within the larger racial history that envelops all Southerners. As I delved into the story to try to tell it, I realized that it entailed meaning and consequences beyond a curious family.

That is why I tell this story in the Celtic fashion. I tell about real Texans involved in a real murder with a real trial and real consequences. For the sake of coherence and meaning, I use fiction to replace facts that have evaporated with the lapse of more than seven decades.

I tell the story in the Celtic fashion, with this exception: I do not want to judge Depression-era East Austin African-Americans and West Austin whites. Technology and three-quarters of a century of astonishing social change have taken me too far from their distinct languages, their unique senses of self and community.

I hope that my rendering of this story, as a substitute, adequately presents the kaleidoscope of issues for those competent to judge. If those judges can use what I present to praise, blame, or condemn, the story has done its job. In fact, if they do so, the story will cease to be mine, for they will indelibly imprint it, and, henceforward, the story will be theirs to tell.

To construct this story, I have employed every resource available, from newspaper accounts and court records to interviews with anyone I could find who was connected. I have not altered one established fact. The quotations from the Austin newspapers, the confession, and the trial accounts are directly from the record. Because the archives of the *Corsicana Sun* were destroyed in a fire, the editorial from that newspaper is my contrivance. The newspaper account of the Austin mob scene is also my fabrication. To develop the story coherently, I have taken the liberty of creating dialogue throughout; I have introduced minor fictional characters (Tucker and Ellie Childs) to make a point; and I have created biographies for those historical figures (Raymond Brooks, for instance) who fill archetypical roles.

Regrettably, by the time I got interested in the story, all the participants and adult witnesses were dead, and someone in the Allison family had destroyed all related documents. Except for Albert Allison Jr.'s high school yearbooks; a few references in my grandmother's private notebook, *Worms*; and scraps out of the childhood memories of Kenneth Allison and Elizabeth Kerr, we have nothing.

Just after his brother was killed, Kenneth remembers that his father said, "I have to get down to Austin to stop a lynching." The dead boy's older first cousin, Elizabeth, recalls a few incidents when growing up with him. She also remembers my grandfather's remark that politics had influenced the outcome.

The story—at least, as I see it—became a lesson in the nature of justice requisite to enable disparate peoples to live harmoniously in close proximity. As well, the narrative imposes on each of us a unique American responsibility to transcend the confines of our native cultures—as rich as they may be, as proud of them as we may be—to recognize the "others." I do not mean *tolerance*" (such a patronizing word); I mean *recognition.* I mean consciously according the others the subjectivity we accord our own siblings and cousins. I mean comprehending that everyone of a different race, with different speech, and different beliefs is human in the same way we are human; that they are just as "chosen" by God as—tacitly or explicitly—we all believe that we are. Of course, "being human like us" means that, just like us, different humans may be good or evil. In fact, judging good or evil acts against a transcendent, rational standard is the kind of American justice for which this narrative begs.

Prologue

1932 was marked by titanic political and social clashes, the aftershocks of which were felt throughout the remainder of the century. This story reflects many of those clashes, which in Texas boiled down to cotton, the "Negro question," and Prohibition.

Cotton was in a crisis of overproduction brought on by the demand created by World War I. It was caught in a tug-of-war between those who wanted government intervention to alleviate the depressed prices versus those who wanted to let market forces work through the crisis. My grandfather, a cotton landlord and the dead boy's father, was in the thick of this argument. He favored intervention. As a result, he had become a target of powerful interests that felt threatened by potential government involvement.

Fifty years had elapsed since the end of Reconstruction, and Texas still wrestled with its racial dilemma. Bitter memories echoed in the lore of white Texans, who often attributed their poverty to the Yankee and African-American predations of that era. Some of the boy-warriors who had returned to Texas from the disease and gore of the Civil War were still living. They still told their stories, still imparted to future generations their sacred mission of vengeance and redemption. They told how, during long marches and heated battle, starving and diseased, they had clung to memories of boyhood homes afloat in an endless sea of white cotton. They told how their hearts sank when gaunt parents in ragged clothes greeted them on the steps of crumbling shacks in the middle of weedy fields. Then the Yankee occupation came, followed by the state police and the Freedman's Bureau. As the oppression worsened, so did the frequency of nightmares in which ghostly comrades in gray beckoned the boys back to the battlefield. So they rearmed, fought again, and drove the Yankees away. Then they exacted Southern justice.

For the next forty years, these veterans and their descendents reimposed white authority and supremacy on the land and mercilessly punished all who resisted. As evidenced by the following digest of 1932 Austin newspaper accounts, Texas, black and white, succumbed.

The Austin Statesman, April 29, 1932: 99-YEAR PENALTY IS GIVEN NEGRO FOR ATTACK. Ninety-nine years for a Dallas Negro who threatened a white prostitute. She said she went with him because the light-skinned man looked like a "Spaniard."

The Austin Statesman, May 29, 1932: NEGRO WHO SLEW TEXAS FARMER EXECUTED. James Williams, a thirty-year-old Negro, executed in Huntsville's new electric chair for killing a seventy-year-old white farmer.

The Austin Statesman, August 5, 1932: TWO NEGRO KILLERS PAY DEATH DEBT—electrocuted for killing Frank Kempf, a white Lockhart dairyman.

Austin American, July 28, 1932: NEGRO DIES IN TEXAS CHAIR FOR ATTACKING GIRL. Charley Grogan, "burly" Beaumont Negro, died in the electric chair for criminally attacking a white girl. Despite Grogan's denial, the jury took five minutes to decide his fate.

Austin American, July 23, 1932: HOUNDS CATCH NEGRO AFTER THIRTY MILE CHASE. Cleveland Davis was wanted for robbing a Houston man and assaulting his white female companion.

The Austin Statesman, January 7, 1932: GOVERNOR STERLING REFUSES CLEMENCY FOR IRA MCKEE AND A NEGRO DUE TO DIE THE ELECTRIC CHAIR. The Governor said equal justice means that both should pay equally for the crime of murder, even if the Negro's victim was one of his "own kind." "Can we have a law for a white man and another for a negro?" the governor asked.

The Austin Statesman, June 10, 1932: COURT DELAYS EXECUTION OF 7 NEGROES. The Alabama Supreme Court delayed the scheduled execution of seven Negroes for attacking two white girls pending action of the United States Supreme Court. The Negroes had been convicted in a speedy trial after authorities had snatched them from a lynch mob in Scottsboro.

The Austin Statesman, July 16, 1932: ARKANSAS MOB LYNCHES NEGRO. An angry Crockett, Arkansas, crowd took Frank Tucker, twenty-four, from the local jail and hanged him from a pole in the town's business section. He had been accused of inflicting a near-fatal razor cut on a bank guard during a failed robbery attempt.

By 1932, white Texans had settled the "Negro question"—at least to their satisfaction—but Prohibition was another matter. It had produced such a rise in bootleggers and gangsters and had caused such a general undermining of respect for the law that Texas was threatened with dangerous erosion in civility and order, and the sentiment for repeal was strong.

Notwithstanding, Prohibition also afforded a unique opportunity for Depression-era African-Texans. The authorities had shut down west Austin's infamous "Guy's Town." But they cared little what the African-American district called East Austin did behind its black curtain, nor did the curfew that kept East Austin from going west after sundown prevent whites from coming east. For this reason, while so-called progressive Texas leaders fretted about lynching and Jim Crow, enterprising African-Texans went to work.

1932 East Austin was the five-square-mile, segregated home for the thousands of maids and yardmen who daily went by foot and bus to manicure west-side lawns, clean west-side houses, cook west-side meals, and raise west-side children. East Austin had churches—shaking, loud churches that demanded respectful behavior, tithes, and brotherhood. East Austin had schools and colleges, which, despite few books and impoverished teachers, pursued education with fervor. East Austin had undertakers, grocery stores, hair stylists, cafés, service garages, and pawnshops. But East Austin had never had a lawyer, had never had a movie theater, had never had a car dealer, a jeweler, or a department store. It would not have dared. These were west Austin businesses. Most of East Austin's streets were dirt tracks, although a couple of the main roads were paved with baseball-size limestone rocks. East Austin's sewers were insufficient to prevent cholera and typhoid from joining syphilis in providing the undertaker with a steady stream of business. East Austin was just beginning to get electricity, but the streets on a moonless night were still so dark that "haints" continually sprang surprises. And even though East Austin had never had a library or a post office, someday it might, or so the white bosses had promised.

In the early 1920s, East Austin resident Perry Rhambo gave up his job at the Stephen F. Austin Hotel, where for years he had been a porter. He took his considerable savings from pimping and bought the largest house in East Austin. The girls and bootleggers came with him—together with the cowboys, university students, lobbyists, and politicians. Soon East Austin nights teemed with life—vibrant, exotic life. Perry Rhambo had given Prohibition-era East Austin "hootchie-kootchie," and hootchie-kootchie helped feed East Austin in hard times. In Prohibition-era East Austin, business, gambling, religion, moonshine, home life, whoremongering, education, stealing, voodoo, and blues music comfortably merged with one another. Little girls grew up around the corner from houses where ladies wore underwear in public; while, a block away on East Austin's one tree-lined street, Huston and Tillotson professors had afternoon teas, conducted recitals, read poetry, and held seminars. Unlike other Texas "Negro Districts," East Austin's vice managed not to threaten the lives or the sensibilities of decent folk. Here, the families, businesses, churches, and schools imposed a demand for unusual self-control on the hootchie-kootchie culture. And that culture responded by making a special effort to protect the professors, the proper ladies, and the little girls.

Perry Rhambo owned the largest bordello in East Austin, a dozen satellite whorehouses, and East Austin's largest barbershop. His brother, Nathan, owned the funeral parlor, a burial insurance company, and the lottery racket called "policy." To expand his insurance and lottery empire, he needed literate agents, so he employed most of the professionals living in East Austin, including most of the Huston and Tillotson professors. They were all grateful for the additional income. Nathan was also the kingpin of the East Austin vote machine, which he controlled through the churches; and he was Treasurer of the Texas Negro Undertakers Association, which gave him the central Texas marketing outlets for "policy." Both brothers gave generously to the Ebenezer Third Baptist Church, the Rising Star Baptist Church, and to various funds for the less fortunate.

The Rhambos were the overlords of East Austin.

One night in late June 1932, a young African-American lured Nathan Rhambo from his funeral parlor on a ruse. The next morning Rhambo's mutilated body was found in the back of his Buick, parked on a roadside 150 miles from Austin. Three weeks later, at the intersection of Seventh and Chicon Streets in the heart of East Austin, Charles Johnson, a senior Rhambo agent, killed Albert Allison Jr., an unarmed white youth.

Both murders were sensations in Austin. Nathan Rhambo was a sufficiently prominent African-American for the white power structure to pursue with unusual diligence. Some viewed that pursuit as progress.

But the black-on-white killing threatened to return Texas justice to the vigilante days from which it was barely emerging. In hard times, fearful people tend to escape to the comfort of the old ways. In 1932, a depressed, nostalgic central Texas needed only a small spark to ignite an old rage.

Charles Johnson provided that spark.

1

Friday, July 8, 1932

510 N. 25th Street, Corsicana, Texas

Midnight telephone calls usually came from one of the Allison's two oldest daughters, so Mabel crawled out of bed, went downstairs to answer, and then called out to Albert that it was R. C. Granberry.

Granberry was an old friend who worked for the Texas Railroad Commission in Austin and who was active in Governor Sterling's reelection campaign. Because the race was in the final three weeks, Albert was not surprised to receive a late-night request for his time or his money. "I know I'm getting close to sixty when these calls start becoming a nuisance," he thought.

"What's up at this time of night, R. C.?" Albert almost yawned. He passed his left hand through the silver hairs that tried to cover his mostly bald head.

"I have bad news, Albert," R. C. responded in a strangely cracking voice. "Your boy, my boy, Sonny Mayes, and the young Cobb boy got into trouble over in East Austin tonight. Albert Jr. was shot. He never had a chance."

Albert had felt his stomach begin to tighten; his temples started pulsating.

"Wha—What did he say? Son shot? Never had a chance?" Albert caught Mabel's worried look. He felt his face breaking uncontrollably. "Is he—?" the father asked, turning wet eyes toward his wife.

"Albert," said R. C. quietly, "your boy is dead."

Mabel grabbed her husband's hand, her grip steel hard. Her cry was almost a whisper, "What? What?"

Softly, evenly, without hesitation, "Honey, R. C. says Son's been shot and killed."

Mabel collapsed into the wooden, high-backed chair against the wall. Her cry filled the room. Albert knelt and grasped her hand, the phone still in the other hand.

"Where is he, R. C.?"

"At Brackenridge Hospital for now, Albert."

"How are the other boys?" Albert had asked perfunctorily, his mind and emotions swirling.

"Derden Wofford was wounded, but he'll recover. Bob Cobb is here; want to speak to him?"

Albert whispered, "Okay," and wondered, "Who is Derden Wofford?"

"Uncle Albert?" a shaky small voice.

"What happened, Bob?"

The seventeen-year-old managed to say, "A nigger ran us off the road—and then he came back around and started shooting. Some of us could run, but Cousin Albert was behind the wheel and couldn't get out. The nigger drove right up to the car and shot."

The senior Allison flinched at the word *nigger,* but his mind raced past his nephew's uncharacteristic crudeness. 'Negro? Where in the hell…?' he thought.

Still stunned, Albert's mind worked to put events in order. When he had returned from the Democratic Convention in Chicago the previous Sunday, Mabel had told him that Son had taken a week off from his job at Lone Star Gas Company in Dallas. The boy and a friend were going to Galveston to celebrate the Fourth on the beaches. On their way back, they were to make a two-hundred-mile detour through Austin to pick up two of Mabel's nephews, who were visiting Granberry's son.

Albert then managed to say, "Robert, boy, you be brave. Let me speak to Mr. Granberry. After that, call your father."

"R. C., I can hardly think," Albert said to his old friend. "I have to take care of Mabel. I'll talk to you later. Would you mind putting up my nephew until we decide what to do?" Albert put the phone down before R. C. could make assurances.

'Son dead?' Albert's mind whirled. "'Shot by a Negro! My God, what can I say to Mabel? To the family? What was Son doing?'

At that moment fourteen-year-old Eloise came down the stairs, "Papa, what's the matter?"

'Is she old enough? Am I right to tell her right now?' he thought.

Quietly, warmly, "It's about Son, honey. The phone call said that he's been killed."

His youngest daughter cried, "Albert?" and erupted so intensely that she did not see her father lose control as he put his arms around the exhausted, bewildered mother.

Albert Allison knew himself to this extent: under stress, he survived by doing. After getting a grip on the nausea and sea of emotions enveloping him, he told

Eloise to take the Ford and find her sixteen-year-old brother Lod, who was play-ing clarinet at a roughneck hangout on east Seventh Avenue. Albert then called Brackenridge Hospital in Austin. The duty physician told him that his son was already dead when the other boys brought him into the hospital. She had no idea who had shot the boy or the weapon employed.

Before Albert could call the Travis County Sheriff, Texas Ranger Earl McWil-liams called. He explained that the five boys (five?) had seemed to have been involved in an incident with a "nigger" in East Austin, the colored section of town. McWilliams said that they had no one in custody, but they had clues, and he promised that no Ranger, policeman, or deputy would sleep until the killer was arrested.

In McWilliams's voice, Albert heard those chilling inflections, the ones that put teeth into placid drawls when Southern men became serious about Negroes. That the Ranger's tone thinly veiled the old vengeance was bad enough; that the Ranger presumed Albert would be party to the code was worse.

"Ranger McWilliams, when you arrest this fellow," Albert replied without hesitation, "I want to talk to him. Maybe the law won't allow it; maybe it will. Please make sure the Negro's available, in case the judge says I can see him."

Albert had no desire to see the killer; he had reacted instinctively to dampen McWilliams's enthusiasm for "traditional" justice. But Albert had no idea how he would feel about "justice" after he had digested the news.

During Albert's conversation with the Ranger, Lod and Eloise arrived and ran to Mabel. Albert noted that little Ken, their ten-year-old, was lying on the living room couch, sleepy, quiet. After Albert had put down the telephone, he called to Lod, his son—not Son, but still his good son—and spoke to him like a man.

"I want you to stay with your mother to help with Eloise and Ken until I get back from Austin. Don't go to the farm; the work can wait. Just be with your mother. Don't talk to anyone about this except your sisters. Do you understand?"

Fighting back tears, Lod nodded, "Yes, Papa."

In reality, Albert knew Lod's job would amount to obeying Evelyn, Albert and Mabel's oldest daughter, who with her husband, Ed M., soon rushed in and took charge.

Albert was relieved to see Ed M. He deeply respected his son-in-law's unas-suming strength and pure Southern gentility, traits so valuable at a time like this. After embracing them, Albert went upstairs to pack. He had to get on the road to Austin. He had to leave.

On the Road to Austin

Hoping that the gas station operator would think he was merely wiping away the perspiration of a hot July night, Albert Allison used his handkerchief to flick away tears still intermittently welling up. He had rattled the disgruntled man out of bed; but, to Albert's relief, he asked no questions. When the man had filled the Buick's tank and wiped the windshield, Albert thanked him, gave him $3 for his trouble, managed a "Thanks, Fred," and drove away leaving the half-asleep man none the wiser. Envisioning the morning's *Corsicana Sun,* Albert muttered to himself that the operator and everyone else would know soon enough.

Before he was three miles along the Waco Highway, he convulsed, pulled over, and broke into tears.

After ten minutes or so, Albert forced himself to peer over the steering wheel at the road ahead. Sweat poured from his brow, the back of his shirt stuck to the car seat, and suffocation forced his breathing into short asthmatic gasps. Head-lights were coming toward him. Breathing hard, he pushed the ignition button, put the Buick into gear, and eased onto the highway. He had to be in Austin; his firstborn son needed him. As he settled into driving, his thoughts worked through a swirl of images and situations.

"Damn, this *could* set off a lynching. God knows, Negroes have been lynched for far less. Far less," he repeated to himself angrily.

A sudden rage exploded through knotted agony and guilt, and just as suddenly the rage ebbed into a terrible ache. 'I am his Papa!' he screamed inside. 'How can I protect him?'

Again, tears streamed down the reddened wrinkles in his furrowed face. He did not wipe them off; nor did he stop the car. He was nearing Waco. For a moment, he wondered if he should have left his family when everyone was still in such shock and despair.

In Waco, Albert turned the Buick south onto Highway 81. Few cars were on the road. It occurred to Albert that except for the hour before Granberry's tele-phone call, he had been awake since five thirty the previous morning. But his anxiety and the cooling wind blowing through the open window kept him alert. Only as he approached the town of Temple did he consider how abruptly he had made his departure. He did not even think to ask anyone to make the 150-mile trip with him. 'But maybe I should be alone,' he thought. 'At least I can indulge my own grief away from the others. This is time for just Son and me. My, that boy could be aggravating, but he gave me unbounded joy.'

◆   ◆   ◆

A summer's night in 1919. Albert and Son, then five years old, were caught in the west Texas desert without shelter in a furious thunderstorm. The wind blew so hard that great horizontal sheets of water cascaded in front of them without touching the ground. Lightning blistered the night sky sending cannon cracks across the desert. And there was Son sleeping in the protective fold of Albert's arms, peacefully unaware of the terror gripping his father.

Albert had taken Son on a trip to New Mexico, and during the trip home, he had left the slow Texas & Pacific train at a west Texas stop in order to cross ten miles of wild terrain to catch the faster Orient Railroad express. Some people said he should never have done it with a five-year-old boy, especially so close to sunset.

'Hogwash to them. The plan would have worked if the ranch house had been where it was supposed to be. Anyhow, though disheveled and weather-worn, we still got home a day before that rickety Texas & Western would have delivered us.'

'How the boy slept,' Albert mused. Son's complete serenity in the terrible storm had given Albert a new, awesome sense of fatherhood. Even when the coyotes howled after the storm passed, the boy was utterly confident that his papa would let no harm come to him; and that confidence filled the father with even more love.

◆   ◆   ◆

But Albert could not always protect that boy. The time had come when Son had had to seek his own manhood. Still, Albert could not help but wonder if Mabel and he should have kept Son under their wings a little longer. Maybe buying him that open-top Chevrolet had been a mistake.

Feeling his eyes getting heavy, Albert slowed the Buick and pulled to the side of the road. No cars, no lights anywhere in sight, but the moon gave the windless, hot landscape a yellowish tint. Albert got out of the car, lit a cigarette, stretched, and walked around. The night heat soon forced him to resume driving, but he was refreshed enough to proceed. His thoughts again turned to Son.

The boy was high-spirited—not mean, not bad, but creative and carefree. Having never been seriously disciplined, he acted as if he had a natural right to test the limits. People who knew him called him a prankster. Indeed, in both his junior and senior years, his high school classmates had created a special place for him among the school personalities—"Most Mischievous."

Albert then paused, 'He was the boy who thought of the high jinks that would often get the others in trouble. But they all liked him; he was sunshine and smiles.'

Not that Son didn't cause embarrassment; he had deeply distressed his mother when he was ten or so, a summer evening on his Uncle Stanley and Aunt Bunny's front porch, rocking in the swing with his eleven-year-old cousin. According to Mabel, a tired black man had walked along the street in front of the house, making his way from a hard day mowing and digging in white folks' gardens. As the man passed barely out of sight, Son's shrill voice pierced the evening air, "*Nigger.*" Mabel later told Albert that she and Bunny had run from the kitchen and scolded the boy, but he seemed not to understand. Elizabeth said that the word—a forbidden word in the family—had blasted from Albert with no warning. Son told Mabel that the word just came out of him for no reason. She said that he had tried to act contrite, but from Mabel's tone, Albert knew that Son had not been convincing.

Approaching 4 AM, Highway 81 merged into a familiar but eerily quiet Main Street—the town of Temple—a little more than an hour from Austin. Albert stopped under a streetlight to clean the bug-spattered windshield and smoke another cigarette. Watching the smoke trail toward the light, thoughts about Son and that word twisted through Albert's mind.

'When I was a boy, my family commonly used it, even in front of Negroes; but even my father—the Gettysburg veteran—used it less as he grew older. He said that like everything else the Yankee's touched, the word became corrupted when they took it up.' Certainly no Allison in Albert's memory spat the word with nearly the same venom as they hissed into the word *Yankee.* Images of soldiers on the family's Leon County farm marauding for clothes, chickens, and hogs took over Albert's mind. He sometimes thought he actually remembered ugly, drunken louts in blue cursing his mother in funny dialects, knocking over fences and pots, grabbing the squealing pigs; but he knew really that he remembered only his mother's oft-told stories.

'Well, *Yankee* was one thing, but that word was accursed. I always admonished my children not to use "Klan" talk they picked up on the school grounds, but Mabel and I could not protect them entirely.'

After he started off again, he thought, 'Thank God, the Klan has become a pariah.'

As Albert drove through Belton, phrases began to course repeatedly through his consciousness: "He was shot, Albert." "Never had a chance." "A Negro shot him, Uncle Albert."

'*Why?*' Albert's mind screamed. 'They said that Albert and four other boys were in the car. Why would a Negro shoot into Son's car?'

'Boys had been stirring up trouble on the Corsicana's east side lately,' thought Albert. Bored by summer days and hot nights, too much to drink at the illegal taverns that served oil camps and farm hands: youth, idleness, and alcohol combined for big trouble. But Son was not that sort. He had been to prep school, and, even though his asthma kept him out of the Naval Academy, he still would be in college this fall. He wouldn't run around with that kind of crowd.

The morning lights of Salado loomed ahead.

Albert frowned. Mabel's sisters had encouraged him to buy that car for Son. They were not fools, but they had soft spots for their charming nephew. In the summer of 1931, their brother Delmore, one of the founders of Lone Star Gas Company, had employed Son at the company's Dallas office, pending the boy's entrance into the Naval Academy. Mabel had arranged for Son to stay with his unmarried aunts. In time, he easily charmed them into persuading the senior Allison to buy the car. 'Of course,' Albert involuntarily grinned, 'Son had figured that as long as I thought he needed the car, he might as well have a car that suited him; and I had gone along. I bought that Chevrolet touring car, removable top, suitable for Texas weather. And, yes, a little snazzy.'

'But someone shot him in that car,' thought Albert as he passed through Georgetown. Albert's mind forged a vicious, black specter—big, muscular eyes, wild with the hate he had seen from time to time in the city jail. Perhaps the Negro was drunk. Perhaps he was dressed in the flashy sporting gear that young bucks like Alice Stewart's boy Carl had taken to wearing. Earlier that week, the *Sun* reported that Stewart had confessed to killing a prominent Austin Negro they found just outside Dawson. Suddenly Albert had an image of Carl's parents—an undertaker who disappeared a few years ago, and his wife, Alice, who was more than just a funeral director's wife. She had taken to wearing a high silver hat and long red robes, and she had somehow convinced East Side darkies that her funeral business equipped her with special powers, which she used to control their votes in city elections. The business certainly enabled her to buy and control their poll taxes.

Albert's mind then went to an evening session at Chicago's Drake Hotel bar just the previous week. Texas Democratic Convention delegates told bawdy jokes, horse-traded, had a few arguments, and shared Prohibition bourbon. Eventually, as usual, the session got around to the "Negro problem." But this year, with the Roosevelt New Yorkers in charge, it was debated a little more intensely. No matter how obnoxious, the New Yorkers would have big jobs in the new administration; and the implications were not lost on jittery Texas politicians. Truth be told, Albert wasn't sorry. He had become persuaded that Texas needed a nudge to get rid of Jim Crow.

The discussion that night had concerned Negro voting in the Texas Democratic Primary, a hot topic because the traditionally Republican Negroes were showing overwhelming support for Roosevelt. Albert had expressed his opinion that the Democratic Party should open its doors. He vividly recalled the stern looks he had received and the comment, "Over my dead body," from John Patterson, the long-time chairman of the Travis County Democratic Party.

Albert also recalled his old friend Bill Tarver's muted grin. Holding Governor Sterling's proxy had made Bill the de facto head of the Texas delegation, a position that tested every ounce of his political skill. Bill was a famous dry, and the delegation was mostly anti-Prohibition. But, despite a demonstration by Prohibition supporters in which fists were thrown, Bill had succeeded in holding the delegation together sufficiently to get John Nance Garner on the ticket with Roosevelt. Albert knew that Bill appreciated Albert's standing up for the unpopular views on race they both shared, but which Bill dare not express.

As Albert drove, he began to wonder what his political allies would think. 'What should he himself think? Was God also mumbling "nigger lover" behind his back? Did God unleash a black devil to remind Allison of His intent for Creation? Is the Negro race destined forever to be too primitive to warrant citizenship?'

The sign said Travis County, and Albert finally saw the lighted Capitol Dome glimmering on the horizon. The window breeze of the speeding Buick cooled the 5 AM morning, with a temperature still in the high eighties, and dried Albert's perspiration and tears.

For the first time in almost nineteen years, the sun rose on a world with no Son. For the first time in nineteen years, that smiling, curious consciousness would not make the world a happy, thrilling experience full of mischievous delights.

When the sun last went down, the Allison family was into its evening mode, lounging on the sun porch, drinking lemonade, watching little Ken chase lightning bugs, listening to Caruso on the Victrola. 'What was Son doing at that time?' pondered Albert. 'Having dinner at the Granberry's? What deadly decision had directed my son into the Negro's gun sight?'

Until midnight of July 8, 1932, Mabel and Albert Allison, their family, their extended family, and their community were characterized in part by Son—by his antics, his wit, and his name. From midnight, the manner of the boy's death would forever taint that characterization with horror and pain. And a gnawing dread in the recesses of Albert's conscience vaguely whispered, 'Shame, shame.'

2

Friday, July 8, 1932, East Austin

7 PM. Sixty-year-old Charlie Johnson washed off the day's sweat and put on his church clothes. After a long day immersed in paperwork tedium, he looked forward to spending a quiet Bible study evening with his longtime companion, Miss Annie Davis.

The atmosphere in Nathan Rhambo's office at the funeral home had been getting him down—the heat, the stale air, the downcast mood of the employees, especially the stuffed screech owl. Occasionally, from the corner of his eye, Charlie had seen the damned owl with its beak open, silently warning of impending doom. Working with Everett Rhambo, Nathan's son, was also getting to Charlie. The young man was just plain slow.

'Well, I owe the Rhambos something,' he reminded himself. 'I guess I have to put up with that place until Everett gets a grip.'

Still, when Nathan's brother, Perry, first asked Charlie to help keep Nathan's businesses going, he had held back. Whoever was responsible for killing Nathan might be after Charlie, too, and he did not want to make himself an easy target. But Perry's offer was too good, so Charlie decided to be a tough target. He found his old bone-handled Colt .45 in his cedar chest, took it to the gunsmith for oiling and cleaning, and bought a box of bullets.

Charlie finished dressing, removed the pistol from the drawer of his bedside nightstand, checked to make sure it was loaded, and walked out of the house to his car. After cranking up the Model T, he placed the gun in the glove compartment, took another look at himself in the rearview mirror, and slowly edged his way along unpaved roads to Annie's little duplex house on Chestnut Street.

Annie was freshness itself, almost pretty, with a flower in her bonnet. She was shorter than five-foot-six-inch Charlie, whose slight frame appeared even smaller when walking beside her ample body. He took from her hand the wicker basket bursting with that special fried chicken aroma.

Nobody thought it odd that Charlie and Annie went as a couple. He was not married; she likewise. After Charlie came to town in 1910, they had had a daughter together. After the little girl had grown up, married, and moved to Denver, both Annie and Charlie had received letters describing how she could swim in the pools and drink out of most water fountains. But the mountains and the snow depressed her, and her no-count man depressed her even more. Charlie never gave much thought to marrying Annie. They were friends, he reckoned, damned good friends. But that was all. And she did not seem anxious to get married, either. That's why the subject had not come up in almost twenty years. 'A man sixty and a woman almost fifty waste their time talkin' about what's not going to be,' Charlie mused.

As soon as Johnson's Model T sputtered from Annie's house, she got straight to point, "You hear about that Carl Stewart?"

Johnson shuddered, "I heard." He glanced at the glove compartment door that concealed the pistol and asked, "Why would somebody from Corsicana want to do that to Mister Rhambo?" His voice got higher through the short sentence.

"Brother Johnson, you knows it's a set-up for something no good. Ain't no Texas Ranger going to chase down a colored boy that kill a colored man like they chase down that Carl Stewart unless there's something else no good."

"No ma'am."

"Everybody say that Stewart's a patsy, that old Rhambo was fooling with a white woman and the husband pay that boy to lure Rhambo away."

'She's fishing about Rhambo's affair with the sheriff's wife, of course,' Charlie thought, 'just fishing.' Annie knew that Charlie was acquainted in a personal way with white girls Perry Rhambo recruited to service the politicians and big shots that frequented his hotel. 'Maybe it would be all right,' thought Charlie, 'if they think that a jealous white man killed Nathan, or the Klan killed him, or white political bosses, or something like that.'

After all, Coley White was the sheriff; and his wife did have a fling with Nathan when she worked for Perry, even if it was long before Coley ever met her. No doubt Sheriff White could have got Nathan if he had a mind to. No doubt everybody noticed Mrs. White at Nathan's funeral, standing alone, as beautiful as ever, dressed in black, and hardly acknowledging her friends from the old days. But nobody stopped to think that while the sheriff made enemies in white West Austin by shutting down small stills and jailing petty bootleggers, he allowed old Perry's hootchie-kootchie hotel to operate wide open.

'This time it's "whites only" that get kicked by the law,' Charlie chuckled to himself. Also, Coley protected Nathan from the white San Antonio gang that tried to muscle into Nathan's East Austin numbers racket a few years back—not a likely action from a man wild with jealousy. Whatever old Coley knew about his wife, he was not the man who put that Carl Stewart up to killing Nathan.

'No,' Charlie conjectured, 'that boy was put up to killing Nathan by the folks that were after Nathan ever since he used the undertaker association to run numbers. Hell, Alice Stewart might have blamed Rhambo, even me, for her husband's disappearance. Somehow that San Antonio bunch got her son Carl to lure Rhambo away to the place where they killed him, and then they stuck the boy with the body and the blame. No doubt the boy was involved somehow; no doubt he tried to drive Rhambo's Buick all the way back to Corsicana with Rhambo's beat-up body in it. Annie's right about one thing. That gang must've had connections. Those Texas Rangers never work overtime to catch a colored for killing a colored, much less spend a week sweating out a confession. Somebody was real anxious to see that Carl Stewart got all the blame.

As Charlie guided the Model T to the parking space in front of the Rising Star Baptist Church, he asked Annie if she had heard that the woman behind Nathan's murder was the wife of a lawman.

"No, I ain't heard," her grave voice was tinged with titillation.

'Hell,' thought Charlie, 'of course she'd heard. That was all them women talked about for years.'

"Why, Miss Davis, I hear that Mrs. Sheriff herself was a visitor to Neches Street more than once."

"Ahh," Annie breathed, as if she had something to ponder for a few days. The couple walked into the small church and happily greeted their friends.

Although cramped in a hot room and seated on uncomfortable wooden chairs, Charlie, Annie, and a dozen fellow students of Reverend Adam Black's Bible study joked and laughed through Annie's fried chicken, the small talk, and the week's gossip. When the students had finally put down the last of the peach cobbler, Reverend Black rose, made a few routine announcements, and introduced that week's guest speaker, the head minister of the Ebenezer Third Baptist Church.

The summer at the Ebenezer Church had not been a happy one. In May, white boys wielding a banana tree from an open-top car had hospitalized a member of his congregation. On Wednesday, white vandals had thrown rocks at the church during choir practice, and a few choristers were cut by shattered glass.

The week before, he had buried Nathan Rhambo, a deacon of his church, a close friend and a major benefactor.

"My friends, I'm here tonight with the heaviest of hearts. Two weeks ago our great and noble friend Nathan W. Rhambo went to the Lord at the hands of a heinous killer or killers. Who can fill the shoes of that giant?"

"Lord save Mister Rhambo. Yes sir," Charlie and Annie said in unison.

"If that's not enough, every week this summer, sometimes twice or more a week, East Austin get raided by white boys that ride our streets like wild demons. They hurt our old folks, throw rotten fruit at our ladies, chuck rocks at our churches, and call us bad names. And what do we do?"

After the dumfounded silence, he repeated, "I say, fellow Baptists, as good Christian children of the Lord, what do we do?"

The visiting reverend did not wait for the answer, "Well, lots of folks think we have got to turn the other cheek like our Lord Jesus His own Self told us to do. We just let the killers come to our houses and ask us to go on an errand of mercy and then get us out in the country and kill us dead. And then we tell the killers—if they be white as icing on a wedding cake or black as a moonless night—we tell the killers to keep on killing if it makes 'em feel good. Is that right? Is that why we turn the other cheek, brothers and sisters?"

"Why, no sir," Annie Davis reacted immediately.

"Well, well, Sister Davis. You mean we don't go to slaughter like sheep? That we have to stand up to evil? Like David stand up to Goliath? Like Samson stand up to the Palestines?"

"Amen. Amen"

"And when the marauders rampage through our community, do we just say, 'Howdy, thank you kindly for hitting me in my new dress with that rotten plum?' Do we just say, 'Bless you for throwing the rock that break the window of the Ebenezer Church, spraying one of our choir ladies with glass so bad she like to bleed to death?' Do we say, 'Please boys, act like the KKK and run poor, quiet colored folk down right on the streets?'"

"No, sir, but what do we do?" several members of the meeting cried.

The preacher was driving Charlie into unwanted visits with his conscience. His mother once told him that she and his daddy left their east Texas white family for central Texas, where the Union occupying army provided the best protection from vengeful rebels. They took a tenancy on a forty-acre cotton farm that provided the young freedman a tumbledown shack, a mule, a plow, and seed. After the Union army left, the landlord sold the land to the couple on good terms. Charlie's mother said that the white man had been impressed that the former butler and lady's maid had somehow successfully made the transition to field labor against large odds. Once secure on their own property, the Johnsons planned to live out their lives planting and picking cotton, bearing children, and spending Wednesday evenings and most Sundays at church.

Charlie recalled those hot summer days picking cotton beside his parents, brothers, and sisters, feeling faint, always thirsty, but never faltering. He would never forget the morning his father so proudly drove his own wagon, heaped with his own cotton from his own farm, headed for the gin. Nor would he forget his father's serious but determined face as he arrived back with the wagon still heaped with cotton. The ginner had offered him half the going rate, so he would take the load to another ginner the next day.

But that night the hooded riders had come.

Charlie's mother had jolted her children awake, screaming, "Run! Run! Run to the fields and hide!" Terrified, panting, stumbling, Charlie saw ghosts on horseback waving torches, shouting, and shooting guns over his shoulder. Suddenly he ran upon an old tree stump. He crawled behind it, shut his eyes tightly, and made himself smaller and smaller…until he was invisible. But he could not block out the light of the flames that engulfed their house or his father's piercing screams or his mother's guttural cries of utter desolation.

Charlie stayed invisible behind that stump until the sun rose. When he finally looked out, he saw the stark silhouettes of his mother, brothers, and sisters standing by his father's charred remains. That afternoon, when the preacher took Charlie in his arms and prayed for his daddy, Charlie could not cry, could not even whimper. When he was older his mother told him that every day for almost a month he had sat in the church, the family's shelter, staring at the door with unblinking eyes and an open mouth. There is horror in the world, he had learned; best find a safe tree stump and stay behind it

For the rest of Charlie's life, when the world got rough, he searched for his psychic tree stump. Everybody who knew Charlie Johnson knew he had no use for confrontation.

When white troublemakers were around, Charlie had managed to find a way to ignore them. The night the "baseballer" knocked an old man into the ditch, Charlie might have heard the cars racing through the streets, but he didn't think so. Wednesday night, Charlie might have heard the glass shattering at the Ebenezer Church. But the next morning, when told how flying shards cut several singers, he just shook his head and went about his business. What more could he do? Two weeks before, he might have heard the commotion as three white boys standing in an open top car threw juicy peaches at men, women, and children walking leisurely around East Austin's streets. Charlie might have heard, but he did not think so.

Yet, Charlie knew that not all East Austin was so intentionally blinkered. He knew that maids and yardmen complained to their white folks.

Annie, for instance, had worked for a big-time lawyer for years. She had raised his children and now his grandchildren. She cooked most of the food the lawyer had eaten in his lifetime. She had nursed him and his children through fevers, poxes, poison ivy, and broken bones. 'You bet,' thought Charlie, 'that white man got an earful.'

Mr. Will Fuller, assistant undertaker at Tear's Funeral Home, had told Charlie that Fuller's sister-in-law, who was president of the Baptist women, had complained straight to the mayor and the chief of police. 'But Mrs. Fuller's just a riled up old lady,' Charlie protested inwardly. Most men sulked until the riders went away. Charlie crouched behind his psychic tree stump.

"Well, let us think on it."

The reverend's "think" broke into Johnson's reverie.

"What did old Gideon do when the Midianites rampage through his land? I'll tell you: he rampage back, brothers and sisters. I know this ain't the kind of Bible lesson you was expecting, but these times call for something different. A little while back my dear friend Nathan Rhambo gave me this poem that a Negro named Claude McKay wrote in nineteen hundred and nineteen following a spate of bloody race wars. Y'all remember those days? Permit me to read.

> "If we must die, let it not be like hogs
> Hunted and penned in an inglorious spot,
> While round us bark the mad and hungry dogs,
> Making their mark at our accursèd lot
> If we must die, O let us nobly die,
> So that our precious blood may not be shed
> In vain; then even the monsters we defy
> Shall be constrained to honor us though dead!
> O kinsmen! we must meet the common foe!
> Though far outnumbered let us show us brave,
> And for their thousand blows, deal one deathblow!
> What though before us lies the open grave?

Like men we'll face the murderous, cowardly pack,
Pressed to the wall, dying, but fighting back!

"Thank y'all for listening. I'll say amen to Mr. McKay and turn the meeting back to Reverend Black."

"Thank you, Brother. Your words make us realize what we have to do," said Reverend Adam Black.

"Let us pray."

After Reverend Black said amen, Charlie and Annie said their good-byes and drove to Perry's hotel for their weekly drink. It was 9 PM. Ten years ago they would have returned to one of their houses for comfortable lovemaking, but these days most of the time a drink was comfort enough.

As Charlie drove, he looked hesitantly at Annie, who made no effort to hide her enthusiasm for the evening's sermon. He wondered if she thought that the preacher was saying old Charlie had to do something about those white rowdies.

'Not likely,' he shrugged. 'Nobody think that be Charlie's job. Not that preacher, not Reverend Black, and sure not Miss Annie.'

Charlie was normally quiet, so Annie took no notice when he said nothing as she rambled on without stopping for a breath. The preacher had excited her so much Charlie thought she might explode in indignation. His own thoughts could not escape the preacher's words, either.

"And for their thousand blows, deal one death blow," Charlie mumbled. Annie seemed not to hear.

'That's what the preacher say,' he thought. 'It's like a call for the Army. Why'd he look at me? It was like I wasn't doing the Lord's will. Hell, if that old fool thinks I'm going to go looking for trouble, he's crazy. Not me. Not old Charlie.'

Charlie turned the Model T from Chicon Street onto Seventh, stopped in front of Perry's, grabbed his clarinet case, and escorted Annie to their usual seats at the bar. Like most early summer evenings, Perry's was full of older folks who enjoyed the music and a little dancing. Youngsters and whites would not arrive for at least an hour, so they had a little time to enjoy themselves in relative peace. Charlie ordered two glasses of shine from Perry's own still and handed Annie hers. After he tossed back his shot, he cleared his throat and sauntered to the bandstand. For the next half hour, Charlie jammed, letting that special "something" rise from his soul. Through the smoke, old spirits, praising God in harmony and time, swayed with Annie and some of Perry's girls. Close on the heels of the blues, Charlie revved up the jazz, and agile couples began a frantic dance to complement the music and the rhythm in their souls. After a few minutes Annie glided her ample body to the bandstand with Charlie's second and last glass. When he finished it, he shook a couple of hands, wiped his forehead with his handkerchief, put his clarinet in the case, took Annie's arm, and departed.

It was after 10:30 PM when he returned her to her doorstep and headed for home in a mellow mood.

As Charlie proceeded south on Chicon Street, headlights and screeching tires swerved out of Eighth Street just a hundred feet in front of him. He slammed on his brakes, skidded by the car, struggled to right his Model T, and stopped. In his rearview mirror he made out an open-top car stopped in the ditch. White men were out of their car, milling around. Instinctively, Charlie jumped out of the Model T, motor still running.

"Y'all all right?" he yelled.

One of them shouted back, "Goddamned black bastard. Where'd you learn to drive?"

Then a thud punched Charlie's shoulder, followed by a sharp ache.

"Rock the son-of-a-bitch! Knock his head off!"

Rocks clunked on Charlie's car. Another grazed his forehead. He jumped in his Model T and began to drive off. Then he heard a crack that sounded like a bullet ricocheting off the car body. As his car gathered speed, Charlie reached into his glove compartment, removed the loaded Colt .45, and set it on the passenger seat.

Within moments Charlie heard the roar of a car passing him on the left. White riders were standing on the sideboards, fists shaking, twisted mouths shouting cuss words. The open-top car sped to the corner of Seventh and Chicon Street, about a half a block further on, and it stopped under a light. As the Model T slowly approached the corner, Charlie again saw that the men were milling around the car. A tall fellow stood upright from the front car seat and threw a rock that hit Charlie's windshield. The faint whisper of a mantra began in his ear: "For their thousand blows, deal one death blow"

Charlie knew better than to stop his car. He drove to the corner, turned right onto Seventh, and tried to speed away. Two rocks hit the car. The whisper became a little louder: 'For their thousand blows, deal one death blow.' A loud crack pierced through the engine noise.

'That's a rifle sure enough,' Charlie thought. 'The San Antonio crowd; it's got to be.' His first instinct was to run, but he had slunk all his life. 'I ain't going to be slaughtered like no hog.' The mantra in his ear became louder, 'For their thousand blows, deal one death blow.'

He was fifty yards past the corner by the time he stopped. The poet's words found Charlie's voice. "For their thousand blows, deal one death blow," he said aloud, biting on each word.

'Hell no! Old Charlie ain't running no more,' he thought. He turned the car and headed back to the corner. His right hand curled around the white-boned handle of the revolver; his right thumb lay on the cock. He saw three men run from the car toward the electric substation on the corner.

"Deal one death blow!" he was shouting.

As he drove close to the open car, he pointed the pistol, fired, and drove on. This time he turned right on Chicon Street. He heard shouts and more cussing. A rock struck a window so hard the glass cracked, but he heard no more rifle shots. When he looked back, he saw that the open-top car was still parked. Evidently the pistol shot made the whites think twice about the chase, and suddenly Charlie was calm.

Totally spent by the effects of the moonshine and the stress of the attack by the San Antonio mob, Charlie drove to his house on Salina Street, parked his car in the shed, grabbed the pistol, and went inside. Still wary that the gang might find him, he removed the empty casing, took a new bullet from the drawer of his bed-stand, and inserted it into the chamber. Then he undressed and lay down on his small bed. Despite the hot, breezeless room, he fell asleep immediately.

But his nerves gave him little relief. Through fits and starts of, waking at every slight rustle, Charlie dreamed of torch-carrying nightriders pursuing him down Chicon Street; he saw Alice Stewart, hand-in-hand with her son Carl, smile large with enormous white teeth beckoning to him to join Nathan Rhambo. He watched Rhambo in his top hat float through East Austin streets wielding that long pole, and he heard a swish as the stuffed screech owl in Rhambo's office spread its wings. Finally, after the risen sun signaled safety, he fell into a deep sleep.

3

Bill Tarver, West Austin

Ringing brought Bill Tarver into semi-consciousness, and he felt Esther nudging him hard. "Telephone, Bill. Get the phone."

He rolled out of the sweaty bed and headed down the dark hall of his small single-level house toward the wall phone. Bill Jr., in his boxer shorts, got to it first. "It's Mr. Granberry, Dad."

As the sixteen-year-old ambled back to bed, Bill heard Granberry's familiar voice, "Bill, there's been a terrible tragedy. I thought you'd want to know right away. Albert Allison's boy, Albert Jr., was in town tonight. He was killed by a negrah."

"Oh my God," Tarver gasped. Images of the Allisons took over his mind. The Tarvers and Allisons had been close friends for more than twenty years, from the days when Tarver was practicing law in Corsicana with Mabel's father, the late Judge Lodowick Cobb, probably the most important man in his and Albert's lives.

"Albert Jr.," Granberry continued, "was in his car with my boy Harry, Sonny Mayes, Bob Cobb, and Derden Wofford. The boys say the negrah just drove up and shot him. I'm not sure what else happened, except that the shot wounded Derden. None of the other boys were hurt."

"What's the time, R. C.?"

"It's about 2 AM. I called Albert just after midnight. He's on his way."

Tarver's senses sharpened. He was due in Houston at noon to make a campaign speech. But Albert and Mabel…Tarver's eyes fixed on the glass-fronted bookshelves that housed the set of law books that Judge Cobb had willed to him. The campaign would have to be put on hold.

Granberry had said that Albert was on his way, Tarver's thoughts raced on. That means that Albert would be in Austin about five.

"R. C., you were right to call me, and I thank you for it. As soon as I get hold of myself, I want to make a few phone calls. I'll get to the hospital as soon as I can."

As Tarver was about to say good-bye, a feeling of dread came over him. "Negro," Granberry had said "Negro."

"R. C., you say he was killed by a Negro? Where?"

"Yes sir. That's what the boys said. Over in East Austin."

"Have we got him? What in the world were those boys doing in East Austin?"

'As if everybody doesn't know what boys do in East Austin,' thought Tarver immediately.

"Don't think they've caught him, and we're still trying to figure out what the boys was up to. Sheriff's deputies are here, and a Ranger's been nosing around. He talked to Albert on the telephone, I think."

Tarver shuddered.

"See you soon, R. C." The tears were welling up.

Tarver turned to face Esther and his son, both very much awake, both alert to a tragedy. "Young Albert Allison was in town last night."

"I seen him, Pop," piped in Bill Jr.

The older Tarver stopped. "Really? How so?"

"Him and his cousin Bob Cobb was with Harry Granberry at House Park field last night. They watched the ball games. What happened, Pop?"

"You see any trouble, Son?" asked Tarver, wincing at the boy's grammar, but too preoccupied to provoke yet another argument.

"Naw, sir. After the game I talked to 'em for a while, standing around Albert's car. Then I walked on home. We was talking and cutting up. That's all. Derden Wofford was with 'em; he was goin' on about a test ride. Albert was hankering to show off his car, I guess. What happened?"

"Mr. Granberry said Albert was shot and killed last night—by a Negro."

Esther stopped fanning herself, "Oh God, poor Mabel, poor little child."

The wide-eyed boy sputtered, "There weren't no nig—Negroes around there, Pop."

The elder Tarver gave his son a hard look, "Think about everything you saw last night. We'll talk later."

Tarver turned to Esther and gave her a hug then wearily shuffled to the bedroom.

"I'll have to call our political friends," he mumbled to himself. "They'll want to be at the hospital when Albert arrives, and they'll lend a little heft in getting the law to marshal everything it's got to find this Negro before all hell breaks loose."

'House Park field at night,' Bill thought as he undressed and went into the bathroom, 'baseball under the lights.'

Some people did argue that those lights would be the source of trouble, that the boys would leave the field too late at night, in too much a mood for excitement and mischief. Even though Bill had supported the installation of the lights, he could not deny that embarrassing incidents had sometimes followed the games, especially big games, especially victory celebrations after big games. An image of Bill Jr. celebrating with his Austin High teammates by heading to East Austin after last May's championship game flashed into Bill's mind. At the time, he had just smiled; his boy was undergoing a rite of passage.

'Yep, and that had been Derden's doing,' Bill recalled, as the night of the great game reeled through his mind. Tarver had joined five thousand fans to watch Derden Wofford take the mound for his last game in an Austin High uniform. In April, *The Austin Statesman* had declared Derden "incontestably the best twirler in Central Texas and rated as the best in the state by many observers." That night, he faced Thomas Jefferson High, San Antonio's undefeated city champion. Austin had lost only to the University of Texas freshmen that season and had won ten straight.

The game had brought out most of Austin's leading citizens. The young assistant district attorney, James P. Hart, shook Tarver's hand. He was a candidate for the big job. His father, James H. Hart, senior partner of Austin's premier law firm, was with him. They sat with Henry Brooks, the retiring incumbent district attorney whom Hart wanted to succeed. Sheriff Coley White had sat not too far from Tarver. The sheriff had introduced Tarver to a young deputy named Homer Thornberry and a Texas Ranger named Earl McWilliams. Tarver remembered that Thornberry had said he had taken the night off from studying for his law school term exams. John Patterson, the Travis County Democratic Party chairman and the elder Jim Hart's law partner, had sat three rows in front of Tarver with the famous defense attorney Warren Moore.

At the end of the evening, Tarver was a little disappointed that his son, Bill, did not get into the game, but, like everyone else in the stands, he was enthralled by the best pitching performance he possibly would ever see.

With sniper accuracy inning after inning, the lanky, six-foot Wofford coiled tightly bound sinews and spat lightning, followed by a turn of the head to relieve a stream of brown juice. Balls whacked so hard into the catcher's mitt that as the innings passed, the big Thomas Jefferson batters cringed further from the plate.

That's when Wofford started to paint the corner off-speed—strike three, or a dribbler to the infield, or a pop fly. In the top of the ninth inning, when the second Jefferson batter was out, five thousand fans rose in a frenzy. Derden had struck out seventeen and had issued just one walk. As Jefferson's twenty-eighth batter took his stance, Derden's arm zipped its hundredth pitch, a strike; then pitch one hundred and one—crack—a line drive to the shortstop. He scooped the ball out of the dust and threw to first. Out!—a no hitter! The stands stormed the field, the team swarmed over Derden. Laughing and whooping, he was on the ground, then on shoulders in a triumphant parade.

After the final pitch, Bill Tarver, still in the stands, was content to watch the crowd sweep the grimy, red-faced boys from the diamond toward the parking lot. Bill saw a large, grinning boy in a baseball uniform sitting on top of the back seat of an open-top Ford holding a six-foot banana tree that he must have yanked from the ground at the edge of the park. He saw a few teammates throw Wofford into the back. Other boys had piled into an old Dodge. With the Ford in the lead, the cars sped out of House Park field emitting rebel yells and war whoops. They tore onto West Street down to Eleventh, then turned left to East Austin.

Bill and everyone else expected their red-blooded victors to do a little hell-raising, and they knew that East Austin was just the place for it. Bill also realized that his son was with a noisy bunch, but they were only noisy—not rowdy, not mean. They would stay out of trouble; Tarver was sure of it.

But a week or so after that night, Sheriff White had told him that the boys had upset folks in East Austin enough for them to complain. "Our boys need to be taught the difference between hell-raising and real trouble," the Sheriff had said. "We've got it pretty good with the Negroes right now. But stuff like that could ruin it for everybody."

As Tarver was shaving, he wondered if the same sort of thing had happened with Albert Jr. Derden Wofford was certainly a common factor. Bill guessed that Derden had introduced his new friends to East Austin and this time found big trouble. "'But,' thought Bill, 'young Allison did not need a lot of leading to find trouble. Albert and Mabel have always had a blind spot for that boy's mischievousness.' Tarver chuckled as a few of Albert's antics came to mind: they were harmless, some were funny, some were damned aggravating. 'That boy,' Tarver sighed, as he was looking in his dressing mirror. He had known Albert Jr. almost as well as he had known his own son.

The word *mischievous* repeated itself in Tarver's mind. The word used for young Allison had always been *mischievous*—not *mean*, not *vicious*, not *menacing*, not even *threatening*. No, by *mischievous* folks meant "a prankster who would tease you, then look you in the eye and wink gleefully at your mild discomfort." Most victims simply went along with the fun and enjoyed a good laugh at themselves. Young Allison had a way of helping people see the comedy in their daily drudge, and sometimes, Tarver knew, the folly of their hypocrisy. In fact, people sought his company. He teased, yes; but he knew the limits; and he wasn't hurtful, at least to friends. To be around him was fun; his spirit and energy refreshed your mood, and sometimes his way of looking at the world made you a little more comfortable with yourself. And once in a while, with exquisite timing, he would shock folks into more laughter and livelier fellowship by daring the limits of decency. By calling Albert Jr. "mischievous," folks in Corsicana hinted that he was encumbered by fewer boundaries than other boys. They hinted at a spoiled lad born to middle-aged parents, successful in all they had done, including rearing two remarkable daughters, but who panicked about the male heir, the namesake. So when he came, they loved him too much to rein in his exuberance for the game he played against the world. And in 1918 when the telegram arrived that Private Perry Allison, their ward and nephew, just eighteen, had died in France, they clung to four-year-old Albert Arthur Allison Jr. even tighter, indulged him even more, and rebuked him even less. Bill Tarver saw it; his wife, Esther, saw it; everybody but Albert and Mabel saw it.

Smart and mischievous, everybody said that Albert Jr. was smart, too. How his father strutted when he discovered that his son had the family faculty for numbers. Albert could not help but brag how during breakfast his son and he "danced in tandem to numbers confounded in labyrinths but harmonized by fast-moving mental feet that pranced to a delightful necessary truth." That was how Albert put it, or something like it, and the boy must have had a knack. Congressman Luther Johnson had told Bill that young Allison would make a fine engineer, and he had offered to sponsor the boy for an Annapolis appointment. Bill knew Albert well enough to know that Albert was taken by the vision of his son in dress whites, standing erect with the family in church, smiling graciously over the congregation before embarking on benign adventures for his country.

By indulging his own harmless fantasies, Albert had overindulged the boy. No, young Allison did not die from a tragic mixture of brains and mischievousness, but perhaps being indulged too much entailed a little bit of tragic consequence.

'Poor Albert,' thought Tarver, 'for the rest of his life he'll be burdened with the knowledge that he had bought the touring car and equipped the boy with a little too much swagger.'

Mischievous, smart, and indulged. A combustible mixture not in itself lethal, just troubling until the boy lived long enough to be thwarted by the realities from which his parents had shielded him. 'On the other hand, if these ingredients were not bubbling last night,' Tarver thought, 'he may not have driven the boys to East Austin. He may not have, but he probably would have.' Many less venturesome boys with snazzy cars had been cajoled into driving friends to Rhambo's hotel for beer—and a peek at the bawdy girls. "Hootch" and "kootch" the Austin High boys had whooped after Derden's no-hitter, and they had returned home without a scratch.

After young Allison had failed his Annapolis physical in May, Bill had heard folks say they had sensed a change in him. He seemed a little vulnerable. His mischievousness and carelessness seemed a little exaggerated, as if another, sadder, wiser boy, lurked beneath the smiling, impish *persona* to which he had accustomed his world. For a Texas boy bred to be the family-first at a prestigious university, the family-first to pursue a prestigious career away from the dirt farms and the merchandise stores, to be in the pristine white uniform of the United States Navy, disqualification from Annapolis must have been a disqualification from life.

'Mischievous, smart, indulged, and disqualified,' Tarver mused. 'Now this just might have been a lethally combustible mixture.'

After Bill Tarver finished dressing, he called Texas Ranger Captain Frank Hamer, who said that he had already assigned one of his top men and that he, personally, would stay close to the case. Sheriff White likewise was on top of things. He was mobilizing all his people to work with the Austin police. Tarver marveled that neither man sounded sleepy or even the least bothered by his intrusion at that hour. He could not say the same for Albert's good friends, the Texas Agriculture Commissioner and the Texas Land Commissioner. But once they got over the shock, they committed to being at Brackenridge Hospital by 5 AM. Tarver did not have to tell them that their support would help both Albert and the community through a trying day.

4

Brackenridge Hospital

Raymond Brooks had been out too late with his capital press colleagues. When his wife called him to the hallway telephone, the desk sergeant on the other end of the line had to say it a couple of times before it registered: a Negro had shot Derden Wofford and killed another boy.

"No," the Sergeant had responded to Brooks's perfunctory questions. Derden's not hurt bad; and no, they hadn't caught the Negro; and no, they had no identity. The dead boy? About eighteen years old, from out of town. He and three other boys were with Derden. The sergeant said the detectives were interviewing Wofford and the other boys at Brackenridge.

Brooks yawned his thanks and threw on his clothes. This was the first black-on-white killing in Austin since he had arrived in town a decade ago. If Austin was on the brink of a race riot, as the senior news reporter for the Austin American and Austin Statesman, the two dailies owned by Mr. Charles Marsh, Brooks wanted the story. Besides, whatever happened, sports stars like Wofford always made good copy.

Forty-five minutes later at the hospital, Brooks inspected Wofford's badly bruised left arm and listened while the pitcher huffed about a Negro who drove by the boys and fired point-blank into their car. A detective subsequently told Brooks that the bullet that had bruised Wofford had penetrated through the entire body of the dead boy, who was the son of Albert Allison of Corsicana.

'Of course,' Brooks thought, 'that explains why Captain Frank Hamer from the Texas Rangers has been here, why so many Sheriff's deputies and Austin police are moving in and out, and why big-name politicians are meandering around before 5 AM on a Saturday morning. This is a much bigger story than a wounded baseball star.'

Brooks knew that Allison was a wealthy, influential cotton landlord, well-known for his work to establish two-year county colleges and for his recent leadership in the cotton moratorium movement. Brooks clearly remembered Allison's masterful argument for his cotton acreage control program before the Texas Senate the previous September. Over the loud objections of the cotton brokers, he had persuaded Governor Sterling to call a special session; and, then, he had persuaded the Senate to enact legislation so flawed that it was at first ignored as unenforceable, and then overturned by the courts.

'Notwithstanding,' thought Brooks, 'the man impressed a lot of hard-nosed people. Hell, in spite of the Texas cotton fiasco, just a couple of weeks ago he somehow persuaded the national Democratic Party to endorse a national cotton moratorium.

'So, Bill Tarver, Chairman of the Insurance Commission, got out of bed to be here for him, as has the Texas Agriculture Commissioner and the Texas Land Commissioner.

'These men are here not just to comfort their friend,' thought Brooks. 'They're on duty. They may have important offices; but their paramount duty is to defend the Southern way of life. Just their presence is a message to every peace officer in Travis County. If a Negro wounding Derden Wofford is enough to spark riots in Austin, what will killing Albert Allison's son do?'

Brooks nodded at his assessment. 'Protecting our way of life is every white man's business.'

It was certainly Raymond Brooks's business. The papers owner, Mr. Charles Marsh, had made it Brooks's business. He had explicitly made it Brooks's business. But in truth, Brooks had not needed to be told.

From the time Raymond Brooks had first written copy for the Waco Tribune, he had laced his stories with words, descriptions, and anecdotes that buttressed Jim Crow, justified the measures that defended Jim Crow, and forgave the occasional excesses of Jim Crow. Brooks had grown up in Falls County as the grandson of original settlers who had arrived with a few slaves, a few children, a wagonload of furniture, and a confidence that they would succeed as well as their forebears had done in Tennessee. And despite lawlessness, Indian raids, and the unforgiving Texas climate, they did succeed. Three of their sons never returned from the War for Southern Independence, and those who did return had to bear the ignominy and poverty imposed by Reconstruction. But, in the way they overcame adversity, and, through the lives of their children, they did succeed.

Like many Texas boys of the late nineteenth century, Brooks was born to redeem the South. That meant participating in the struggle to overcome the sun, the Yankees, insects, outlaws, thunderstorms, varmints, carpetbaggers, lawyers, and Negroes. It meant learning Texas lore and Southern virtue from bitter lips. It meant baptism into the community of the saved. It meant blood brotherhood in the white tribe.

Because Brooks had a knack for reading and writing, he was occasionally relieved of farm tedium to help with the church news bulletin, to read folks' personal letters, even to read wills and deeds. Eventually these talents enabled him to find employment as a printer's helper at the newspaper in nearby Waco. Within a year, he was writing copy. By the time he was twenty-one, he was the paper's city reporter. He had also become active in the First Baptist Church and started attending Wednesday night Temperance Society meetings to be in the same room with a girl named Gladys. He had little luck with her; but at those meetings he did meet and become good friends with a young lawyer named Henry Brooks. (No relation, as far as either knew, but they called each other "cousin," anyway.) Finally, in his fourth year of ostensible temperance, Gladys noticed Raymond. By the end of that year, they were married.

Just after the World War, "Cousin" Henry Brooks took a job with the attorney general's office in Austin, where, after a few years, the powers-that-be asked him to run for district attorney. Five years later, Henry showed Mr. Charles Marsh articles describing Waco's outrage at a Negro's "assault" on a young girl, written under Raymond's byline. Mr. Marsh owned both the morning *Austin American* and the evening *Austin Statesman.* While careful not to support mob violence, Raymond had sympathetically implied that Waco had obeyed an ancient code above the civil law, that for the sake of the Southern woman, the immutable will of the people justly trumped Caesar's law. Mr. Marsh had been so impressed that he offered Raymond three times his wage at the *Tribune.* Mr. Marsh had told Raymond that he did not expect mob violence in the state capital; but he did want his papers to reflect, even advocate, the virtue of racial "place," and to justify Austin's emphatic enforcement of it.

As grim-faced officials paraded purposefully about the halls of Brackenridge Hospital waiting for Mr. Allison to arrive, Brooks contemplated the possibility of an Austin riot and its ramifications.

'That mob in Waco had had a heart, a heart that beat with animal rhythm. Of course, I sure as hell didn't write about it that way,' he thought. He recalled the young farming couple standing in the middle of the mob, directly in front of the courthouse. Both were breathing in short, hard gasps. The sweat rolled off them; their faces were flushed, mouths contorted. From underneath a sunbonnet the woman's narrow eyes focused steadily on the cordon of officers standing before the courthouse door. Brooks figured at the time that both had partaken of the moonshine being passed around. When he had introduced himself, the man said breathlessly that they had just helped the daddy get rid of one "nigger" that maybe raped his little girl, now they were going to get the "nigger" the sheriff arrested the day before, and then they were going to get the "nigger" the Rangers were bringing in from Corsicana. The young man said that the victim described her assailant as "tall, black, and had a gold tooth," and all three fit the description.

Earlier in the day, a deputy had told Brooks that when the sheriff arrested the second Negro fitting the girl's description, instead of taking him to jail, the sheriff had taken him to the girl's house for identification. The girl took one look and screamed. Her father took out his gun and shot the Negro dead on the spot. Within minutes, the mob that had gathered outside the girl's house had taken the body, hung it from a pecan tree, and set it afire. The mob then proceeded to the courthouse, where Brooks and the young couple stood.

The young farmer, who had introduced himself as Tucker Childs, was earnest, hard, sure of himself, and certain of his duty. Childs had said that he and his family farmed a share just south of Waco and that he worked as a car mechanic when they needed extra cash. Brooks remembered that Tuck had talked in hushed tones, as if he were trying not to be distracted. He had seemed to be watching for a sign or listening for a signal. His wife Ellie stared at the courthouse citadel through the smoke of a corncob pipe she held in the hand of her right arm, which was folded over her obvious condition. Brooks would never forget this woman. As he and Tuck talked, she aimed steely blue eyes at the courthouse door. After a few minutes, as if obeying a command, she began to sway gently from side-to-side. Brooks noticed that several of the men and women in the crowd glanced in Ellie's direction from time to time, as if seeking approval. As the crowd grew (Brooks estimated a thousand), people pushed closer together. Almost imperceptibly at first, the men and women began to sway with Ellie. Soon the whole mob moved in unison side-to-side. Even Brooks was caught up in it. Suddenly, he saw Ellie turn her head toward the swaying Tuck and nod toward the courthouse. He heard her breathe quietly, "Okay." Tuck nodded, and the swaying gradually became an irresistible surge forward. The protective cordon at the courthouse door soon melted into the surge, the doors broke open, and the people's justice was underway. Brooks managed to avoid being carried along and soon lost sight of the couple. Within thirty minutes, a black body was swinging from the old hanging tree.

After the mob had cut down the body and tied it to the back of a car to be towed through colored town, Brooks caught sight of Tuck and Ellie strolling in the courthouse square hand-in-hand, smiling, light footed. The burden of blood-duty was lifted, he surmised. The Sheriff later told him that the Rangers coming from Corsicana had freed their suspect when they had heard about the lynchings. They figured that the guilty man had paid.

Six months later, shortly before Brooks moved to Austin, he happened upon the couple doing Saturday shopping in Waco. Tuck remembered Brooks; Brooks remembered Ellie. Brooks noted that like all who spent hard lives in the blistering sun, they were aging quickly. She was carrying an infant and holding hands with a little girl.

"Howdy, Mr. Newspaper. Nice to see you, again," her voice was so soft.

Brooks felt something: an attraction. Those eyes, their fix; they beckoned you to please her. They commanded you to please her.

After a few words, Brooks impulsively invited them for a cold drink at the drugstore. He said he was doing a story, and they might help him. He could tell Tuck was flattered; Ellie was only a little more reticent. On the way, a boy and girl came out of a dime store, waved at Tuck, called him "daddy," and joined the three adults and the little girl. Walking fast, the pack overtook an old Negro slowly ambling with a cane.

Ellie spat, "Move out of the way, nigger."

The old man half-stumbled into the street, "Yes ma'am, I's sorry." Brooks remembered that no one paid attention.

With iced lemonade and ice cream on the table, the Childs talked casually about their lives. 'If they had ever had dreams,' thought Brooks, 'the sun had incinerated them; and the burden of the cotton and the kids had scattered the ashes.' He visualized a little shack, on stump supports, peeling white paint, broken porch step, rocking chairs, the smell of burnt pork fat, everywhere dirty children. Tuck farmed the one hundred and sixty acres on a quarter-share with his landlord, and worked part-time as a mechanic. Ellie, who said she was expecting again, tended the children, the house, the chickens, and the little vegetable garden. She said her little girl would soon be old enough to help pick cotton. Deteriorating prices, crop liens, and no options put them, like everyone else, in a squeeze. But they spoke strongly, even optimistically; they were secure in Jesus, in their identity, and in each other.

When the conversation turned to the day of the lynching, Ellie spoke first. "Mr. Brooks, we all got a duty. Them niggers is looking for anyway they can to move in on us. We reckon that ever' decent white man and woman owe it to our daddies and their daddies and to our little girls to stop 'em cold."

She told Brooks that while her daddy was dying from tuberculosis, in convulsions, blood dripping from the corner of his mouth, he had gripped her arm with all his might and made her promise that she would "not let the niggers do to us like the Yankees did."

"I promised Daddy on his deathbed that I'd fight 'em to my last breath."

Tuck told how his pa's landlord evicted them from the tenancy when his pa demanded a two-fifths share. As the family was loading its belongings on the oxcart, a wagon appeared on the horizon heading toward the little house they were vacating. When they saw who was in that wagon, Tuck's pa went into a rage Tuck never forgot—"that landlord replaced us with niggers." Not only that, as the Childs family made its way down the road, it had to endure the humiliation of passing close by the "nigger" wagon. Tuck said with a sneer that he later heard a rumor that to teach the landlord a little loyalty some "boys" had burnt out the "niggers." Tuck intimated that the rumor had relieved some of the hurt, but Brooks knew that a man like Tuck Childs would never forgive.

Ten years had elapsed since that Saturday encounter, but to Brooks it seemed as fresh as yesterday. 'These politicians and lawmen are awaiting the arrival of the landlord Allison, whose boy is dead at the hands of a Negro,' thought Brooks. 'I wonder what Ellie Childs would say.'

Just before Tuck and Ellie had said their good-byes, Ellie drank the last of her lemonade, dipped her snuff, gave a silent sneeze, then fixed her magic eyes on Brooks, "Landlords on one side of us; niggers on the other. The landlords is worse. They let greed get in the way of duty. They hold the niggers over our heads, and they got the politicians bought. Look what happened to old Governor Ferguson when he tried to give us a three-fifths. Can't keep old Jim down, though. At least he's one politician who admits he's in it to take what he can. Can't help but like him, even if he is against the Klan."

"'Well,' thought Brooks, 'here it is ten years later and old Jim is still fighting to take what he can, and this time all the old Klan people are behind him.'

Brooks had never joined the Klan; but Tuck and Ellie Childs obviously had, along with just about everybody else in McLennan County. He wondered if Tuck had been part of that bunch that had tarred and feathered the adulterous white couple caught in that Waco hotel room.

Brooks caught himself shaking his head, 'Well, the Klan's gone but not old Jim and Ma Ferguson. It's amazing that Jim could be disgraced, impeached, and thrown out of the Governor's office; then seven years later run his wife for Governor and win; then be disgraced and defeated for reelection; then six years after that have Ma running this strong race to defeat Ross Sterling. Jim's railing against landlords like Allison, again. Like a lot of politicians, he's making scapegoats of the governor, landlords, Negroes, rich folks, and Hoover; and terrified tenant farmers are listening again. Given the mood of the country, central Texas just might forgive the killer of a rich landlord's son. But would it forgive a Negro who killed a white boy? Would it forgive the Negro who harmed Derden Wofford?'

'Nope,' Brooks answered his own question, 'not if the cry of blood-duty is heard in the farmyards, churches, speakeasies, and living rooms.'

And, State Capitol or not, Brooks figured that the message would be heeded.

The police detective finally walked out of the room where the boys were held and waved at Brooks, "They're all yours, old buddy."

"Thanks, I'll get to you later."

Derden Wofford sat on a bench next to three boys Brooks did not recognize. Wofford's upper left arm was bandaged, and he was wearing a dirty, ragged baseball uniform. When he looked up, Brooks detected a trace of that defiant sneer that Derden was famous for showing hapless batters. The other boys barely turned their heads. A man introduced himself as R. C. Granberry and said he was the redheaded boy's father. From the haze and the overflowing ashtrays in the room, Brooks could tell that Granberry and one or two of the boys had been chain-smoking.

Granberry told Brooks that one of the boys, Robert Cobb, a cousin of young Allison, and another cousin who was not there, had come down from Dallas to fish with Granberry's son, Harry. Allison and his friend "Sonny" Mayes had arrived in the afternoon from Galveston to take the Dallas boys home the next day. With four extra boys staying the night, to get a little peace after dinner, Granberry said his wife and he suggested that Harry show the boys the University of Texas and then take in a night baseball game at House Field Park. The boys left soon after dinner in Allison's car.

Granberry motioned to the redheaded boy, who looked to be sixteen or seventeen, and introduced him to Brooks.

"Tell Mr. Brooks what you told me, Harry."

The boy was still tearful; but he nodded and hesitantly said, "Well, we walked around the Texas campus because Albert was going to start here in September. Then we went over to House Park to see what baseball games we could watch."

Brooks saw Harry glance at Wofford, who was talking to the boy next to him. He had a wad of tobacco in his cheek.

"We was sitting in the bleachers," Harry continued, "and after a while we started talking about things to do after the game. I was the only one from Austin, and I didn't know much; so I thought I'd ask Derden, who was playing for the Magnolia team. Between innings I went down to the field, and Derden said that after the game he'd be glad to show the Dallas boys around."

Harry yawned, paused, and looked at his father, who said, "Go on, Harry. The man ain't going to hit you."

Harry continued with a lowered voice, "After the game, we met Derden on the field, and he said he knew just where to take care of his terrible thirst. Albert said it sounded like a fine idea, and we walked over to Albert's touring car. Derden jumped into the front, and the rest of us got in the back."

In response to Brooks's look, Harry commented, "I reckon we drove out of House Park a little before ten thirty. Derden was telling Albert where to drive, and within a few minutes we was in East Austin. At first, Derden showed us places, like a hotel he thought was pretty famous and the colored college. But it was real dark, and the roads was rough; and I guess Albert liked to drive too fast. Before we knew it, we was on a dirt road with little houses on each side and soon came to a dead end. When Albert drove into a driveway to turn around, the car lights and our yee-hawing must've bothered people in the house because they turned their lights on and yelled. Old Derden yelled back, and Albert sped out of there.

"We suddenly came to an intersection with Chicon Street, which I guess Albert didn't see, and Derden started yelling for Albert to take a right."

Harry's voice had become louder, and the other boys had started listening. As Harry was describing the drive, the boy sitting next to Wofford joined Harry and his father. Mr. Granberry introduced him as "Sonny" Mayes, the boy who had made the trip with Allison.

Harry continued, "The car was going too fast to make an easy turn, so when Albert turned, we skidded some; but there was a T Model Ford that seemed to swerve at us, so Albert had to run into the ditch across Chicon."

Brooks was forming an impression of the boys who been in the car with Derden. Allison was likely a hotshot rich boy who had been in his share of harmless trouble. Harry was one of those boys who went along for the ride. His father had told Brooks that he worked for the Railroad Commission, not a wealthy man. This "Sonny" Mayes did not carry himself like a rich boy, either. But he was no roughneck. These were not the usual cowboys and mechanics that ran with Derden and his crowd.

Brooks saw that the baseball player was sitting alone, so he thanked Harry and Mr. Granberry and moved over to the bench where Wofford was sitting and chewing. Like a lot of athletes, Wofford could be surly and untalkative; but he would be on page one that morning, and Brooks wanted his side of the story.

"Rough night, eh Derden?" Brooks said.

"Shit, Mr. Brooks, it's terrible. I don't know if I'll be able to pitch anymore."

Brooks had met Derden when he attended Austin High's games with the *Statesman* sportswriters. One of them told Brooks that after Derden's father died, his mother had kept him out of school for a couple of years to help with the farm. Derden's detractors said that he looked good only because he threw against boys two or more years younger. But Brooks heard many people knowledgeable about baseball swear that Derden's stuff would beat anybody. 'To them,' Brooks thought, 'and most of Austin, Derden's a genuine hero. What in the world are they going to do when they hear that Derden's been shot by a Negro?'

Brooks took the place on the bench next to Derden. He lit a cigarette and asked Derden if his arm was permanently damaged.

"Naw. It's just a bruise, really. I guess the bullet was pretty well slowed down by going through Allison's body. Thank God it ain't my throwin' arm."

"You mean the shooter hit both you and Allison with the same bullet?" Brooks asked.

"I guess so," said Wofford. "The policeman found the bullet. He just showed it to me."

Brooks said, "Damn. One shot, two down."

Then, after a moment, Brooks asked, "How'd you boys get in this fix, Derden?"

"Well, I guess I heard Harry tell you that the nigger ran us into a ditch on Chicon Street."

"Something like that," said Brooks.

"Well, after the car came to stop, Allison got out and inspected his car. He was really worried, scared that if the car was damaged, his old man would skin him. Then Harry yelled that the Model T stopped and that a nigger was coming at us. I jumped out of the car and saw this guy walking to us. He was hollering something, and I hollered back for him to get on out of there, that we didn't want no trouble. He didn't leave, so I picked up a couple of rocks—you know those limestone rocks they paved Chicon with—and chucked them at him. Some of the other boys did the same thing.

"Then we heard the Model T crank up and start to drive off; to make sure it kept driving I uncorked high heat with a rock the size of a hardball."

Sonny Mayes had returned to the bench and was sitting next to Brooks. He interrupted Derden to say that when the rock hit the Model T, it made a hell of a crack. He obviously meant to give Derden a compliment.

Derden smiled with a sneer and said, "I figured it did the job. Anyhow, Allison spotted a street light at the corner of Seventh and Chicon, by the power station, and wanted to move the car there so he could take a better look at it. We pushed the car out of the ditch, and Allison got it started. After we stopped at the light, Allison inspected the car and was a lot happier. We all got in the car, and was ready to leave, when one of the boys shouted out, 'Here he comes, again.'"

Mayes said, "That was Bob Cobb, Mr. Brooks." He pointed at the boy sitting at the other end of the bench, "Allison's cousin."

"When we saw the car coming," Mayes added, "I guess we panicked. Me, Bob, and Harry jumped out of the car and ran behind the substation. I thought Derden and Albert did, too."

"But," Derden picked up the thread, "we were in the front seat and couldn't jump out so quick. Before you could say 'Jack Robinson,' that Model T was on us. Allison and me just sat there. I remember a black face, a pistol pointing out the window, then a flash and a loud bang. My left arm was burning. I jumped out of the car and picked up a rock with my right hand and threw it at the car as it sped away. I heard it connect."

Brooks looked at Mayes, "What did you boys do?"

"When we heard the shot—I could tell it was a shot—we ran back to the car. Derden was walking around, cussing, and holding his arm. He tore off his shirt for us to look at his wound. Then I noticed Albert still in the front seat. He was slumped over the wheel." Mayes voice started to choke. He wiped away a tear and looked at Wofford.

Derden said, "Sonny here saw that Allison was out and that blood was oozing from his left shoulder. That's when we knew we had to get help quick. Sonny and Harry moved Allison out of the driver's seat, and I gave Sonny directions to drive here."

'So they were marauding a little,' thought Raymond Brooks. He had heard that Negroes had been complaining about white hell-raising in East Austin. 'These boys finally made somebody mad—somebody with a gun, probably a pimp that works for Perry Rhambo.'

Bill Tarver wanted to be resolute, but the Rangers and politicians were going on about "crackdowns" in East Austin and other Negro communities. They wanted to teach the blacks another lesson about harming whites. They felt that by being tough the governor would quell white fury enough to head off the vigilantes. Tarver, however, knew that so-called crackdowns, though comforting to some in the white community, would not improve the situation.

'For God's sake,' Tarver suddenly thought, 'I hope Albert somehow maintains his composure. I hope he can keep a grip on his commitment to civility. If he arrives in a fury, he could personally spark a riot.

'In fact,' the thought suddenly occurred to Tarver, 'whether or not Albert is bent on vengeance, with Derden Wofford injured as well as young Allison dead, to save East Austin from the kind of riot that damn near destroyed Sherman a couple of years ago, the police had better apprehend the killer quickly.'

Complicating Tarver's assessment was a bothersome feeling stemming from his son's demeanor that morning. Bill said that he had seen Albert Jr. at House Park field after the ball game, that Albert seemed to be showing off his new touring car, and that Derden Wofford was hankering for a test ride. That was it. When mentioning Wofford, the boy had averted his eyes and made a strange face. Tarver had thought Bill was reacting to the news about Albert, but then he recalled Austin High's team celebration after Derden's no-hitter last May, and that reminded him that he had not yet confronted young Bill with the comments he had heard about the boys' behavior that night. 'Was Bill recollecting something those boys did? Did he connect their behavior to this tragedy?' Tarver felt a nudge of inexplicable guilt.

Albert Allison found Brackenridge Hospital easily. He walked through the main door, identified himself to the desk attendant, and, heart in throat, asked for the duty doctor. Before she could approach, Bill Tarver, the Land and Agriculture Commissioners, and a few other six footers rushed from the waiting room and enveloped their five-foot six-inch friend. Albert waved at R. C. Granberry and acknowledged the reporters, who stood respectfully in the background. In the waiting room law officers were talking to the four boys, one of whom stepped out of the room and walked carefully to Albert, who extended his arms.

Exhausted, frightened, seventeen-year-old Robert Cobb sobbed dryly in Albert's embrace, "Uncle Albert, Daddy's coming down with Uncle Stanley."

"That's fine, boy. We'll talk later. I want to visit with a few folks for a while."

He turned to the three commissioners. "I'll never be able to thank y'all enough for your kindness and concern." Nodding to the waiting room, "I can see already that the law is being diligent. Any news of who did this?"

Tarver shook his head, "This will be the biggest manhunt in Austin history, Albert. The killer will be arrested. Have no fear."

The Land Commissioner added, "Albert, none of us will rest until this animal is brought to justice."

And the Agriculture Commissioner whispered, "Amen." The vehemence was unmistakable.

Tarver said that Captain Hamer had assigned Earl McWilliams, a Ranger with experience in the colored community, and that Sheriff White had assured him that every available deputy would be on the job before sunup.

Albert nodded, "Ranger McWilliams called me, Bill. He seemed pretty aggressive. I hope he isn't going to take the wrong measures, if you know what I mean."

Albert knew that Tarver knew. Bill said he had already mentioned to Sheriff White that the governor was concerned about heavy-handed police work. The sheriff had told Bill that he was aware of the problem and that he had assigned a young, levelheaded deputy who was a part-time law student, who had experience in East Austin, and who had a way with the Negroes. White was sure he was the right man to keep a Ranger or cop from being a one-man lynch mob.

Albert stolidly nodded at this information and said to his friends, "After I see my boy, I'd appreciate your company when I visit the place where it happened."

Each nodded. Then Albert turned to the lady in doctor's garb, standing a few feet away with a city policeman and a young deputy, later introduced as Homer Thornberry.

Before she could speak, the city detective standing close by said, "Mr. Allison, we need you to identify the bo...boy...your son."

Albert heard the word, the attempt at sensitivity; but he was jarred nonetheless—"the body." His precious son, his own extension of being, a version of the meaning of his own existence had overnight become not Albert Arthur Allison Jr., an identity, creature of God, a Texan imbued with the mysterious majesty of a special new race, a vestibule of his mother's love—but a mere object, an artifact, a body.

Nodding in response to the detective, Albert looked at the doctor.

"Sorry about these interruptions, Doctor, Ma'am."

She smiled wearily, "As I told you last night, Mr. Allison, your son passed before he arrived here. We were obliged to call Cooks Funeral Home to ensure proper treatment. He is there now."

Albert nodded numb understanding.

"Mr. Allison, it may comfort you to know that the boy went without pain."

After a few more words, Albert nodded tearfully and thanked the doctor. The detective offered to take the father to the funeral home.

To the reporters who were beginning to push a little with their questions, Albert summoned his political skill enough to say, "Thank you, gentlemen. Right now, I know less than anyone about my son's death. I'm sure the sheriff'll keep you informed."

Albert had been awake for twenty-four hours; events and words began to blur.

"Where are the boys?" he asked no one in particular. "I'd like a word with the boys before we go to the funeral home."

The policeman guided the father to the waiting room, where the boys were seated on a bench with a few adults.

"Hello Sonny…Bob."

Both said a quiet, "Howdy, sir."

Looking at a disheveled redheaded boy sitting next to R. C. Granberry, he said, "That you, Harry? You've grown. How all you boys have grown."

Next to Harry Granberry, the father saw a tall, thin, unsmiling specter in a dirty, bloodstained baseball uniform. After looking Albert straight in the eye, the specter turned its head to the left to stare at its bandaged left shoulder.

Harry said, "This here is Derden Wofford, Mr. Allison. He was shot, too."

Albert understood that Wofford had been sitting next to Son when the shot was fired. The doctor had said that the bullet had entered Son's left shoulder, passed entirely through his torso, exited the right shoulder, and had hit the fleshy part of Wofford's left shoulder. The police had found the bullet in the front seat.

"What happened, boys?" Albert's red-streaked eyes leveled steadily on Harry Granberry, who looked hesitantly at Wofford.

Wofford did not hesitate, "We was cruising around Austin in Albert's car after the ball game and got turned around over in East Austin. As we turned out of a street to a main road, this Model T come up on our side of the road and forced us into a ditch and stopped a little ways ahead of us. We thought a bunch of niggers was looking for trouble, so we threw some rocks to scare them off. They drove off, and we went down the road to a light to inspect the car. That was when they drove back to us, and, the next thing I know, I hear this loud bang and feel a sting in my left shoulder. I was sitting next to Albert, who was behind the steering wheel. After the shot I jumped out of the car. Sonny seen that Albert just slumped; then I seen his shoulder. We couldn't bring him to. My shoulder hurt awful…We drove here as quick as we could."

Albert could only acknowledge Wofford by nodding. He turned abruptly and walked away in the company of his friends and the police. To Tarver he said, "I'm dog tired, but I know I won't sleep until I see where my boy drew his last breath on earth. After I go to the funeral home, I want to see the place."

The Agriculture Commissioner said, "Albert, this is awful hard. I'm sorry more than you know. You know your friends in this town will do whatever we can to see that justice is done."

The father gripped his old ally's arm as they walked from the hospital. "That's all any man can ask."

At that moment, Albert looked back to see newspapermen talking to the young man in the bloody baseball uniform. 'That's the boy who shared a bullet with Son,' the father thought grimly.

'White, he is so pale,' thought Albert. 'Where is the suntanned body at the end of a cane pole? So still. Where are the quick legs that chased lightning bugs? Twinkling eyes, sweet smile. Breakfast table gags; the newest jokes. He may have been mischievous, but he always sparked.'

'Oh God,' Albert cried silently. 'God gave Abraham a son late in life. Like old Abraham, I lived in complete faith that, despite the miscarriages, God would one day bless Mabel and me with a son—not a son to establish nations, just a son to carry on our tiny part in God's story. Then, that September day in 1913, our blessing from God burst into the world. It wasn't my hundredth year; but, as a man past forty, I could feel Abraham's joy and relief.'

Albert looked at Son so still on the cold, bare table. Standing poised, knife in hand, for all Abraham knew, God had taken his boy, too. It was just a matter of the final thrust. God had given Abraham and Albert their boys, and then for His own reasons He wanted them back. At that moment, at the instant before the angel came, at the instant that Abraham knew that Isaac was gone, God had united Abraham and Albert in the archetypical anguish.

But Abraham's faith saved Isaac.

'Where is the angel today? Oh God, I have faith, I suffer mightily for You. Why, oh, why did you not send the angel to save my boy, too? Is my faith not enough? How did I so offend that You would smite me with a black devil in a black car?'

Shoulders hunched. Albert silently wept and nodded to the detective, "Yes he's my boy; he's Albert Allison Jr."

'But where is the angel?' his thoughts trailed on.

"May I see the wound?" the father asked the undertaker.

"The bullet went through his entire body, sir…into his left shoulder," he lifted the sheet and pointed to a black wound, "and out his right shoulder….The doctor says he met our Maker immediately, sir."

"He didn't suffer," the undertaker added the overused but meaningful words of comfort.

Taking a signal from the father's silence, the undertaker and detective returned to the anteroom where the father's friends waited.

Albert remained alone in his reverie.

'Poor, poor child. If only he had been admitted to Annapolis, he would not be here now. But his damned asthma….He was so disappointed. All of us were. Or maybe if I hadn't bought him that car, he wouldn't be here. Or maybe if I'd been home to stop him from going to Galveston, he'd have been at our Fourth of July picnic, and not here.'

Thus the guilty ifs began to hang on Albert's conscience like anchor chains.

Reluctantly, the father turned from his boy. After ascertaining arrangements to take the boy back to Corsicana, he walked alone to the car where the others waited. Time to go to work.

It was about 6 AM, Saturday, July 9, 1932. The killer was still at large.

Taking care to avoid the ditch beside the rock-paved road, Bill Tarver parked behind Sheriff White's car. The men emerged from the car and walked to Sheriff White and the young deputy who had been at the hospital. Bill noted that Albert was beginning to look very tired. White dust from the limestone paving rocks covered the men's shoes.

"This is colored town, Sheriff. What were the boys doing in colored town?" Albert asked.

"We're not sure why they was over here, sir. White boys come over to go to what folks over here call 'hootchie-kootchie bars.' Right, Homer?" The sheriff briefly glanced at his deputy.

"I haven't talked to the boys myself, but I understand they said they was just driving around. One thing, though, Mr. Allison, Derden Wofford's about the best baseball pitcher in Texas. If he hit that negrah's car with one of these rocks, he had to make an impression. We should be able to find a Model T with small dents in it."

Then the sheriff waved his arm along the north-south street, "This here is Chicon Street. There's the electric substation." He was pointing to a structure on the corner of Seventh and Chicon Streets. "The shooting happened around there."

Albert looked around, slowly, intently; it seemed to Bill that he was mentally photographing the scene. Occasionally, Albert would take out his handkerchief and wipe his eyes. A few cars drove by slowly; the drivers could not avoid staring at the official cars and uniforms.

"Skid marks over here," the young deputy called Homer soon announced, pointing to the west side of Chicon opposite Eighth Street.

Albert walked to that spot and followed the marks to a spot in the ditch where tire and skid marks clearly depressed the weeds. Contemplating, dabbing his eyes again, he turned away from his inspection. He seemed to be resigned.

"Seems the boys drove out of there," Tarver said, pointing to the unmarked dirt road the sheriff called Eighth Street. "They must've turned right and somehow skidded all the way across Chicon Street into this ditch on the left. The other car must've stopped down there."

"Seems so, Bill," commented John McDonald.

"But," Deputy Thornberry recalled, "the boys said they were attacked at the substation further down at Seventh and Chicon."

The sheriff suggested the entourage drive two hundred yards south to the intersection of Seventh and Chicon Streets.

At the substation the tire disturbances were plain. "The car was parked here," the sheriff said quietly.

Everyone respectfully gave the father room.

Bill Tarver bowed his head. 'Life is so fragile,' he thought. 'Just eight hours ago, right here, a mere instant sent young Allison into oblivion.'

After a few moments, Albert said that he had seen enough. He thanked the sheriff and the deputies, and Bill drove Albert and the commissioners back to Brackenridge Hospital. Bill then took Albert to his house to await developments.

Two blocks from the substation at the little house on Salina Street, Charlie Johnson was in a deep, peaceful sleep.

5

Worms

Mabel Cobb Allison escaped July afternoons by writing in the reading room. There, shaded air breezed through two large windows to provide enough relief from the heat to accommodate her muses. Most days she wrote long, thoughtful letters to friends and relatives or cajoling, persuasive letters to children in camps or colleges. She knew from reactions that her correspondents delighted in her word-craft and discomforting common sense. Some days she recorded the rhymes that invaded her reveries, sometimes sentimental, sometimes sardonic, always loving. These rhymes no one read; these she carefully filed in the rhyme book labeled "Worms," which she locked away in her desk drawer.

The night before, after Albert had departed and after the shocked family had drifted off in chairs and couches around the living room and porch, Mabel had finally managed to find her way to the bedroom. Her sleep was full of Son, bright and happy; but when she awoke, she felt such an ineffable emptiness that she knew she had become a smaller version of the self that she had been. Son was her fulfillment; he had vindicated the life she had chosen when she met Albert.

Following a haphazard breakfast with no help from the absent housekeeper and laundress, Emma, Mabel's children and relations allowed her a few minutes alone in the reading room. As she opened the desk drawer to remove "Worms," words and rhymes flooded her tired mind. For a time she toyed with the jumble of images and fondled a few words, but, they did not satisfy, so she rested her pen.

Mabel had worried about Albert's late-night drive, but nothing would stop him. Typically, within minutes of Granberry's telephone call, he had become a whirlwind of activity: issuing orders while dressing, demanding coffee, and then, as soon as Evelyn and Ed M. arrived, speeding off. He had not even asked Ed M. to go with him.

The call to Evelyn's younger sister, Juliet, had been awful. Evelyn was still hysterical, and little Eloise could not talk. 'Thank goodness Juliet's young husband is strong and sensible,' thought Mabel. He had assured Mabel that they would get there as soon as possible. Later he called back to confirm their arrival by train from Chicago on Sunday morning.

Albert did not call until after seven that morning. He said he was calling from Bill Tarver's home and had not yet been to bed. He sounded exhausted. That she expected, but to hear him so subdued bothered Mabel. Albert was always so defiant in adversity. He told her that his political friends, especially Bill, had greatly comforted him, and that he had talked to Bob Cobb. Albert supposed that Delmore, Rob's father, was on his way. Albert's voice trembled as he told her about the place where Son last drew breath. Mabel heard herself moan when he described the scene at the funeral home. The boys, he had said, had been driving in Son's Chevrolet in the colored part of town and had some kind of altercation with a Negro driving a Model T Ford. The Negro had shot into the car. Every lawman in central Texas was hunting for him. Then, Albert told Mabel that more than anything at that moment he wanted to hold her in his arms and mourn their boy. He would be home by nightfall.

Mabel ached for her Albert, too. They had held each other during her miscarriages; they had held each other when the telegram arrived saying that poor Perry had been killed while guarding a train the day after Armistice; and they had clung to each other each time one of their parents died. And such different parents—Albert's father, Arthur, the unreconstructed Confederate merchant with his three-eighths Indian wife, and Mabel's father, Lodowick Cobb, the reconstructed Southern judge with his Yankee wife. 'What would they have said about their grandson's demise? Would Arthur Allison instigate a lynching like he did for the Negro that killed Albert's brother Andrew?' Mabel shuddered as the memory of that Thanksgiving in 1895 came back like a terrible omen.

She was sixteen-years old, attending the Sherman Normal School for Girls, and had returned to Groesbeck for the Thanksgiving holiday. Her brother, Delmore, had met her at the train station, and they had barely exchanged pleasantries before he announced that a Negro had killed Albert Allison's big brother Andy the previous week. Mabel had had only a passing acquaintance with the Allison family, mainly from church, where the previous summer Albert had paid her enough attention to evoke a little teasing from Delmore.

When Delmore first mentioned Andrew's killing, she had been horrified about Andrew and sorry for the Allison family, but her feelings turned to confusion and revulsion as Delmore explained further. Arthur Allison—Andrew and Albert's father—had led a mob that removed the Negro from the jail and had taken him to a lynching tree outside of town. Delmore said that their father, the judge, was still fuming.

Judge Cobb was actually between offices at the time, having completed his two terms as Limestone County Judge and not yet having been elected District Judge. But he was still a force for civility in the community, and Mabel knew that nothing sent him into a rage like lynching.

That Thanksgiving Day, after helping clean up from the meal, Mabel walked onto the porch where her father and Delmore were talking. Her father glanced at her and turned back to his son. Speaking a little louder so that she could hear, Judge Cobb confirmed what Mabel's sister Bunny had told her earlier. The judge had been in his office the morning that the Negro had killed Andrew Allison. He had heard the screams and shouts and walked out to see a mob forming around a terrified Negro. When the judge approached the crowd, he saw two bodies on the ground; Andrew was dead from a gunshot, and a small black boy had obviously been badly beaten. Judge Cobb had immediately leapt onto a wagon and asked the men to bring the Negro to him. The judge said he held his breath while they fidgeted, but someone called him "Judge," and that gave him a stamp of author-ity, so they did as told. The judge then managed to lead the Negro, whose name was Parsons, through the mob to the sheriff, who had finally arrived. The judge said Parsons had cried over and over that Andrew had killed his boy. Apparently Andrew had caught the boy pilfering from his wagon and had pistol-whipped him.

The sheriff took custody of Parsons and placed him in the jailhouse. But the sheriff was conveniently absent when his old friend Arthur Allison arrived that night with a torchlight mob.

'That was how Andrew forever would be remembered,' thought Mabel. 'Par-sons's ugly, unjust lynching is the ugly, unjust final act in the ugly, final chapter of Andrew Allison's life. Is that to be Son's story? Would Judge Lodowick Cobb have treated the black killer of his grandson with the fairness for which he was famous?' Mabel was not sure of anything at that moment; but she knew that if they caught the Negro, she would have to think about these matters. So would Albert. 'What would Son want?' she thought. 'Does it matter?'

In that moment of reverie, Mabel almost heard her son say "Mama, don't be sad. Let it be. Just smile, and think of me."

When Son had left home to prepare for Annapolis at Marion Military Insti-tute in Alabama, the one thing Mabel missed was his happy, whistling morning departures for school. "Bye, Mama. I'm throwing you a kiss that'll last you all day"; then to the boys waiting in the front for the group-walk to school, "Hey! I'll race you!" When he arrived home from school, usually late, usually a little mussed from a scuffle or some such mischief, he often brought a bouquet of wild-flowers for his "favorite mama." He could charm, he could spark, he could lead.

'He could have,' Mabel sighed, and the tears came again. Without Son, the world was grayness, dread, meaninglessness.

'But,' she remonstrated to herself, 'I still have wonderful Albert, five wonderful children, and two beautiful granddaughters.'

Mabel had married Albert almost thirty-two years before in Groesbeck, Texas, after a courtship defying both sets of disapproving parents. Judge Cobb and Mabel's mother had no use for Arthur Allison's stubborn affinity for the old South. Arthur Allison hated Yankees so much he had refused to attend church after the Methodist conference sent a young man from Ohio to be Groesbeck's new preacher. One could only imagine what Arthur thought about Mabel's mother, born and raised in Iowa, or even Mabel herself, the daughter of a Yankee. He was always civil and courteous to them, but never charming, as Mabel knew he could be.

But Albert was not his father's son, at least with respect to Negroes, the South, and the old Confederacy; and over time Mabel's father warmed to him. "He got me with mathematics," Judge Cobb had said at the family dinner table the day Mabel turned eighteen. "Your beau is an expert mathematician; he figured out for himself that immutable, rational laws govern both nature and human nature, and that the most civilized people are those whose actions are most compatible with reason and the law." In those days, the judge spoke in such profundities; but at that moment Mabel had not heard the courtroom philosophy. Instead, she had heard her father saying, "If you love him, I approve." Her private thrill gave her such a blush that little sister Bunny broke out with her infectious laugh, bringing the entire dinner table to one of those rare joyous moments.

Albert was Limestone County's official surveyor at the time; four years before, Harvard University had awarded him the George Peabody Medal for Mathematics.

'Indeed,' Mabel mused, 'Albert's a mathematician, and I'm sure he made numerous computations on how to please the judge.'

At that birthday dinner, one of Mabel's siblings teasingly asked the judge, infamous for his faulty personal financial accounts, if he, too, was a mathematician. But their father did not respond with the witty, self-deprecating comeback the family expected. Instead, he became serious and said that in a way he was a mathematician, just as young Albert had said. Then the judge started talking about his youth, about how his being the son of Methodist missionaries to Arkansas Choctaws firmly wedded him to the law.

"First," the judge said, wagging his finger just a little, "my parents, who opposed slavery (though they bought slaves to keep families together), taught me that the essence of respect for God was to respect the law.

"Second," he said, looking warmly at the opposite end of the table, "your mother gave me the backbone not to waver from my deepest sense of justice. Third, my own experience showed me the utter savagery of life without the law. In fact, both your mother and I know it too well."

Then, after hesitating, the judge spoke evenly. "I'm going to tell them, Eva. They must know, and they must never forget."

Mabel never forgot. And as she mourned for her lost son that morning, the judge's words flooded back and pounded on her as if to instruct her. She wondered if the judge had sent an angel to steel her for the days ahead.

At the end of the Civil War, young Lodowick Cobb had helped his parents deed the farm to their ex-slaves on which they had been living while his parents had run their school for Choctaw girls in another part of Arkansas. That was when young Cobb had found that he had a knack for handling tedious procedures and paperwork.

Reconstruction had imposed civility on most of Arkansas; but in the remote Ozarks where the Cobbs lived, breakdown of civil authority had driven whites, blacks, and Indians into a savage war of all against all. That viciousness convinced Cobb that to protect lives and property, all men must be brought to heel under the law. For him, that meant the eternal, immutable law of the scriptures, which gives existence coherence and meaning, and which necessarily supersedes the will of the mob majority. Individuals, young Cobb had decided, could govern themselves; and a majority could govern their communities. But neither an individual nor a majority could govern justly outside the law.

By 1876, when the Yankees left, Cobb had secured his law degree from Vanderbilt University and had served two terms in Arkansas's Reconstruction legislature. He did not run for reelection that year because a one-armed Confederate major wanted the job, and that was fine with him. He had done his duty; his law practice in Harrisburg thrived; and, besides, his young wife was pregnant.

In those days, the judge told his family, he and their mother had every reason to be optimistic. He said he had even thought he could come back to politics in the future.

Then one March Saturday in 1877, Lodowick was in town when a mob dragged a young Negro, accused of molesting a white girl, from the city jail.

Mabel clearly remembered how her father warmed to the story as his lips curled, his eyelids narrowed, and his voice mockingly took on familiar country accents.

"At first, the subdued churchgoing townsfolk and farmers were just curious. 'Hey Ma, lookee at those men headed for the jail. Let's have a look, Jethro. Why, they got a nigger. He the one that leered on the Campbell gal? Look at that animal son-of-a-bitch. There's old Campbell with a whip. Goldarn. That nigger's going to be red meat. Yee-haw!'

"So Jethro and Ma and hundreds of others set aside their afternoon plans for the important work of community justice.

"Well, I jumped on a fruit box nearby and tried to speak, but someone knocked me off, and before I could get to my feet, a young man I did not recognize laughed and swung a boot into my ribs, grunting 'nigger-loving lawyer.' A young lady spat tobacco juice on me. Confused, disgusted, embarrassed, I could do nothing but stumble the two blocks home."

At this point in his story the Judge had paused. For a full minute he looked at each of his children, and then his eyes rested on their mother, who nodded with pursed lips. As if in resignation, the judge raised his eyebrows slightly, sighed, and continued.

"Two hours later, your mama and I still heard screams pierce the general din created by a moonshine-heated mob. With terrible frivolity, they responded to the occasion with a banjo band and a quartet singing 'Old Dan Tucker.' The stench permeating the night breeze brought us to tears. Your Mama's rage made her so sick she could not leave her bed for two days.

"We couldn't go to church the next day. On Monday, my partners avoided me. I was a pariah. Two days later they made their offer. I accepted. I told them that we would be leaving Harrisburg.

"We decided to move to Groesbeck because we thought Texas was far enough away from the hatred of the War to be free from lynching and such. By the time we arrived in 1878, however, we found a seething hatred leftover from Reconstruction. And, with the military gone, the old rebels had taken strong measures to reestablish Southern control. Only, unlike Arkansas, the Groesbeck Negroes were fighting back. We had moved into the middle of a vicious, underground race war."

Nonetheless, the young lawyer had quickly established a thriving practice. Six years after arriving, he was elected county judge. After serving three terms, the Democratic State Convention nominated him for district judge. Soon after, he and the family moved the thirty-five miles to Corsicana, where the district court was located. By then Albert and Mabel were married.

Mabel was not sure when Emma had slipped into the reading room. Mabel must have had her head on her reading desk when she felt the bony calloused hand of this little black maid who had attached herself to the family.

"Honey, I is so sorry." Her face bore an unfamiliar, terrible look, her voice croaked painfully, "I is so sad, I be crying ever since I hear."

"Thank you, Emma," Mabel replied.

"It's that ol' owl," Emma said. "I try to choke him, but it don't work, and now poor Son be dead." As she spoke the final words, she broke into sobs.

The mention of the owl jarred Mabel. Emma had long entertained the Allison household with stories of the haints and devils that frequented her world. So when about two weeks before, Emma had become increasingly agitated about a screech owl in the neighborhood, Mabel humored her by listening with feigned seriousness. As the owl's distinctive, mournful cry seemed each night to be closer to the Allison house, Emma became more agitated. Late one afternoon Mabel spotted her scattering coffee grounds around the perimeter of the house and the bases of the backyard trees. When Mabel inquired what she was doing, Emma explained that used coffee grounds would keep the screech owl away, and that if the owl were to get into the premises, some member of the family would surely die.

A few days later, Emma told Mabel, "That ol' screech owl got hisself in this yard last night, but I choke him before he get a chance to screech."

When Mabel asked how she managed this feat, Emma replied, that "I just turn my pocket-wrong-side out and throw a little salt on the fire and it sure choke him every time."

The family had had a good chuckle when Mabel related the newest Emma story. But as Emma talked that morning, Mabel tried to recall if she had heard the owl's screech after she and Albert had retired the night before. She involuntarily shivered. She recalled nothing. But Mabel Cobb Allison was a sensible woman. She emphatically assured Emma that neither she nor the owl was responsible—that Son died as result of a terrible tragedy. That was all.

Looking at Mabel as if pitying her lack of comprehension, Emma shook her head and began to whimper. Mabel rose from her chair to cradle the desperate little woman in her arms.

6

The Arrest

After the father and his friends had left the scene of the murder, Homer Thornberry and a montage of peace officers from various agencies waited there for instructions for the next step.

Standing next to Homer, a deputy took a long drag on a cigarette and surveyed the quiet neighborhood surrounding the intersection. "The newspaper's hitting the west side about now," he said. "That's gonna stir up a lot of trouble. Sheriff White don't just want to catch the killer. They're getting every officer in the county over here to give them old Klan boys pause before heading this way." Homer pursed his lips. 'God, I pray we're enough,' he thought.

After a few minutes, Sheriff White walked over to Homer's group and said that he planned to return soon to the courthouse to face whatever mobs might collect there.

"Ranger Earl McWilliams is in charge," he told them. "I want y'all to be fully cooperative and to remain close to him."

Homer saw White's eyes flick in his direction. He realized the sheriff had caught his frown. As the sheriff walked from the group, he motioned for Homer to follow.

Out of the others' hearing, the sheriff said, "Homer, I know McWilliams' reputation, and I'm worried as hell that he'll really make a mess. That's why I want you to stick by him. I want you to make sure he don't start busting heads or molesting people. You understand? I know he's been a lawman since before you were born. Don't let that scare you. You understand?"

Thornberry nodded.

The sheriff held his eyes for another ten seconds, then said, "Okay. Look, that dead boy's daddy has a lot of big-shot friends. Believe me, by now the governor hisself is taking a special interest. Him and Mr. Tarver have a lot of confidence in Captain Hamer; that's why the Rangers have moved in on the situation. Captain Hamer has a lot of confidence in McWilliams. That's why he insisted that

McWilliams be in charge of the search. Wasn't no use talking about race riots or anything. I hope to God we find the killer before sundown."

Homer's mind flicked to the horrible consequences—everybody knew about Sherman and Waco. He linked his eyes to the sheriff's steady gaze and nodded. The sheriff told Homer that McWilliams and a constable had left the hospital a few hours ago to check the outlying Negro communities to see if they could spot any Model Ts recently battered by rocks. If they had no luck, they were due to rendezvous at this spot before 8 AM.

The time was just before eight.

"Okay," the sheriff concluded. "I can't wait any longer. I got to go. Who knows, maybe McWilliams found the killer."

Homer understood Sheriff White's concerns only too well. Earlier in the year he and McWilliams had been friendly enough to spend time together drinking beer at the icehouse and going to a few ball games. In fact, they saw Derden Wofford pitch that no-hitter a couple of months ago. ('That Derden has a way of bringing old Earl and me together,' Thornberry thought wryly). At the time, McWilliams, a bachelor, had only recently joined the Rangers after serving twenty-some years as a deputy down in Bexar County. Soon after arriving in Austin, he had looked up Homer. He said that he was a "sort of Mexican-Negro specialist" and that he had heard that Homer had the same reputation. This was news to Homer, but he went along with it. 'Better to be a specialist at something than just a part-time law student,' he had thought. But Homer knew his reputation was not entirely undeserved. He had been on a number of calls to East Austin, mainly to collar cowboys getting out of hand in the hootchie-kootchie bars. He had spent enough time there to develop respect for the way its people lived. Sure, they had clubs and whorehouses; of course, they were ignorant and poor. But most worked every day and went to church every Sunday, trying to find an honest way to fit into a white world that rejected them. They encountered this world with a grace, wit, and good humor that would do credit to whites in these awful Depression times. He guessed East Austin must have appreciated his attitude because they had opened up to him when he needed help and had not hid very much behind that famous black wall of silence.

Homer had no illusions about the meaning of McWilliams's "specialty." When McWilliams was a deputy in San Antonio, he reportedly apprehended or killed dozens of murderers and bandits in parts of town his colleagues dared not enter. As a result of four legendary, Hollywood-style shoot-outs, he carried in his right thigh the lead badge of battle that caused his slight limp. At first, such ruggedness and daring impressed Homer; but McWilliams also impressed the young deputy with stories that strongly hinted at graft and brutality at the expense of the barrio residents. Partly because Homer stopped thinking of McWilliams as a worthy colleague, partly because McWilliams seemed to detect Homer's discomfort, their friendship had been cooling for some time.

That friendship had gone into deep freeze about ten days earlier at the icehouse. During their evening beer time, McWilliams had bragged to Homer and a group of policemen about how he extracted the confession from the young Corsicana Negro accused of killing the East Austin undertaker, Nathan Rhambo. Homer had cringed as McWilliams chuckled about taking the boy from Corsicana to Waco to Austin and back to Corsicana, about sleep deprivation, beating with fists and rubber hoses, hanging by the wrists, and water torture. None of the officers had smiled. McWilliams had grinned weakly, then forced a laugh, and sneered that, to finish the boy off, he talked the Corsicana sheriff into arresting the boy's mother as an accessory and telling the boy she faced twenty-five years. Homer would never forget McWilliams's face when Homer remarked with his own sneer that anybody who could stand that treatment for eight days was probably innocent. Thornberry had punctuated that remark by pinging a well-aimed wad of tobacco juice at the spittoon.

'Well,' Homer said to himself, 'I guess the sheriff must know what he is asking. God, help us find that killer quick.'

McWilliams arrived at the rendezvous a few minutes after eight, accompanied by a deputy constable. Thornberry and his fellow officers immediately gathered around. After McWilliams asserted that he was in charge of the search for "that murdering black devil," he said that he and the constable had thoroughly covered possible hideouts in the county and found nothing.

"Sure," he declared, "the killer might have hightailed it like that Corsicana nigger did after he killed that undertaker, Rhambo. But the chances are the boy is still in East Austin. Our job this morning is to turn the place upside-down to find out."

Looking straight at Homer, McWilliams said, "Men, everybody knows that tension's been building over here this summer, and we've all heard rumors that the niggers are getting ready to start a fight. Now it looks like they've gone and done it. To stop 'em, we have got to show who's boss. We have got to catch this boy and make the niggers see what happens when they kill one of us."

The officers said nothing, not even a grunt; some shuffled their feet; all their faces hardened.

"There was a lot of noise last night," McWilliams continued. "Cars was skidding around—one or more gunshots, shouting, and rocks being thrown."

McWilliams pointed to the little houses and shacks on the east side of Chicon Street, "Somebody must've heard something. You deputies go talk to these people. Constable, let's you and me have word at Rhambo's hotel."

Then, "One more thing. Keep your eye out for that Model T. Derden Wofford and the other boys threw rocks so it may have some marks, especially if Derden connected."

Each deputy took a different street. Uninvited, Homer followed the Ranger and the constable to Rhambo's. Other than a set jaw and a short dark stare at the younger man, McWilliams showed no sign that he was bothered. Homer likewise said nothing. As the officers approached the door of the hotel, Homer remembered a police officer at the hospital telling him that Derden Wofford had said that the boys had come to the east side to get beer. 'Mr. Allison will not be pleased if his son is implicated in beer,' Homer mused. 'Won't look so good if the boys were beered up and raising hell in colored town.'

Rhambo's hotel bar had probably closed at two or three that morning, but the officers knew that the bartender and some of the ladies stayed there; so they knocked loudly. Soon an angry, sleepy, black woman of considerable girth threw open the door, ready to yell until she saw the three uniformed white men wearing stars. Wrapping the bright red robe more completely around her, she backed and waited.

Thornberry spoke, "Morning, Daisy"

"Morning to you, Sheriff."

"We want to ask you a few questions. Where's Perry?"

"Mister Perry's been holding up at the farm since Mister Nathan was killed. Come on in."

The three officers followed the large woman into the bar, which reeked of stale beer and used tobacco.

McWilliams barked, "Wake everybody. Get them in the bar."

Thornberry added, "Especially Johnny. Get Johnny here now."

They got no argument. She went to the back of the large room and started yelling into the cubicles. Soon Johnny, the bartender, and half a dozen disheveled, robed women were standing in the bar. A few minutes later, a bare-chested cowboy, carrying boots and wearing his sweaty hat, sheepishly crept through the bar area to the door. The officers ignored him.

Before McWilliams could say anything, Thornberry nodded at the disappearing cowboy and asked, "Any other white boys in here last night?"

"Course they was," replied Johnny. "You know white boys in here most every night, Sheriff."

"Any of them in a baseball uniform; say, after ten o'clock?"

Silence. Thornberry could see Johnny and the others contemplating: 'Where's this going to take us? Is some poor brother in trouble?'

Johnny answered, "Not last night, Sheriff. Sometimes a whole bunch of baseballers come here, but not last night."

The constable was taking notes. McWilliams and Thornberry exchanged glances.

McWilliams asked, "Any y'all see anything…last night. Out on the street, Chicon Street."

Again, silence. Heads shook. Nothing.

"Except for a couple of cowboys who bloodied each other, nothing happened. No knifing, no bad fighting, and nothing outdoors. Just music and girling with the usual folks and cowboys." Johnny's gold front tooth shone out of his slight grin.

"Who y'all know that's got a Model T?"

Silence. Then Johnny spoke again, "Nobody here, Sheriff. We ain't got no cars. Mister Rhambo, he drive a Buick."

"Any of you know anybody in East Austin with a Model T?"

Blank looks. The code was taking over. If they did know, they wouldn't say.

McWilliams narrowed his eyes, tightened his lips, "How many times y'all see this many laws working together? Y'all will hear soon enough that there's more officers out in the neighborhood asking questions. We're looking for a negrah in a Model T, and we're going to find him. You know what that means. It'll be real hard on anybody who don't tell us what we need to know. Understand?"

Smiles vanished behind grinning white teeth and eyes widened in mock fear signaling the ancient defiance.

"Yes sir. No sir, we don't story. Anybody knows anything about a Model T is going to tell you, Sheriff. Sure enough."

McWilliams looked at Thornberry, "Let's go."

To Johnny and the girls, "Y'all think hard. We'll be back to get answers. Nobody wants trouble. Understand?"

As the officers headed for the door, Thornberry caught Johnny's eye, which held his in silent understanding. It was approaching half past eight. People were now reading about the murder in the *Austin American*. Thornberry wondered how many men had already been to their gun cabinet. Time was running out.

Back at the rendezvous point, a deputy reported that a few people had complained about white boys raising hell. One household had complained about bright headlights shining into folks' houses. One lady said she had heard shouting and cars late last night, but no gunshot.

As another deputy was about to report, McWilliams broke in, "Well, I'll be doggone. Lookee here." He immediately straightened his posture and folded his arms. Thornberry turned to see Johnny on the other side of the street ambling in their direction. As he approached, Johnny waved but made no move toward them. McWilliams motioned for him to come to them. Johnny made an exaggerated gesture of surprise and submission, then sulked across the street.

Thornberry almost smiled at the obvious acting. 'He's sending a message,' Thornberry thought. 'Folks in the houses would see the law leaning hard on one more brother. "Maybe a Friday night killing," they were guessing. "But seems more than that—all these lawmen," a husband would say to his wife. "Old Johnny's in the wrong place," she would respond. "He's going to catch hell."'

"You thought of something there, Johnny?" McWilliams asked.

"Might be, Sheriff. It's them white boys. They be coming by most every week. Sometimes they stay, sometimes they buy some beers and go. One baseballer, he always throw a rock at the door when they drive away. I guess he want to show us that he can throw real strong. When that rock hits the bar door it crack like a gun."

Johnny was confirming the officers' suspicions. The boys were doing more than driving around East Austin, and Derden Wofford must have been one of the hell-raisers causing complaints from East Austin residents. But, Homer knew, the bartender had not come to them to tell them that.

McWilliams asked, "You the one with the Model T, Johnny?"

"Naw Sir! Taint this poor nigger. Only a few people in East Austin got Model T's. Course you knows them—like old Charlie Johnson."

"Charlie Johnson?" queried the Ranger. "Who's Charlie Johnson?"

"He be that old teacher that worked for Mister Nathan Rhambo."

Homer noted that McWilliams almost jumped at Johnny. 'Could last night and Nathan Rhambo be linked somehow?' he wondered. Like his fellow officers, Thornberry assumed young Allison's killer was a young buck, probably a bootlegger or pimp (had enough money for a car): mustache, pomaded hair, handy with a switchblade, meaner than hell. "Old teacher" did not fit, but the association with the late Nathan Rhambo was too compelling not to follow up.

"Where does Charlie Johnson live, Johnny? Who else has a Model T?" a deputy asked.

"Boss, I don't think I knows where Charlie live. I don't know who the Model T'ers is, either. Maybe old Charlie Johnson ain't a Model T'er. Nobody going to live long in East Austin that know anything more."

'Well, he knows, of course,' thought Homer. 'Johnny's worked up the courage to come to us, but he's just realized that he's close to crossing a dangerous line. The wrong move one way, and East Austin'll punish him. The wrong move the other way, and the Ranger'll beat him. He's afraid, and he's shutting down.'

Thornberry knew that if McWilliams leaned on the Negro or took him in, the entire east side would shut down, and Charlie Johnson would be hidden for a long time. Without another thought, Homer took Johnny by the arm and led him away from McWilliams and the other officers. He motioned for the others to leave him and Johnny alone, and then quickly reassured the bartender.

"Nobody's going to lay a hand on you, Johnny. I personally guarantee it. We just need your help."

McWilliams, caught by surprise, stayed still for a moment, but only a moment. Hitching his britches, McWilliams made a move toward Thornberry and Johnny. Thornberry threw up his hand, palm out, facing McWilliams like a traffic cop ordering a car to stop. McWilliams stopped. Then Thornberry tried a tactic with Johnny that McWilliams himself had taught him a couple of months before.

"What about a Mexican, Johnny? Would a Mexican know where Johnson lives? Would a Mexican tell us if he knows anybody who owns a Model T?"

"Meskin? Why there's a few Meskins that lives around here." Johnny's eyes got wide, "Sure enough there's a Meskin in the bar last night. There two, three hours."

Johnny realized that Homer had tossed him a lifeline.

"Name's Frank Ruiz or something like that. He say he be in a rooming house over at Salina and Second Street. He talk big, like he know all about East Austin."

"We can find this Ruiz's rooming house on Salina Street?"

"Yes sir. There's two, three Salina Streets. This Salina is by Second Street."

"Stay here, Johnny," Thornberry ordered.

He walked back to the other officers and faced McWilliams squarely, "He's given us a lead, and I'll check it out. It won't take much time. Leave Johnny where he is until I get back."

For a moment, Homer thought McWilliams might remind him who was in charge; but the Ranger just spluttered and gestured that Homer should get going.

Just before 9 AM, Homer drove down the rock-paved Chicon Street to Second Street and turned right. He bumped along the dirt road until it intersected with another dirt road with a wooden post designating "Salina Street." He turned onto it and stopped in front of a lot full of weeds. When he surveyed the street, his heart gave a mild leap: 'Well, I'll be dog.' A Model T Ford was parked in an open shed two houses down on the other side of the street. 'Thanks, Mr. Frank Ruiz,' he chuckled to himself. He walked over to inspect, and he saw immediately that its windshield had been broken and that it had been dented by something like rocks. The telltale white chalk marks meant that they were recently caused. He checked the address: 205 Salina Street. When driving back to the rendezvous area, Homer saw an empty *Austin American* delivery truck heading west on Seventh Avenue.

Saturday morning, July 9, 1932. The *Austin American's* banner headline slapped a waking Austin in the face:

NEGRO SHOOTS YOUNG MAN TO DEATH
Derden Wofford Is Wounded by Bullet Fatal to Dallas Man

Worried politicians, university professors, and businessmen wondered if the city's time had come. The Depression was hitting hard; the Fergusons were threatening at the polls; and the heat was oppressive. Now Negroes have started killing whites. "Better check the gun cabinet," the community said in unison. "Derden Wofford of all people."

Attorney Mae Yelderman looked over the breakfast table at her husband Bill and asked rhetorically, "Why did the *American* have to put it that way? 'Negro (not a man) shoots young man (innocence) to death (Negro equal vicious animal).' God, what a paper!"

> *Albert Allison, 18, of Dallas was shot to death shortly after 11 PM by a negro who drove alongside a car driven by Allison in the 600 block of Chicon Street, in which rode Derden Wofford, Austin high school student and baseball pitcher.*

The Dallas boy's name was familiar only to politicians and some employees of the Department of Agriculture. But Derden Wofford was a famous athlete. He had pitched that no-hitter in the championship game. "Shot in the arm by a colored," the indignant chorus sang. "We can't let the coloreds shoot down the cream of our youth like this."

> *Wofford was injured in the left arm by a .45 caliber bullet which went through the body of young Allison. Other persons in the car besides Allison and Wofford were*

Robert Cobb of Dallas, John Mayes of Corsicana and Harry Granberry, 1610 West Avenue, Austin.

Cobb was in Austin on a vacation while Allison and Mayes were stopping overnight en route to Dallas from a vacation trip in Galveston.

According to information given by City Det. Ted Klaus, the boys had been driving in the eastern section of the city, when Allison, unfamiliar with the streets, drove into a blind alley on East Eighth street. They turned into Chicon street when the negro approached in his car and drove them into a ditch.

"Yep," the chorus chanted, "they was catting around. Boys been catting around in East Austin since Prohibition. This Negro must have been drunk and mad, probably about a woman. First time a white boy's been killed in East Austin. Lot's of coloreds killed in Saturday-night knifings, but never a white boy. By God, he'll be the last one, too. These coloreds are getting fresh and need to be taught a lesson. The sheriff better be getting up a posse."

Negro Followed Them

He stopped a short distance further on and words were exchanged between him and the boys. The boys continued on their way down Chicon to the city power plant substation in the 600 block. They stopped there to see if their car had been damaged when it went into the ditch, Klaus said.

The Negro circled the block, drove alongside the youths' car and fired a bullet at Allison, who was sitting at the wheel. The negro escaped.

Allison's companions took him to Brackenridge Hospital but he was dead when they reached the place. His body was taken charge by the Cook Funeral home and the boy's father, A. A. Allison, who resides in Corsicana, was notified by R. C. Granberry, of 1610 West Avenue, of the killing.

Fired at Close Range

The bullet, Det. Klaus said, was fired not more than three feet from Allison. It entered his left arm, continued through his body, exited the right arm, and struck Wofford in the left arm. Wofford's wound, however, is not serious.

Police early Saturday morning had spread throughout the city searching for the killer, but had no trace of him.

The chorus cried that the war had started, and every man must do his part. Head for the courthouse to help old Coley White find that mad dog killer. Find him before he kills again, before they get the idea they can kill white folks just like they kill each other.

Travis County Democratic Party Chairman John Patterson leaned back in his chair, cup of coffee in hand, and looked at the name again. 'Of all things, Albert

Allison's boy. Albert was one of the nigger-lovers in Chicago. Bet he'll be spitting blood now." Patterson's thoughts raced, 'Damn, must've been an out-of-town darky, like the one that killed Rhambo. Coley mishandles this, and he's beat for sure.'

James Pinckney Hart, the assistant district attorney and candidate for district attorney, read the article once, then again, and then he called the sheriff at the courthouse.

"What about this killing, Coley?"

"Pretty much as the paper says, Jim. According to the boys with him, the Negro drove right up to the car and fired almost point blank. The police even found the bullet in the car."

"How we doing on finding the killer?"

"Right now every Ranger, sheriff's deputy, constable, and policeman in this county is working on it—mainly in East Austin. We're stopping every Model T with a black driver. If we don't come up with something quick, we'll have a lot of help I don't want. Some of the old Klan are sitting on their cars outside right now. But it's not those fools I'm worried about. Many good folk blame the negrahs for this Depression. Something like this could spark these people to take out their hurts on East Austin."

The sheriff paused; Hart said nothing.

Then the sheriff said, "Maybe you and Henry should come on down here."

"I'll call Henry and see you soon."

Jim Hart hung up. Henry Brooks was retiring from the district attorney's job because of times like this. Then, for just an instant, Hart wondered if he was a fool to be talked into running for the job.

By 8 AM, an unusually large crowd of black men and boys had gathered at Delashwah's Drug Store on East Sixth Street. Amid nervous sips of Delashwah's famous coffee, old men fretted over childhood memories of the white fury. Young men flicked their knives.

"That fool don't just kill any white boy. Damn, he killed the boy of the governor's best friend. That old governor is going to have to kill a hundred of us to make up to that boy's daddy."

"Hell, you knows those boys was aiming for trouble. They throw rocks, hit people, run us off the road, and call us names. No police ever do a thing. Bet the whites stop now, even if the sheriff don't kill any of us."

"I heard they's looking for Jim Boudreau. They say him's the only nigger crazy and mean enough to shoot that gun."

"Hell, bet you a week's pay that the killer was on the prowl looking for Perry Rhambo. He just happen to run into them white boys and decide to use the gun on them instead."

"Lord, lord, there're five, six them police cars down the road around Chicon."

On the streetcar, maids riding to their jobs in west-side homes said, "White boys at it again. Now one's dead. Somebody can't take it no more. Now we're all in for it."

"My Henry say 'taint a East Austin man. The killer be out of town, like that boy who killed old Rhambo."

"Hell, I don't care if they burn us out. About time we stood up to them white devils."

"I'm gonna tell my lady that she and the boss got to do something. I don't care if we not supposed to talk about white and black things. This summer them boys've gone too far. Now one of them's dead, and we're going to catch hell for something that's not our doing. My lady going to hear about it from me, even if she's not supposed to."

Homer Thornberry sped back to the rendezvous point at Chicon and Seventh Streets and jumped out of the car. The officers were talking to several Negroes. Johnny was standing away from the group and alone. Thornberry glanced at him and smiled.

Taking McWilliams aside, Thornberry said, "Earl, we may have him. There's a Model T parked in front of 205 Salina. It's marked pretty good; could've been pelted by rocks."

McWilliams immediately said to the officers, "Let's go. Constable, dismiss these folks for now. You and the deputies follow us."

Minutes later, two official cars turned off Second Street and pulled up in front of the yard full of weeds. Across the street the officers could see a Model T parked in an open shed beside a small frame house. With weapons in hand, the officers got out of their cars and walked to the shed.

"Yep. This car's been hit with rocks." McWilliams said to Homer. "There's a hell of a dent in the right rear, and residue of white dust in several marks—probably from a limestone rock. That's got to be from Derden."

Without a word the officers moved toward the small house.

"We have no warrant. We can't just break this door down," Thornberry reminded them.

McWilliams said, "What we going to do? Say, please?"

The other officers frowned. Homer did not respond. He went to the door and knocked loudly.

It was about 9 AM.

"Just a minute. Who's there?" came from behind the door.

"Open immediately. It's the sheriff," Thornberry had his Smith & Wesson cocked and ready. The other officers were aiming their pieces. They had to assume that the voice came from an armed killer. After a long moment, a short, slight, balding, light brown man, adjusting his glasses, opened the door. He was still in boxer shorts.

"Yes sir, Sheriff?" Then he saw the guns, "Oh Lord save me...blessed Jesus."

"We are here to ask you a few questions. Can we come in?" Thornberry asked.

"Sure enough, Sheriff, ya'll come on," the frightened man said, "What's the trouble?"

Homer edged into the small living room with the other four officers right behind him, guns cocked. Shades still covered the windows. A few books were open on a bare wooden table. One small toss rug was in the middle of the floor, and a well-worn stuffed chair was by a window. A card table was covered in papers that looked like coupons. Through a doorway they saw a nightstand next to a single unmade bed in a small bedroom. To the right, a door opened to a small kitchen.

McWilliams asked the man his name.

"Why, it's Charlie Johnson, sir. Can I help y'all?"

"Anybody else home? Where's your wife?"

"Nobody here but me, Sheriff. Ain't married. I be alone."

"That your car in the shed, Charlie?"

"Yes sir."

"You drive it last night?"

"Yes sir. To the church."

"Any trouble with anybody?"

"Just white fellows throwing rocks, Sheriff. One hit me right here," pointing at his forehead, "but it's really nothing."

"You own a gun, Charlie?"

Quietly, "Yes sir."

Homer noted a change in Johnson's demeanor and thought, 'He knows we're on to him.'

"Let me see it," McWilliams continued.

"It's in the nightstand drawer in the bedroom."

A deputy retrieved the bone-handled Colt .45 pistol. An empty cartridge was loose in the drawer. A quick sniff verified that the gun had been fired recently.

McWilliams waved his own pistol at Johnson and snapped, "You murderer! Prepare yourself for the hanging tree."

Before McWilliams could do more, Homer Thornberry deftly yanked Johnson away and started to tie his hands behind him. "You're under arrest, Charlie. We're taking you to jail."

"What's the matter, Sheriff?" Johnson's voice was a quiet plea.

"You fired that gun last night, didn't you, Charlie? You went after those white boys and shot them, didn't you?" Thornberry said.

"They threw rocks at me and chase me. I fired the gun to scare them. Didn't hurt nobody."

To his fellow officers, Homer said, "Earl and I are taking Charlie in. Y'all stay here and gather evidence. I'll send someone over to get fingerprints and take pictures."

From then on, nobody talked. After Johnson dressed, Thornberry tied his hands again. With Johnson between him and McWilliams, they walked from the house to the Ranger's car.

Homer noticed that a small crowd of silent witnesses had gathered just far enough away not to be obtrusive.

Thornberry drove and McWilliams sat in the back with Johnson. After a few minutes, in the rearview mirror, Thornberry spotted brass knuckles enveloped in McWilliams right fist. He was nudging Johnson's left arm with them.

"Do you want to tell us about it, Charlie?"

"Tain't nothing to tell, Sheriff," Johnson's voice audibly quivered. "Them white men almost run me off the road, then they was rocking me and cussing me. I thought they was after me to kill me sure. So I drove by their car and fired one shot. I only wanted to scare them. Then I come on home. That's it."

Making an exaggerated turn of his shoulders to look back at McWilliams, Thornberry said, "Well, Earl, congratulations. Everybody said you were the specialist, and now you've proved it again."

"Thanks, Deputy," oblivious to Thornberry's sarcasm.

But the Ranger put the brass knuckles away, and barked at Johnson, "You just remember that you confessed in front of two officers of the law, boy."

Just before ten, the officers hustled Johnson through the growing crowd milling around the courthouse. "That the killer?" one burly man shouted. "Let us at him." The crowd moved forward, but the officers were inside before any real threat could develop. They immediately ushered Johnson upstairs to the sheriff's office, and McWilliams announced, "Well, Charlie here says he done it. Ain't that right, Charlie?"

Thornberry thought the interrogation was remarkably straightforward. Johnson no longer acted afraid. In fact, for a doomed man, he was unusually self-possessed. Not cocky, not defiant, not angry, just concerned. He seemed to be a man at peace with himself. During the interrogation, the more the pressure mounted, the more dignified he seemed to be.

By eleven o'clock, Johnson had signed a confession. The sheriff had Thornberry take Johnson to Judge Frank Tannehill, where Assistant District Attorney Hart had Johnson formally arraigned for murder in the first degree and committed to the county jail pending a grand jury hearing. At noon, Sheriff White held a press conference in which he handed out carbon copies of Johnson's confession.

July 9, 1932

I, Charlie Johnson, after having been duly warned by Coley C. White, Sheriff, the person to whom this confession is made, First, that I do not have to make a confession at all and Second, that any statement made may be used in evidence against me on my trial for the offense concerning which the confession is herein made, wish to freely and voluntarily state the following facts without any compulsion or persuasion of any kind being used on me, and for the sole and only reason that the facts stated are true, vis:

That on the night of July 8th, A.D. 1932, I attended a Bible School entertainment (at the Annie Davis home on Chestnut Street, scratched out) in Austin Travis County, Texas, at the Rising Star Church, after the entertainment I took Mrs. Annie Davis home on Chestnut Street, then I went to Fourteenth Street and from Fourteenth Street to Chicon and from Chicon Street on over to Tenth St., some boys in a car coming up the street with the top down crossed in front of me so close they lost control of the car and ran into a ditch. They got out of the car and began to throw rocks at me. I drove on ahead and they caught up with me at Seventh Street and began to chunk rocks at me again. I had my .45 pistol, which the officers recovered at my home, on the seat of my automobile. When the boys began to chunk rocks at me at the corner of Seventh Street and Chicon Street, again, I shot at the one driving the car. I then went straight on home and went to bed. I looked back and saw that they had evidently lost control of the automobile they were driving as it ran upon the curb, this was immediately after I fired the shot at them. About Nine o'clock the morning of July 9th, A.D. 1932, Paul Blair, Jack Newman, Arthur Cowery, Ranger R. E. McWilliams and Homer Thornberry came to my house and arrested me and I turned over to them the gun and the empty shell which was on a table, and which I took out of the gun last night after I got home. This statement I have made is

true and I am guilty of firing the shot and wish to plead guilty and ask the
mercy of the Court, I further wish to state that after I fired the shot, the boys
again threw rocks at me. All of this happened in Austin, Travis County Texas,

/s/ Chas. E. Johnson

Witnesses
/s/ Coley C. White
/s/ R. E. McWilliams
/s/ Ben T. Morrall, Jr.

In response to reporters' questions, the sheriff replied: "This incident happened between the five boys and Charles Johnson only. No one else was involved. We anticipate no trouble from anyone white or black on this matter."

"We understand that some people are outraged and want to take Johnson right now. But it ain't going to happen in Austin, not in the shadow of the State Capitol, not with me here."

"Yes, I'm confident we'll be able to hold Johnson here. There's no need to take him to another county for safety."

Homer Thornberry prayed that the sheriff would not have to eat his words.

7

Encounters

Hiyah Pop, laughed the eighteen-year old with twinkling blue eyes. What are you doing here? We're having a fine old time. They had a big party in Galveston. You remember. You would've liked the fireworks. Hey Pop, I guess I'll not be seeing you much, but don't worry. I'm in a safe place, and I know you loved me.

Suddenly the father was talking to a sandy-haired, ten-year-old: Son, your mama tells me that you shouted a bad word at that yardman. Didn't mean nothing, Papa. I just called him "nigger." Mama already bawled me out. I won't do it again, Pop. I promise, replied the ten-year-old.

Then the eighteen-year-old was back. Yeah, Pop, no more. We were in colored town, but I didn't shout "nigger." Ha-ha, Pop. Nope, Pop. The others? Maybe, Pop. There comes a Model T, Pop. Oh Papa, the driver's face is so black, so mean, his white teeth in a wild smile as he points the gun! BAM! Where am I, Papa? Why did you let me get here? Come get me, Papa. I don't like it here.

I'll get you, Son. Get up from that slab and let's go.

Lookee here, Pop. It's Granddad Allison. He got here before I was born, but he's taken me to his heart. The familiar face in the familiar white suit and white broad-brimmed hat came into view. He looked suntanned and fifty. Hello, boy, now you've done it, too. You've gone and got your oldest son killed by a darky, just like I did. See, your brother Andrew's here, too.

Two figures emerged arm in arm from behind the figure of Albert's father, who had become a tired, sad old man, dressed in the new Confederate uniform that he wore to the reunion barbecues. One figure was Andrew, Albert's older brother, dressed in chaps and a high-peaked hat. The other was Andrew's son Perry, born after Andrew was killed on a Groesbeck street. Perry was dressed in the World War I Army uniform he was wearing when he had been killed in France.

Howdy, Uncle Albert. Say hello to Aunt Mabel.

I will, dear Perry, the dreamer said.

Albert's older brother, his jaw now missing, said nothing as the dreamer pled with their father. What should I do, Father? Tell me what to do.

Justice, boy, Justice, said the old Confederate.

But what is that, what is justice? the dreamer asked the ancient question.

You know the answer, boy. Remember Groesbeck and the white man's duty.

"Albert, time to get up. Delmore and Stanley are here," Bill Tarver was shaking his shoulder. The room was already heavy with midday heat. After Albert washed and dressed, he went into the Tarver living room to greet his brothers-in-law, who had just arrived from Dallas. Delmore, Mabel's brother, was young Robert Cobb's father. Stanley was one of Albert's closest friends and married to Mabel's sister, Bunny. His son Stanley Jr., had not gone with the boys the night before. The men told Albert that they had stopped by Cooks Funeral Home, but Son was already on his way to Corsicana. Stanley added that Albert's son-in-law had already made arrangements with Corsicana's First Methodist Church to have services at 5 PM the next day, Sunday. Before the father could react, Bill Tarver came into the room.

"They've made an arrest, gentlemen," he announced. "He's confessed."

Albert was jarred by the size of the crowd at the courthouse. Tarver had said he had hoped that the arrest would dampen folks' enthusiasm for vengeance. But too many grim faces suggested that Tarver's hopes were far-fetched. As the four men walked through the crowd toward the deputies guarding the courthouse door, one man with a rifle slung over his shoulder said, "Y'all are late. They got him. Don't need us no more."

Tarver replied with evident relief, "Yep, the party's over. Everybody can go home." But another armed man said, "Hell, lots of people'll be here soon. The fun's just beginning."

The deputies opened the door for Albert and his companions and led the men to Sheriff White's office.

After pleasantries and condolences, Bill Tarver said, "Well, you boys made quick work. What have you got?"

"Yes sir," Sheriff White responded, "Everybody with a badge was out there. Arrested the man in his own home about nine o'clock. Woke him up."

The sheriff went to his desk and picked up a paper.

"Here's his confession." He handed it to Albert, who looked at it for a while, said nothing, and passed the paper to Tarver.

District Attorney Brooks told the men that he had dispatched his assistant, James Hart, to ask the judge to convene the Travis County grand jury immediately.

"Gentlemen, I assure you. Justice will be sure and swift."

Brooks then informed Delmore Cobb that his son and John Mayes would be needed as witnesses on Monday. Cobb nodded. He had already mentioned to Albert that he expected to be staying in Austin a few days.

"What about the fellows outside?" Albert asked.

"Mr. Allison," the sheriff replied, "you know those people. They live scared, especially of the coloreds. Something like this gets them stirred for a while, but they come to their senses before they do anything. Except for one tar and feathering in the Klan days, we've not had a lynching or anything like it in Travis County in living memory. And we don't aim to start now."

White spoke the last sentence evenly with emphasis on each word. 'The sheriff's serious about doing this right,' Albert thought. 'That was a prudent warning in case I or my friends have any ideas.'

He nodded in recognition of the sheriff's professionalism and asked, "What do we know about the Negro?"

"Well," said the sheriff, "He's about sixty. Seems not to be married. He says he's a schoolteacher at a colored school out in the county. One of my deputies tells me that folks in East Austin say he's been selling insurance for a number of years."

Again, Albert nodded.

A deputy came into the office to say that the police had no more need of young Allison's Chevrolet. Albert asked his brother-in-law, Stanley Kerr, to take the car back to Corsicana. Stanley responded that, with permission, he and his son would leave immediately so that they could be back at a reasonable hour. He said he thought he ought to be with the family.

As the men rose to leave, Albert lingered in his seat, hat in hand. Henry Brooks, half rising from his seat, sat down again, but the sheriff stood.

"I want to see him," the father said with force in his voice. "I want to see this man face to face."

Albert noticed that Bill Tarver broke eye contact with the sheriff and gazed out the window.

When the sheriff said nothing, Albert continued, "I know it's unusual, but I have no weapon and am in no position otherwise to inflict harm."

Sheriff White looked at Henry Brooks, who shrugged and widened his eyes to signal "why not?"

"All right, Mr. Allison. The deputy will have to search you anyhow; and Mr. Tarver and Mr. Cobb will have to stay here; but you can see him."

The sheriff went to his door and asked Homer Thornberry, who had just reported for duty after a few hours sleep, to step inside the office. Thornberry would escort Albert to Johnson's cell.

◆   ◆   ◆

Heat penetrated every cubic inch of the cellblock. It seared skin-pores and scorched the passageways to the lungs. Charlie Johnson had been lying on his cot, in his underwear, thinking about the taunting from the Stewart boy who was two cells away. "Hey I knows you. You the Rhambo runner. You be Charlie Johnson. Remember Forest Stewart's Funeral Parlor? Remember my daddy? Did you kill my daddy, Charlie? Why they bring you in, Mr. Runner? Did somebody catch you cheating mister white man out of his winnings?"

Charlie tried to ignore Stewart. Another inmate told the young man to shut up. Charlie worried that an official might hear Stewart talking about Johnson's ties to policy. 'How'll it go for me if the law know about my running for Rhambo?' he fretted.

When the young deputy they called Homer came to Johnson's cell and said that the white boy's daddy wanted to see him, the old terror took hold.

"He here? What for?"

Charlie jumped up and pulled on his clothes. His instincts told him to look around the cell for that tree stump.

"Don't worry, Charlie," the deputy said. "He's not going to hurt you. There are plenty who would, but not him, not yet anyhow."

Waiting for the deputy to lead him to the cell, Albert's mind again filled with images of the black beast—hate-filled yellow eyes, a drooling sneer. 'School-teacher, pshaw! Bible study, indeed! Nobody believes it. That time of night? He was honky-tonking, armed and looking for a fight.'

When the deputy signaled Albert to follow, he steeled himself. 'I'm here for my boy. I have to take the measure of the animal that killed my boy.'

Following Deputy Thornberry into the stifling, stinking cellblock, Albert felt the stares of surly black inmates. Then he saw Johnson, almost gasped, and, without a moment's thought, removed his hat. Before him stood a slight man, a man with a light brown complexion, a slightly balding man, a man his own height, a man his own age, a man who stood erect and who looked at him sympathetically, but evenly without averting his eyes.

In that instant, Albert saw himself. 'They said he was a schoolteacher, so was I when I was young. They said he worked in insurance to supplement his income, just as I had worked in my father's store when I taught.'

Albert was looking at a man of dignity, a human being.

After a nervous moment, Johnson spoke. His voice was steady, respectful, but not obsequious, "I'm so sorry about your boy, sir. I be praying for him and you and everybody who loves him." Tears streamed down his face.

Albert could not respond. He wanted to scream, "Why?" But he only gave the man an understanding nod, and brushed aside a tear. After a moment Albert broke eye contact, replaced his hat, and motioned to Thornberry. The other prisoners had remained quiet during the brief encounter; as the father walked away, they rustled loudly, coughed, and murmured. Before the cell door slammed shut, Albert heard one voice, "Well, Mister Rhambo-man, you killed yourself a white—and it looks like a rich one—and to think I only killed myself a Rhambo."

Albert considered himself sufficiently erudite to pinpoint the right word or expression for most events, but he doubted he would ever be able to articulate adequately the sum of impressions that pounded his consciousness during the encounter with Johnson. The words "dignity" and "man" returned to him time and again, together with the unsettling feeling the he and his son's murderer shared a common identity.

Albert did have a word for the growing crowd he and Tarver encountered outside the courthouse.

"I see the makings of a mob," Albert said as they got into Bill's car.

"I'm afraid so," Tarver replied. "But I doubt it will amount to much. The sheriff's a capable man. I'm sure he'll get this thing to run out of steam pretty quick."

Bill Tarver had cancelled both his Houston speech and his Sunday campaign schedule in order to drive to Corsicana that afternoon with Albert. He would stay with his in-laws, attend the funeral Sunday afternoon, and return to Austin by train immediately afterward. He was struck that Albert seemed so subdued after they left the courthouse, and for almost a hundred miles, Bill watched Albert doze feverishly in the passenger seat of the speeding Buick. 'Sure,' Bill thought, 'the man has just had the shock of a lifetime and has had little sleep in almost two days. Why shouldn't he be subdued?' Still, it seemed strange not to see Albert bursting with plans, fidgeting to get on to the next phase. Tarver also wondered what Charlie Johnson was like. Albert had not said a word about him.

As Tarver navigated through Waco, Albert stirred, yawned, and said that he bet Bill could use some shut-eye, too. Albert told Bill to stop at a gas station; he would take over the driving. Then abruptly, he asked, "What do you make of this mess, Bill."

"Well," Bill responded. "No doubt, the boys were out too late and were in the wrong part of town. But seems to me this Johnson way overreacted by firing at the boys…unarmed boys. It was like he was looking for a fight."

"You think the boys could have provoked him into justifiable self-defense?"

'Strange,' thought Tarver. 'Why would Albert be thinking about justification, especially for a Negro who killed his son?'

"Doesn't appear that way to me, Albert, but we know so few facts. One thing we know for sure is that Johnson's a Negro who killed an unarmed white boy."

Albert was quiet for a long minute.

"Bill, Johnson is not a brute. He has an air of dignity about him. Like you would expect from a sixty-year-old teacher. He killed Albert, that is certain, and for that reason I want him to pay. But he is not an animal…" Albert's voice trailed off.

'Teacher. That's what bothered Albert,' Bill thought. 'To Albert, teachers are next to holy men. In speeches he has called them "officers in the war on ignorance" and "missionaries of progress." A Negro might have killed young Allison, but so did a teacher who's a Bible student.'

"I guess I'm confused," Albert continued. "He was my son. Anybody that hurts him I want to tear limb from limb, and that includes a man like Johnson. When I heard that Johnson's a Negro, it somehow made me even angrier. But Johnson's no mean black buck. In another situation, I figure he's a man with whom we could have a sensible conversation."

After turning onto the Corsicana Highway at Bell Mead, Tarver pulled into a gas station. Albert asked the sweaty attendant for the restroom, and Tarver asked for water. When the attendant returned with a cup, he asked if Tarver had heard about that Corsicana boy down in Austin.

Tarver's stomach churned with the all too familiar anger in the man's sun-wrecked face. Tarver's political eye noted that the name on the man's overalls was "Tuck."

He nodded, "Yep, Tuck, terrible thing."

"Calls have gone out all over central Texas. Boys are getting up caravans to head to the Travis Courthouse. Can't let armed niggers gun us down in cold blood, even down in tea-sip town."

Tarver grunted. The last thing he wanted was someone talking like this in Albert's presence. When Albert returned, Tarver had already paid and was in the passenger seat. Albert drove away, and Tarver closed his eyes. But the snarling face of the sunburned mechanic peering back at him prevented sleep.

'They say that old Waco Kluxers were in the Sherman riot a couple of years ago.' Tarver thought. 'Damn, that was terrible. If that mechanic is serious, Sheriff White's going to have a time this weekend.'

Albert dropped Bill Tarver at Bill's in-laws' house and drove to the home that he had left a mere eighteen hours before. Cars were parked down the street. People were everywhere, even in the yard in the sweltering heat. Neighbors, family, and acquaintances had brought heaps of fried chicken, potato salad, pecan pies, biscuits, hominy, and black-eyed peas. Mabel sat on the living room sofa hand in hand with her daughter, Evelyn, surrounded by a half dozen mourning women. Hysterical teenage girls clustered in the dining room with Eloise. Albert's sons—Lod and Ken—sat in the porch swing. Lod's arm was around his younger brother. Older men leaned on the porch railings, shaking their heads, sipping shine, smoking, and sharing stories about Son's escapades. Albert made his way to Mabel and Evelyn, and they fell into one another's arms. The ladies stood back and bowed their heads.

After a moment, Albert said, "Mabel, I'm so tired. I have to go upstairs for a spell. Please tell everyone how much I appreciate their support and concern."

Even though people stayed well into the night, the father did not come downstairs until morning.

8

Charles Johnson

Charles Johnson could not sleep in that strange place, on that strange bed. Through most of the night, Carl Stewart kept up a stream of taunts. "Hey Charlie, those white folks getting plenty worked up. They going to get in here and take you brown ass to the hanging tree. Then you pants be brown with your shit."

"Hey Mister Numbers Man, your old boss in the cold, cold ground, and they think I done it. Well, maybe I did. Maybe I killed that old thief, and maybe you be next. Old Rhambo shit all over himself when he see this boy got him. Maybe I'm in here just so's I can get you, old man.

"Hey Charlie, you remember my daddy? You remember how you sent that killer to my house and lure my daddy to his death? Course, you remember—and I damn sure remember you.

"Charlie, listen to them people outside. They preaching about justice for the white boy—looks like tonight be you last. Hope you be praying hard. Must be the whole city out there howling to rope your ass and chop it up and burn it. Bet they already burn your house and car and wife and children. Too bad, they get you before I does."

Charlie knew better than to respond. At one point, one of the deputies came in and told Stewart to be quiet, but Stewart soon started up again.

And the crowd did worry Charlie.

Charlie had heard the shouts soon after the deputy had brought him to his cell—"Hey, Coley, bring him on out here." "Hey, Sheriff, let's get this over with." As evening approached, the crowd seemed to grow. Periodically, the shouts would start; then Charlie would hear the sounds of somebody preaching. He could not make out the words, but he knew Stewart was right. He knew the crowd was out there to lynch him.

While Charlie lay still in his cot trying not to think of the heat and trying to ignore the mob noise, the young deputy they called Homer came to his cell and said, "Charlie, those folks are blowing off steam about a lot things, not just you. Times is hard for everybody, and people just want to hit out. But they ain't going to get in here, Charlie; don't you worry none. By the way, I seen you play the blues music once when I was checking on some trouble at Perry's. You're pretty good."

"Why, thank you, Sheriff."

Charlie had never met a white man he trusted. That's why he never worked for whites or went to the white sections. But this young man looked him straight in the eye, man to man, like that poor Mr. Allison.

As frightened as he was, as much as Stewart annoyed him, Charlie was most bothered that none of his friends could see him. Of course, they dared not try. But he had left Rhambo's business in limbo, and nobody else knew what to do. Maybe he was going to hang soon and shouldn't care. But he did care. When they buried him, he wanted all his accounts in order. What's more, he had talked to Reverend Black about holding the first drawing of the resurrected lottery at the Rising Star Baptist Church next week. 'Well, that won't happen,' thought Johnson. 'Reverend Black was looking forward to his cut. He'll be disappointed; because I'll be here listening to that Stewart rant—if I ain't been lynched.'

Charlie's thoughts turned to the previous Monday night, July 4, at Perry's having a quiet drink with Louis Lyons. "Colonel," Charlie had said to the man everybody called "Colonel," "I be at Nathan's office all day today. I be there every day and most every night since Perry asked me to. You ever seen that mess? Old Nathan ran 'policy' on scrap paper. They ain't no records—no record of agents, no record of commissions, no record of winnings. He made all that money from all over Texas by the seat of his pants. I tell you something else, Colonel; no matter what Perry say, I just can't do it that way."

"But," Charlie added, "we should kick off again in the week or so."

"Man, I hope so," Louis had responded. "My grocery business can't support us these days. My family got to have that commission. And I tell you something else, Charlie: East Austin need the hope."

◆   ◆   ◆

'Colored folks's "hope" made Nathan Rhambo rich,' Charlie reflected. 'That and their haints and their fear. A $50 win on a policy ticket make a big difference for a week or two. Then they go back to handing our agent a dime or nickel for the hundred-dollar win that never happen. Old Rhambo took their money for their hope, that is, if he hadn't already took it for their fear. Funny how few people knew that Perry and Nathan had been partners in the policy game. I don't think they were partners in many businesses, because Nathan wanted to be as respectable as possible; and old Perry ain't respectable. But I bet they was partners in politics, too. Old Louis was Nathan's main vote man to keep the preachers in line, but everybody know that Perry butter up the big wheel politicians that sneak a drink in his club.'

Charlie chuckled to himself. 'No wonder old Perry would often lift his glass and say, "God bless Baptists and Prohibition." Because of them, the law shut down Austin's infamous "Guys Town." When the girls had no place to work, when the law started chopping up west-side gin joints and harassing west-side speakeasies, the business and the girls came to Perry Rhambo's Hotel and Club in East Austin, the land the white man's law forgot.

'Oh, the law come around often enough—Rangers, deputies like that young Homer fellow, even Sheriff White hisself. But they came more to partake than interfere, though they would become "official" after a killing or a serious fight involving a white boy or white working girl.

'But now Nathan's dead; and since Perry didn't do nothing in "policy" 'cept send his thugs to collect from a cheater once in a while, he had to have someone who knew something about the business run it for him.

'He say, "Charlie you're the teacher; you teach Nathan's son Everett the business. Nathan trusted you enough to run the agents in central and north Texas, and Nathan say you know more about the business than anybody else—besides hisself, of course."

'What could I do? I owe them Rhambos everything—the house, the car, the clarinet. But that don't make old Charlie any more confident. In fact, it make old Charlie plain nervous to have to make decisions with nobody's help. For Louis Lyons's sake, for Everett Rhambo's sake, for the sake of all the agents, for the sake of East Austin's hope, those decisions got to be right. And now I cain't do nothing about 'em.

'Lordy, it's hot in this cell. Hot and still on a never-ending night. Damn! Just thinking of Nathan's agents make me nervous.'

Nathan Rhambo didn't have hotshots selling for him. He had every respectable man in East Austin, including teachers like Charlie and professors at Huston and Tillotson. At first, they just sold Rhambo's burial insurance, and they were glad for the money. Then Nathan and Perry set up the lottery they called "policy," and they let their insurance agents collect for that, too. Later on, Nathan let his original agents bring in new agents under them—small businessmen like Louis Lyons, and doctors and dentists.

'Nathan did a lot for men like me,' thought Charlie.

His mind turned to a day seven or eight years before when Nathan had asked him to help expand the business outside East Austin. Nathan told Charlie that Perry used his influence with a powerful lawyer, who regularly brought his political friends to the club, to help Nathan organize the Texas Negro Undertakers Association. The lawyer made sure the state charter authorized the association to approve the licenses of Negro undertakers and to operate its own insurance company. Nathan planned to use undertakers in colored towns all over Texas to sell the association's insurance (Nathan was a major shareholder); and, while they were at it, he would offer them the opportunity to be policy agents, just like in East Austin. Nathan wanted to focus on the smaller and midsize towns, where the business wasn't already controlled by the Dallas or San Antonio gangsters. He figured Perry's boys could discipline cheaters anywhere in Texas, but he did not want to start a war he would likely lose.

Charlie slowly turned in his bed. The crowd outside the courthouse was singing, but Charlie could not make out a recognizable tune. Stewart continued to shout his insults, but Charlie was becoming inured, and he was exhausted. Then, just as he seemed to be drifting into sleep, a mosquito buzz aimed at his ear and put his mind into a whirl again.

Charlie had always been skeptical about the effectiveness of Perry's boys. Nothing he had seen in eight years caused him to be more confident. Old Nathan's reputation kept East Austin in line, not Perry's boys. Charlie smiled to himself.

Sometime before the war in Europe, when Nathan was still an assistant at Mr. Tears' funeral home, Mr. Tears let out that Nathan was "at home with the dead." That's when folks meeting the young undertaker on the street started giving him a smile and a tip of the hat and then walked a little faster in the other direction. Nathan was a man "at home with the dead," a man who caressed the dead, who prepared the dead for their place with the old folks, who served as their escort through the passage into the other world. Folks would not want to cross him, not even professors, doctors, and teachers. 'Yes,' thought Charlie, 'nobody in East Austin cheat such a man. Nobody cheat old "Papa Labat," 'Recalling the long walking stick with the top hat perched on it that leaned in the corner of Rhambo's office, Charlie smiled at the mystique with which Nathan surrounded himself.

After the war, a New Orleans voodoo priestess who called herself "Madame Lebeaux" came to East Austin and began reading palms. She told some ladies that Nathan looked the picture of Papa Labat, the spirit who used a long walking stick to guide folks to the beyond—and sometimes back. East Austin already knew that Nathan was "at home with the dead." The priestess told them why. And Nathan did his best to make sure they kept thinking it. Off and on, he would take midnight walks through the heart of East Austin wearing that top hat, taking long strutting strides, while wielding the walking stick.

But Charlie could not smile at the stuffed screech owl that Nathan kept on his desk. When Charlie was working in Nathan's office, that owl seemed to watch Charlie's every move. Out of the corner of his eye, Charlie could see the owl nod or grimace or open its mouth to let out a silent screech. Charlie dare not touch the bird, so he had asked Nathan's son Everett to move it. But the young man refused. Nathan had told the boy that the screech owl was the family totem.

"Always respect the screech owl," Everett said Nathan had told him. "He bring the world his death song, but he bring us our wealth and fortune."

'Well, Nathan,' Charlie mentally said to his dead benefactor, 'that owl ain't brought either of us much luck. But it's little wonder we never had cheaters in this town. I wonder if we could convince our runners that old Nathan'll punish cheaters from his grave. I doubt it; but with me in this fix, we'll never get the chance to find out.'

'Anyhow,' Charlie reminded himself, 'undertakers who became our agents in central Texas never give a damn about those things; but they did give a damn about their licenses. So Nathan had himself made the association's treasurer and chairman of the licensing committee.'

The previous Wednesday evening, Charlie and Nathan's son, Everett, had sipped lemonade on the porch of the funeral home with Nathan's employees. Even though there was no undertaking business, the employees managed to keep busy for the pay that Perry promised. They could not stop themselves from talking about the night Nathan was killed.

9:30 PM, June 21, a Rhambo employee had opened the door to a young man dressed in a gray suit and wearing a Panama hat. He asked for Mr. Rhambo.

"He looked about twenty-five or thirty, black as me, and not much taller than you, Charlie," said the woman who answered the door. "And he did ask for 'Mr. Rhambo,' not just 'the undertaker.' But I didn't think nothing of it 'til the sheriff asked me about it."

The woman asked what the young man wanted, and he said he needed Mr. Rhambo to tend to his grandmother.

"He said she'd died in his car, which he had left on the Round Rock road about five miles north of town. He said he couldn't face driving the car with her in it; so he took a taxi here. Mr. Rhambo had been preparing old Mrs. Jackson in the downstairs parlor, and heard me and the young man talking. After Mr. Rhambo came to the door and asked a few questions, one of the embalmers offered to go with the young man and drive the car back. But Mr. Rhambo said he didn't want his embalmer driving. Since the driver had the night off, Mr. Rhambo said he would drive the young stranger out to his car and tend to the poor lady. Mr. Rhambo and the young man left in Mr. Rhambo's Buick, and everybody else went home."

After a pause to sip her lemonade, the woman said, "I thought it was strange that Mr. Rhambo wasn't here when I got to work next morning. But I sure didn't know nothing was wrong until the deputy knock on the door." She glanced at Everett and choked back a tear.

The deputy took all Rhambo's employees to the county jail, where he, the sheriff, and some Rangers spent the entire day and much of the next morning grilling them about their involvement with a Carl Stewart.

"Why hadn't they gone with Mr. Rhambo? How much money did Mr. Rhambo have on him? How much money did the stranger pay them?"

Before too much of the morning had gone by, the deputies turned nice and let them go. The deputies told them to tell everybody that justice would be done for Mr. Rhambo. They told them that Mr. Rhambo's body, all shot and beat-up, was found in the back seat of his wrecked Buick one-hundred-fifty miles away, twenty miles west of Corsicana. They told them that they had arrested this Carl Stewart after he tried to talk the funeral director in nearby Hubbard into driving him to Mexico. Some of these things, the woman admitted, she had heard from the deputies that morning, and some she had got from the newspaper the next day.

"Just think about it, Everett," the woman concluded. "You daddy so big in this town that the sheriff hisself, even the Texas Rangers, drop everything to chase down his killer. Hell, he even make the front page of the newspaper. I know it take more than a week to get that Stewart to confess he do it, but the main thing is that this town sure give you daddy first-class white man's treatment."

Everett's face broke into a reluctant grin.

'Yep,' thought Charlie, 'old Nathan must be strutting all over hell with a smile wider than the Devil. And here I am in this cell listening to his killer and wondering if next week I'll be selling policy for Rhambo in hell. Maybe Carl's daddy and me'll be on the same sales team."

Carl's daddy, named Forest, had been an undertaker in Corsicana and one of the first policy agents Charlie had signed up and trained when he started working central Texas. Things went well for a few years until Forest told Charlie that a local white businessman had asked Forest to switch from "policy" to his lottery. Forest said he suspected that the white man represented a San Antonio syndicate; and he assured Charlie, "they can't offer me enough to make them white gangsters rich." A short time later Forest disappeared. His wife, Alice, said a young man had asked him to help with a grandmother who had died suddenly. Forest went to help and never returned. ('Man, that's a familiar way of getting people,' Charlie thought.) For a long time Alice was convinced Forest had run off with another woman. So, because she knew that Forest would be back begging for forgiveness and because Forest had just hired a qualified embalmer, Alice and her teenage son Carl continued to operate the business. Charlie even worked with Carl for a time teaching him to run numbers. It was during that time that Charlie learned that Alice bought poll taxes for folks on the east side of Corsicana and organized them to vote.

Then, in early 1932, Charlie discovered that Alice had switched her lottery business to the San Antonio syndicate, even though she continued to sell the association's insurance. A month or so later, the Texas Negro Undertakers Association officially notified the Corsicana City Commission that Alice and her son were operating without a license. Because of Alice's political influence, the commissioners gave them ninety days; but neither Alice nor young Carl could pass the exam. Finally, the commission forced her to sell the business to some brothers from Waco who had been recommended by the association.

Charlie shook his head in admiration. As chairman of the association's licensing committee, Rhambo had got Corsicana to shut Alice down. Then, he financed those Waco boys, took a lien on their business, and, of course, made sure they sold policy. Charlie remembered hearing that Alice and Carl had moved out of Corsicana to the country. He also heard that she continued to wield a powerful influence with her votes.

'Well, sure, Alice and Carl Stewart be mad at Nathan,' Charlie thought, 'but the San Antonio boys be madder. Corsicana was not the only town we was keeping them out of. Yep, somehow they spot that Carl as a patsy wanting revenge and get him to lure Rhambo away. And I figured Perry and me be next. If Carl Stewart's words tonight mean anything, I was right.'

Well past midnight, the noise from outside abated considerably, but Stewart babbled on and on about Johnson and his daddy and the way Rhambo killed his daddy. Then, just as Charlie started again to drift off, a screech owl's shriek pierced the quiet; and Stewart's muffled rambling turned into terrified whining. For some reason, the screeching and whining made lullaby music for Charlie; and he went to sleep.

9

Perry Rhambo's Problem

Louis's Model T sped south on the Lockhart highway through the heat waves shimmering up from the pavement to the turnoff to Perry Rhambo's farmhouse. "Man," he muttered, "it's too hot, and I'm too old for all this stuff."

Over the telephone, Perry had sounded madder than Louis had heard him in years. After Perry got through the cuss words, he said he had dreamed something would mess up the deal with Will Fuller. He said he had to have Louis's help to save it, that he'd already arranged for young Dr. Everett Givens to bring Mr. Fuller to the farm later that afternoon. Perry also wanted Louis to bring the afternoon newspaper "right now" so he could read about the killing before Mr. Fuller got there. 'Perry got a lot of time for those dreams,' Louis thought. 'Dreams and crows. Now he say he dream that something like this would happen. How do I get mixed up with his dreams and those crows?'

'But, let's face it,' Louis thought after a moment, 'me and Everett Givens be more'n happy to help Perry.' Louis was a grocer. Everett Givens was a dentist. Both were respectable leading citizens of East Austin. Both badly needed that extra income from the lottery, and Perry's deal with Mr. Fuller would have given Charlie Johnson the backing to get it going again. On top of that, Louis and Dr. Givens were counting on Perry's blessing to take Nathan's commissions from the fees paid by the white politicians for organizing the vote. 'Yes,' thought Louis, 'old Perry's a pain, but me and Everett'll jump when he hollers.'

'But damn it all.' Louis's thoughts continued, 'Just last night me and Everett left our families and came to the farm to witness Perry and Mr. Fuller close the deal. Shame Charlie went to Bible study 'stead being with us. He be the main reason the deal worked. So what if he promised Miss Annie. Everything was set, and now Charlie's made this mess...Or was everything set? What do Perry mean about that dream?'

Louis recalled that at Nathan's funeral, Perry had told him that the crows had come to him the night before and told him that the venerable undertaker, Mister

William Tears, had a licensed assistant who was not only ready to run his own funeral parlor but had the business wits to match Nathan's. A few days later Perry told Louis that the very next day he drove to Mister Tear's funeral parlor and made Mr. Tears a proposition. Perry said that Mister Tears saw the chance to make some money, especially from Nathan's insurance and numbers business. He agreed right there to back that assistant, whose name was Will Fuller. Mister Tears, Perry said, wanted Fuller to take over all Nathan's businesses, and that was just fine with Perry.

But Mr. Tears made a condition. He knew that Charlie was the only man who understood the ins and outs of the insurance and policy businesses; so, he said that for him to back the deal, Charlie would have to agree to work for Fuller. Perry then added his own condition—that young Everett Rhambo be Charlie's assistant so he could learn the businesses and run them for Mr. Fuller someday. Mr. Tears agreed. Perry agreed. Will Fuller agreed. And, within a day or so, Charlie agreed.

"Now I know why Daddy always say never celebrate a deal 'til the money's in the hand," Louis mumbled as he turned onto the dirt road that led to Perry's house.

As Louis approached the house, he was mildly surprised and a little relieved to see a smiling Perry Rhambo sitting comfortably on the front porch smoking a cigar with a tall glass in hand. Louis parked under the ancient live oak with long, outstretched branches that spread over most of the front yard, walked up the porch steps, exchanged the usual loud greetings with Perry, and settled in a chair. Ferris, Perry's "man-who-what-does," handed Louis a tall glass of Perry's best "pre-war" over ice. When Louis made a pointed remark about the shotgun and rifle leaning against a porch railing, Perry laughed and said, "Welcome to Fort Rhambo, Colonel." But Perry's smile turned to a snarl when he saw the headline of the afternoon *Austin Statesman* that Louis handed him.

After a brief look at the front page, Perry set the newspaper aside. "Johnny call me early. He say the Rangers and sheriff search the hotel first thing this morning, and they told him somebody killed a white boy on Chicon last night. He called back a couple of hours later to say that somebody come by the bar and tell him fifteen or twenty police take Charlie off to jail."

Perry heaved a sigh and looked away from Louis toward the cornfield adjacent to the farmyard, "Shit. I knew something would mess up this deal."

Louis sipped his drink; he did not remind Perry that he had already told Louis about the dream. Perry was in a mood to think out loud, and Louis knew that his job was to listen sympathetically.

"Last night," Perry said quietly, "my daddy and mama—old Henry and Miss Lillie—come to me in their crow selves and squawk about some dead white man. Then Nathan join 'em, wearing his top hat and flapping his owl wings. He screech that he be mighty grateful to me for getting Will Fuller to save his businesses and give his boy Everett a chance. Then Nathan screech something about 'the deal ain't done 'til Miss Lillie say so. But don't worry 'cause she'll say how it'll be done, too.'"

Perry paused and turned his head to look at Louis. "Now what do you reckon Nathan mean by that?" he asked.

Louis shrugged and said nothing, but he shuddered a little at the thought of Nathan meaning anything.

"Well, maybe Miz Lillie 'say how' and 'say so' in another dream," Perry went on. "But she don't act like it. I reckon she'll be close by...Daddy, too."

Perry pursed his lips, frowned, set his glass on a table, and picked up the newspaper. Louis realized that Perry was putting off any further talk until the other two men arrived.

Left to his own thoughts, Louis reflected on the fact that he had known Perry and his family for more than fifty years. He well remembered Miss Lillian. Louis, Charlie Johnson, and hundreds of Reconstruction children had suffered mightily in her classrooms. Then, over the years, Louis had watched Nathan build his business empire and Perry make a fortune pimping while portering at Austin's downtown hotels. When white folks went into their Prohibition, he had watched Perry set up his whorehouses and his hootchie-kootchie hotel to fill the demand. And he had been one of the first customers at Perry's barbershop.

'That barbershop,' mused Louis. At first Louis was taken aback when Perry told him that the barbershop was his long-dead parents' idea. "They want their boy to have a respectable business," Perry had said. Then, when Louis had thought about it, he realized that every time Perry had talked about his successes, he had given old Henry and Miss Lillian the credit—especially when he made a success out of some mess or another.

'God knows,' thought Louis. 'Charlie's arrest is a hell of a mess—for Perry, for me, for most of East Austin. But we'll make things right. We got to make things right. And if old Henry and Miz Lillie can help, that's OK with me.'

Louis took another sip, lit the cigar that Perry had given him, and gazed at the cornfield that had briefly occupied Perry's attention. Two crows were flitting through the green cornstalks.

As Lyons pondered the crows, Perry suddenly barked, "Hell, Colonel, them whites wasn't the San Antonio gang; they was just marauding white boys. Good for business on Saturday nights, but trouble—maybe too much trouble. I know about that baseballer. He make trouble at the hotel before, but we ain't never said nothing to the sheriff. Now this—now old Charlie's in jail, and we's up a shitting creek."

Almost everyone in East Austin addressed Louis as "Colonel," a title he picked up as a small boy when he did odd jobs for the Reconstruction Union troops stationed in Austin.

Without waiting for a response, Perry put his head down again, drew on his big cigar, and, eyes fixed on the paper, held out his empty glass. Ferris replaced it in a heartbeat. After a while, Perry turned his head in Louis's direction and asked, "Did you read this, Colonel?"

Louis nodded.

"What do you make of it?"

"I can't figure out what Charlie be doing on Chicon Street so late."

"Johnny say that Charlie and Annie Davis be in the club late, following Bible study," Perry responded.

"But the white boys been making trouble all summer," Louis said. "Maybe they just make Charlie too mad. Course, if they did, it'd be the first time in Charlie's life. Anyhow, he wasn't chased by the folks that killed Nathan—we know that now. But Charlie mighta thought it was them. Hell, if the newspaper's right, it look like he drove at the white boys, shot at them, and then went home and went to bed. Now, if there be one thing I know about Charlie, it be that he get real nervous when something's wrong. Way too nervous to go to bed and go to sleep."

"But no matter what he was thinking," Louis continued, "he's in big trouble now, Perry. Maybe all of us is. I hear a mean crowd is already at the courthouse. One old boy say they yelled at him as he was coming back from his yard work in west Austin. This boy's not a fearful man, but he was shaking bad."

Perry grunted. As his eyes dropped down to the newspaper, he mumbled, "This paper say a Meskin tell on old Charlie. A Meskin? That's one dead Meskin when I find his brown ass."

When Perry finished the article, he held out his empty glass and pointed at Lyons. Ferris arrived with two refills. Without explanation, Perry stood and strode from the porch over to the fence where the two crows were loudly wreaking havoc. Lyons noticed that Perry's head was gently bobbing, as if in conversation, but Lyons did not dare allow himself to think about it. Instead, as he waited for the other men to show up, he thought about the other responsibility that Nathan's murder had suddenly imposed on him and Everett Givens.

'Perry and Charlie think the San Antonio gang put that boy up to killing Nathan,' Louis thought. 'But I ain't so sure. Of course, all the ladies think it be the sheriff 'cause of his wife, but I got a suspicion it could've been them Democrats, 'specially Mr. John Patterson.'

A couple of weeks before Nathan was killed, Nathan had called Louis and Everett Givens to his office to discuss his plan for breaking into the Democratic Party. 'Nathan always be so sure, so determined to get his way,' Louis thought as Nathan's words came back to him.

"Everett," Nathan had begun, addressing himself to the big dentist, "old folks like the Colonel and me have had to live through the bad Klan days and Jim Crow, but we had it better than our daddies and mamas. And we work hard to make things better for you young bucks. But we got to keep moving, keep doing more. When me and Louis figured out how to organize the East Austin vote, we made white men look at us with respect. Now, every time one of 'em want to be on the council or want some tax, they come to us with cash in hand and a few promises they mostly can't keep. Back in '28 they was so afraid that their City Plan won't pass that we make them come through with a few sewers and that electric station at Seventh and Chicon. We had the whip hand then 'cause we could act insulted that the plan make East Austin the official Negro district. Shit, we didn't care about that. But we know they was desperate to get their roads paved, so we act mad and made 'em promise to keep their promises. And, except for the library and a few paved roads and a few sewers, they did."

At that point, Nathan leaned his long body back in the chair. He let those white teeth gleam and said, "We'll get those, too, Everett. The Colonel and me ain't resting 'till we get 'em. And we be mighty proud that you be along to help."

Reliving that moment brought a little smile to Louis's face. Everett had listened like he had never heard this story before.

'That boy's a quick learner,' thought Louis. 'He figure out real quick that Nathan always starts his meetings with a story of his success, and that you better not tell him you hear it all before. Everett had heard it all and more. But Nathan was right: the big man (damn, Everett's big) had come in to the organization at the right time.'

Rhambo's votes had grown from just a hundred in the early twenties to almost a thousand in the last council election. It had become too much for one man to pay all the poll taxes, to pay the preachers, and to get folks to the voting place. And Louis's commission had gotten so large that he couldn't argue at having to split it with Everett. 'Yep, that big man be a godsend. His size, his educated talk, and his deep voice make folks pay attention. Bet he get no arguments when he want to pull a tooth. But Nathan had more on his mind than telling me and Everett that story,' Louis thought.

Louis recalled how Nathan had stopped for a moment, and then had said, "Yep, we know how to deal with the city. But lots of what we need is with the county and even the state of Texas. But since the politics of the county and the state is controlled by the Democrats, organizing for the Republicans and the big election is a waste of time. That's because it ain't even close, and our votes just get lost. Well, the Democrats always have close elections in their primary; and there's some of them that would lay down a lot of cash and some beautiful promises for our vote. I mean right now old Jim Ferguson would be happy to make us rich men."

"Well, guess what," Nathan had said as if he had already taken the former governor's money, "down in San Antonio the mayor is leading a group to get a judge to make the Democrats let coloreds vote down there. They been working the past few years to get evidence that Democrats turn them away from the polls even though they have poll taxes and act good. We got to do the same thing. We got to get the evidence that we have the poll taxes and that we act right so the judge can see we is fit to vote. Now here's what I already done."

That's when Nathan told Louis and Everett that he had gone to see Mr. John Patterson.

"When I told Mr. Patterson that nowadays East Austin like the Democrats more'n the Republicans, he said 'that's real nice, Nathan.' And when I told him we wanted to be good Democrats and vote in the primary, his face frizz up. He say that I know as well as anybody that the Democrats be the white folks party. I just kinda said, 'Yessuh.' And then he thought a little and say who votes in the election is not his decision. That decision is made by the state committee. He say he'd check to be sure what the rules be."

At that point Everett Givens had laughed, looked at Louis, and said, "Now we know why the newspaper says that Mr. Patterson announced that the state committee says that no Negroes are going to vote in the primary this year." Everett had shown Louis the article just the day before. Both had been puzzled that the chairman wanted to make a point that everybody knew already.

"Yessuh, young fellow, now you know," Nathan had said. "And that's step one for the San Antonio lawyer. Next, we got to get someone to vote in the courthouse before the election. They call it 'absentee voting.' It's for folks who plan to be out of town on election day."

'Well, Nathan,' Louis thought sadly, 'you'd be proud of me and Everett. We got Lester Armands lined up to go to the courthouse this Monday to try to get the absentee vote. White folks take to old Lester, so we expect they won't be mean to him. Then Monday afternoon, me and Everett is going to visit with Mr. Patterson ourselves—we going to ask one more time just to let him know that just because you be gone, we ain't giving up. And we have the plans for Election Day (you called it 'step three'), 'cept it'll be me and Everett at the front of the line, and not you. The San Antonio lawyer was here for your funeral and told us what we have to do.'

Despite his suspicion about John Patterson's involvement in Nathan's murder, Louis was determined to do this election right—not only to impress Perry, but also to honor his mentor. 'Maybe they got you, Nathan. But they can't kill us all.'

As Louis pondered the risks he and Everett were taking, he became aware that Perry was still standing by the fence at the cornfield. Perry's head was moving in all directions and his hands were gesticulating at the two crows. They had moved perceptibly closer to the fence and were flitting and squawking like two old women scrapping over a plug of tobacco.

However, the conversation came to a sudden halt when the engine noise of Everett Given's new Ford broke through the squawking. Perry turned abruptly; and, sporting his bright smile and stretching out a welcoming hand, he walked to the driveway with a sprightly gate. He extended exuberant welcomes to Givens and his passenger, Will Fuller. Perry's wild mood swings never ceased to amaze Louis Lyons.

While Ferris served the new arrivals, Givens reported that he, too, heard that a mob was forming around the courthouse. "East Austin's getting edgy," he said. "Everybody's talking about that Sherman mob two years ago."

Perry said, "Shit, nothing like that's gonna happen here. These Austin whites is different to those Sherman crackers."

Then Perry raised his glass in a gesture of greeting and immediately asked, "What you think there, Brother Will?"

'Just like Perry,' thought Louis. 'No beating about the bush. He want to know what Mr. Fuller going to do.'

"Hell, Perry, Charlie's a dead man," Mr. Fuller answered. "Either the mob'll lynch him or the courts'll hang him. No matter why he did it, he killed the son of one of the governor's good friends."

Fuller paused and waited for Perry to say something. After a few seconds of silence, Fuller said, "Look, I figure that Charlie was carrying that gun because he feared what happened to Nathan…like some other folks we know."

Perry smiled.

"Those boys must've hassled him," Fuller continued. "The paper says he ran them into a ditch, but I reckon they were driving crazy like those boys do and tangled with him somehow. Then they started throwing rocks at him; he lost his temper and shot. We know those boys've been making big trouble all summer. My sister-in-law's president of the Baptist women, and she's been to the chief of police about these rockings, especially Ebenezer Church last month. She told that man straight that if they doesn't stop these boys, there's going to be a tragedy. Damn, I hate that woman for being right!"

Fuller concluded that, of course, he would not be taking over Nathan's business.

Perry's eyes narrowed. He asked Fuller if somehow Charlie couldn't help from jail.

"Hell, Perry, Charlie isn't going to be in jail. He's going to be in the ground, after being hung, chopped up, and burnt."

"Well," said Perry, "what if he don't get lynched? Nobody's been lynched in Austin since Charlie Blackshear, and the whites here are big on the law. Hell, man, this is the state capitol, the home of the law. Sure, a crowd's at the courthouse—a crowd is one thing; a lynching is something else."

Fuller shook his head. "Lord, Lord. Perry, if that crowd leaves now, he'll still be hanged by the judge. You ever hear of a Negro that killed a white man that a judge doesn't hang?"

Perry said that, of course, he knew the problem. "But no Negro ever had a lawyer worth a hoot. These days there's lawyers that'll work for us—like those lawyers that are saving the hides of those Scottsboro boys. Maybe we can get one for old Charlie. Maybe he can make a case that those white boys was going to kill Charlie, and Charlie fire that gun to save his own life."

"Read the paper, Perry," Fuller shot back. "About every big shot in government was down at the hospital at five o'clock this morning to see the boy's daddy. Five o'clock in the morning! He's got to be somebody to get those men out of bed at that time. Now you tell me any lawyer will go against that crowd. Even if a lawyer does, the judge'll be so beholden to those big shots, he'll hang Charlie no matter what."

Perry became quiet.

Louis could tell that Perry had realized that Mr. Will Fuller was a man who saw things in black and white—no little shades, no squeeze room—it works or it don't work; it can or it can't; it is or it ain't; and no way Perry was going to get him make a "can't" into a "can."

Perry said, "Well, Will, I understand. No Charlie, no deal. But I hope that if and when you know that you got Charlie, there is a deal."

Fuller shrugged, "Sure. I've got time, but I'm looking for something."

"Well," Perry concluded, "Charlie ain't dead, yet. As long as he's alive, there be hope for the deal. That's why I wanted the Colonel and Dr. Givens to be here. They have a lot to lose if Charlie can't run the lottery. Lot's of people do."

Perry paused and turned his face from Fuller to the crows, now perched on the cornfield fence, "If old Charlie can make it through the next week without being lynched, somehow we're gonna figure this out—and make you a rich man, Will Fuller. Let's all pray real hard tomorrow. But right now let's have a drink and enjoy a little breeze."

Louis purposefully lingered after Mr. Fuller and Dr. Givens had said their good-byes and driven away. He continued to pull on his cigar and sip at the drink, wanting to get a few things clear; but Perry had become silent again, and Louis was not sure if he should discuss the matter further. As soon as Louis's cigar burned to the butt, Perry got up, extended his hand for a good-bye handshake, and led Louis to his old Model T. When the men got to the driveway, Perry grinned and told Louis to look out for white boys.

Louis departed still unsure why Perry wanted him and Everett there that afternoon, but he allowed himself to be hopeful. 'Maybe,' he thought, 'this means that Perry figures that me and Everett be the new political bosses and speak for East Austin like old Nathan used to. Maybe Perry figures that Fuller be impressed that the deal is serious enough for people like us to do what we can to make it happen. Maybe he thinks Fuller'd see that the deal's too important, not just for Fuller personally but for the whole community. Maybe. But how in the world are we going to save Charlie?'

10

Reflections

Neither words, nor hugs, nor bursts of tears numbed her ache. Relief came from the minutia of morning tasks, more that morning—the morning of Son's funeral—than usual, because Emma had not appeared for work.

Because the funeral was at five, Mabel and Albert did not attend morning service; but the children needed the solace, so Lod had taken Eloise and little Ken.

Albert called several times.

When Mabel could find no more work, she went to the reading room and had a quiet moment writing in "Worms."

> *It cannot be—*
> *Do I hear your whistle down the street,*
> *Your footstep on the stair?*
> *It cannot be—*
> *Do I see the twinkle in your eye,*
> *The sun-glint in your hair?*
> *Ah no, my son,*
> *For ever 'fore my aching eyes I see*
> *You—young and tall and fair.*

When the pen rested, she idly turned pages of her notebook until her eyes fell on a little piece she had written about Emma and the screech owl. Mabel sighed. She had told no one about Emma's strange outburst yesterday, but she could not get the episode out of her mind. Then, seeing what she had written a week or so before, sent chills through her: "If the screech owl gets into our yard, somebody in our household would surely die." 'True,' Mabel thought, 'Emma was terrified when it arrived.' As in a trance, she picked up the pen and appended an afterthought to the story:

"We continued to hear the owl's voice nightly, ever seeming to be getting nearer, and Emma was becoming more and more agitated. However, Friday night the screeches suddenly stopped and have not recommenced."

Bill Tarver needed the solace of his religion that morning, but it was not to be. The furious, weather-marked face of the Waco gas station attendant had haunted him all night. During church it kept emerging from the faces of Bill Tarver's old friends. 'Ten years ago,' he thought, 'ridiculous pointed hoods had covered the vengeance forever chiseled into their leathery faces.' They reminded Tarver of the photographs of the soldiers' faces at the moment they jumped from their trenches. 'The boys charged into machine gun fire for their country, for their people, not for the government or for Woodrow Wilson's ideals. They died for their own kind and that's all. Like them, the Waco face would not hesitate to risk death to defend his blood, whether or not the cause was just.' Bill only vaguely heard the Reverend expounding his Sunday morning warnings of certain hell-fire.

Tarver's mind meandered to a December day ten years before, during the final month of his two terms as Navarro County Attorney. Luther Johnson, who had just been elected to his first term in Congress, had insisted that Tarver and Albert Allison accompany him to Streetman, thirty miles south of Corsicana. The local Sheriff was hunkered down in the city jail trying to protect a young Negro accused of raping the town's twenty-year-old schoolteacher, and he had called Johnson for help. By the time they arrived, the crowd of fifteen hundred men and women had bonded with moonshine and revival songs. Without hesitation, the congressman-elect jumped on top of Albert's car and waved both arms for attention, and somebody shouted to give him a chance. The mob relaxed for an instant and listened. Then just as Johnson's oratory seemed to be having affect, the jittery sheriff decided to make a run for it with the prisoner. The spell was broken; and a riot of backfiring cars and motorbikes mingled with angry shouts, curses, and random gunfire. Johnson was jostled from the top of the car. All Bill, Albert, and the congressman-elect could do was to sit in the car and wait until the mob was gone. A few miles out of town, the mob caught up with the sheriff. After a short time, hundreds of cars streamed back to Streetman, one with the bullet-riddled body of the hapless Negro strapped to its hood. The mob hung the body from the town's only lamppost. Then, not entirely satisfied, the mob found another Negro who had made the mistake of mowing a lawn at the wrong time. When his employer rescued him, the mob burned down an empty hotel owned by another black man. Tarver had known some of those people. They were ordinary, hard-working, decent churchgoing citizens. But that December day he had seen them shed their humanity and merge into the soul of the monster.

As Tarver surveyed the congregation, his churning gut told him that the monster was lurking again. Accounts in the Dallas Sunday papers mocked Charles Johnson's confession and clearly intimated that he had killed young Allison wantonly. The *Corsicana Sun*'s lead editorial could not contain its rage:

TRAGEDY IN AUSTIN

On Friday night the brilliant, handsome son of one of Corsicana's finest families was shot to death by a vicious negro killer on the streets of Austin. As reported in this newspaper, the negro and young Albert Allison were in a minor traffic incident that led to an exchange of words. Young Allison and his companions reportedly were lost on unfamiliar streets in the colored part of Austin. Provoked only by this incident and perhaps a few thrown rocks, Charley Johnson's base instinct got the better of him. From within a few feet, he wantonly fired his loaded Colt .45 at the unarmed Allison.

This awful tragedy is but one more example of the great differences between the races. It is one more reminder of the wisdom of segregation. Peace, harmony, friendliness, and understanding are possible only when each race attends its own churches, its own schools, stores, and clubs. But it is also imperative that the race responsible for civil institutions, the white race, be uncompromising in enforcing the rules of civil conduct that apply to us all in whatever part of town. We cannot countenance incivility by negroes in a murderous rage.

Anglo-Saxons have struggled through a long history to learn how to settle disputes based on a system of law and a code of conduct that has become the highest expression of civilized man. The negro has only recently been brought into the civilized family. He still lets primitive vapors and animal instinct settle minor disputes. Poor young Allison was the victim of such an animal. All Corsicana joins the Allison family in this time of mourning. We call upon the people of Austin to vindicate with swift, sure justice the loss of one of our beautiful young sons.

When Tarver returned from church to his father-in-law's house, the *Sun* was folded to the editorial and in plain sight on the coffee table. The Waco face seemed to grimace from it. He flipped the paper over and tried to lose himself in his nephews while his in-laws prepared Sunday lunch.

In the early afternoon, Esther Tarver called Bill from Austin to say that Governor Sterling wanted to talk to him right away. She said that a mob had surrounded the courthouse and that the governor had sounded very concerned. Bill called immediately and was put straight through. The governor said that Sheriff White had come to the mansion that morning. He had told the governor that so far the crowd at the courthouse (numbering a couple of thousand and growing) had rebuked appeals by the district attorney and Ranger Captain Frank Hamer. But, the governor had said, the sheriff and Hamer both thought those folks would listen to the boy's father. The governor wanted to know whether Albert would be willing to help and whether he could get down there before the governor had to call out the National Guard.

"I don't have to remind you of the political consequences, Bill; but I'll use the Guard if trouble starts. I have already ordered it to stand by at Camp Mabry."

Tarver reminded Governor Sterling that the boy's funeral was that afternoon and that the father had had almost no rest since Friday.

"But," Tarver concluded, "Albert's as good a man as you'll ever find. I'll talk to him as soon as I can and let you know."

In East Austin, Louis Lyons and more than a hundred worried churchgoers crammed into little Rising Star Baptist Church that Sunday morning. The singing was unusually loud, the handclapping more vigorous than usual, the shouting more intense. Lyons saw tears on folks' cheeks. Almost no one smiled. The atmosphere was anxious, fearful. 'Reverend Black's got a big job this morning,' Louis thought. From the time Louis had opened his grocery earlier that morning, he had listened as East Austin prepared for the worst. "The mob's just burned the courthouse and is heading east. They're going to burn every house on Chicon Street." "The mob's going to bring old Charlie back in pieces and then kill every boy under twenty…and a few gals, too." "My gun's in the car. When they come, I'll take a few white asses with me."

Louis saw in the way the reverend stood—just a little more hunched than normal—that the poor man was not sure he could do what was necessary for his anxious flock. Louis was not sure, either; and he found himself saying a silent prayer for the good Reverend and for Charlie Johnson, too.

"Brothers and sisters," Reverend Adam Black began quietly, "we must think on trouble, and we must think about the Lord's own chosen people. We must think on the troubles of the Lord's own people, when they was the Pharaoh's slaves down in Egypt, when they toted the bricks in the hot sun, when they drove the oxen, when they built them pyramids. Pharaoh make God's chosen work every day from sunup to sundown, and they be bent and tired and old before their time.

"But that wasn't enough for old Pharaoh. He say to his captains, 'Get in your chariots, go into the town of the Israelites and rock them people and hit them with sticks and throw coconuts at them.' So Pharaoh's soldiers rode through the town and hurt the people and call them bad names. Then the Lord, He take

Moses by the hand and He show Moses an Egyptian man beating on a child of Israel; and Moses cain't stand it no more. Before he know it, the spirit of the Lord move him to ride by that Egyptian man and slay him. Moses slay that Egyptian man that hurt his people, and the Lord, He bless Moses and help him get away from the wrath of Pharaoh. Praise the Lord!"

"Praise the Lord," cried the congregation.

"Now sometimes the Lord send a special man to do His work against the oppressors. Sometimes the Lord look down on the suffering of his people. He look down and see the open cars with wild white boys speeding through the streets and cussing the people and throwing rocks and peaches and watermelons, and He weep for His people. Then one day He remember old Moses, and He say, 'The next time this happens, I'll fill a God-fearing man with My spirit and send him against those night riders.'"

Reverend Black paused for a long moment, the clapping stopped, the congregation became quiet, then beginning in a whisper, rising to a thunderclap the Reverend continued, "and Friday night that's what He done!...Now, Brother Charlie Johnson need our hard praying, our hard begging to the Lord to snatch him from Pharaoh's chains and save him like he save Moses. Hard praying, hard begging of the Lord to save old Charlie and to save us from the vengeful wrath of the Pharaoh and the Egyptians."

Then the Reverend prayed, and the congregation prayed, and then they prayed again.

Sunday, July 10, 1932, *Austin American-Statesman,*

GRAND JURY CALLED TO PROBE KILLING OF WHITE BOY BY NEGRO

"Charles E. Johnson, 60, negro school teacher, was charged with murder in Justice Frank R. Tannehill's court Saturday after his arrest by state rangers and sheriff's officers at his home, 205 Sabine street, in connection with the fatal shooting of Albert A. Allison, 18, of Dallas, at 11 p m. Friday at Seventh and Chicon Streets.

Circumstances surrounding the shooting death of Allison and the wounding of Derden Wofford, Austin high school athlete, will be investigated by the Travis county grand jury called to convene for that purpose at 10 a.m. Monday by Judge J. D. Moore of the 98th district court.

Murder Charge Filed

The charge of murder was filed against Johnson by Sheriff Coley C. White after Johnson made a confession in which he admitted the shooting and after Wofford and other companions of Allison on the fatal car ride in East Austin had identified Johnson in connection with the shooting.

Johnson was arrested at his home at 9 a.m. by State Ranger R. W. McWilliams, Deputy Sheriffs Paul Blair, Jack Newman and Homer Thornberry and Deputy Constable Arthur Cowey. These officers together with State Ranger O. T. Martin and Wofford, Robert Cobb of Dallas, John Mayes of Corsicana and Harry Granberry of Austin, the four companions of Allison when he was shot, will be witnesses before the grand jury session Monday.

Ran Into Ditch

Wofford, in a statement to police Friday night, said Allison, unfamiliar with Austin streets, drove the automobile in which the five boys were riding into a blind alley on East Eighth street. In circling to get back on Chicon, the negro's car coming down a hill, crowded the boy's car into a ditch.

The negro stopped the car a short distance ahead and heated words were exchanged, officers said Wofford told them. The boys, according to City Det. Ted Klaus, had stopped their car near the city electric substation to ascertain whether the car had been damaged.

Continuing Klaus stated, "Allison was at the wheel, another youth was standing on the running board, while Wofford and another youth sat in the front seat with Allison. The bullet entered Allison's left arm, penetrated his body and struck Wofford in the arm. I have the bullet here. It was fired from a .45 calibre pistol."

Officers, in arresting the negro, said he had a .45 calibre pistol with him at the time.

Signed Statement

Sheriff Coley White made public the statement signed by Johnson with Sheriff White, Ranger R. E. McWilliams and Deputy Sheriff Ben Morrall as the witnesses."

Austin attorney May Yelderman read the last paragraph to her attorney husband while he was spooning breakfast grapefruit.

"Another Negro statement without benefit of counsel," she remarked. "Maybe this is the case you and Tass Waterston have been looking for, Bill."

11

Funeral

Five PM, Sunday, July 10, 1932. Men in black suits and ties and women in full black dresses and black hats crowded into the small, stifling sanctuary of Corsicana's First Methodist Church. Before beginning the service, Dr. P. E. Riley stood in the pulpit and surveyed the family in the front pew. Grieving, certainly; shocked, yes; but controlled, so controlled. The boy was murdered. Had the Allisons absorbed the implications, the awful days and nights to come? The *Corsicana Sun* had reported that a Negro shot the boy in the colored part of Austin. Mrs. Allison confirmed as much yesterday. That boy! He could charm anyone; at the same time he was all too ready to cross the line. Could the Allisons' stiffness this afternoon stem from remorse as well as grief? Is there guilt churning underneath those masks?

Over the years, Dr. Riley, an Ohio native, had developed a degree of appreciation for the peculiar attitudes of his Southern flock; but the extreme lengths to which some would go still appalled him. In 1922, the year the Methodist Conference assigned him to Corsicana, race riots and indiscriminate lynching had consumed the area. People still spoke of those times in whispers. The same year the Ku Klux Klan in full regalia marched into one of the reverend's July Sunday services, appealed for votes for its candidate for the U.S. Senate, made a large contribution, and, singing *Onward Christian Soldiers,* marched out. Two years later, during another Klan demonstration, Mr. Allison and his family led the entire congregation to walk out of the church. He recalled young Albert Jr., steadfast and uncharacteristically serious, as he stood and marched beside his mother.

"When tragedy suddenly takes a loved one," Reverend Riley began, "we feel as if our own hearts will never beat the same. In a wisp the world is forever empty; nights around the piano are just a dream; breakfast teasing and baseball games exist only in our nostalgia. The world diminishes into a long, gray winter. Our ache is so unbearable we wonder if we want the world to turn another time."

Dr. Riley paused a heartbeat, just enough for a subtle effect, then he lowered his voice and looked at the Allison pew. "And when we lose a child, we want to lash out at the tragic forces that robbed the future of this miracle we called into life such a short time ago. As brothers and sisters and friends, we ask how a just God could cut down this boy who has hardly begun to live. And when the tragedy appears to have been caused by a monstrous, evil deed, we want to wield the sword of justice in swift retribution."

Pausing briefly, the reverend thought, 'Albert and Mabel Allison are prominent and powerful—Southern to the core. Yet, I have heard Albert speak against lynching and what he calls "mock trials." And Mabel, dear Mabel—Judge L. B. Cobb's daughter. I'll never forget how proudly Bill Tarver said in his eulogy at the judge's funeral that "the blackest of blacks received justice in his courtroom." Now, Albert and Mabel are struck down in the most personal way. They have the wealth and political power to have retribution any way they want it, and the community would applaud. Please God, please help them stay true to the legacy of the old judge.'

"Albert Arthur Allison Junior's short life," the reverend continued, "has left us with such cherished memories. In talking about Albert with his family and friends, it occurred to me that we are so disconsolate because when we think about him, we think about something we learned, something he *gave* us, not something he took. Yes, brothers and sisters, this free-spirited young man, his whims and wit, gave us something about which to smile; but we remember not the smile, we remember the wisdom in the gift. Ironically, I am reminded of the Allison family Sunday dinner table, where Mrs. Riley and I have been guests on numerous occasions. On one occasion eight years ago, Mr. Allison provoked Evelyn and Juliet, home from college, to weigh in on issues of the day. On this day the discussion turned to the war, though it had been over some six years. Albert asked whether American ideals were well-served by our sacrifices. In the midst of the argument, point and counterpoint, a young boy's voice interjected, 'But cousin Perry did a good thing by getting killed, didn't he, Pop?' Some of you might remember Perry Allison, nephew and ward of Albert and Mabel. A volunteer, inspired by youthful idealism, he was killed in France in a terrible accident the day after Armistice. He was just eighteen. I remember the father's answer so well, 'Yes, son, Perry was very young, yet he was called to duty and then to glory.'

Then young Albert Jr. said, "Someday I'll fight for *us*, Papa, and if I die, I'll have a good life, like Cousin Perry.'

"Brothers and sisters, out of the mouths of children," Dr. Riley sighed, "that boy just ten years of age knew better than any of us that the value of a life was measured in its quality, not in its length. He knew that life's value was enhanced through sacrifice for family and loved ones.

"Of course, most of you remember the Albert Jr. who led the others, unnamed here, on many adventures through our backyards and alleys—adventures that often ended in one mess or another. Whether guilty or not, Albert was lead suspect in much of the mischief made in Corsicana until he went away to Marion Military Institute almost two years ago; even then he was lead suspect when high jinks were about. On two occasions the students of Corsicana High voted him 'Most Mischievous.' Given the famous capabilities of his classmates, that honor was some achievement."

Polite laughter. The father and mother managed smiles.

"What else could a boy with such a quick, creative mind be? Not bad, no Lord. Not mean, not vicious, no, no Lord. But, quick of mind and permanently in awe of wonders revealed by lightning-fast insights, he was the first to say, 'Let's give it a try, boys.' Like the great men who gave us a new country dedicated to the wonder of God's freedom, like the great men who have made our lives easier through the wonders of science, Albert tested our standards and tampered with our ways of doings things. Someday he might have led us into new ways to solve depressions and poverty, or to improve travel, or to communicate better, or to save democracy in a world replete with godless dictators."

The preacher then focused on the front pew. Mabel Allison was looking at her son, Lod, the sixteen-year-old sitting to her right. He was staring vacantly. 'Both boys are smart,' the reverend thought, 'like their father.' An image came into his mind of Lod and Albert Jr. at the dinner table quickly adding in their heads the four four-digit numbers tossed to them by their father.

"Mr. and Mrs. Allison, however, have not lost a future leader, they have lost their son, their little boy, whom they nurtured from the womb through heat rash, colic, mumps, chicken pox, bumps, and bruises. Evelyn, Juliet, Lod, Eloise, and little Ken have lost their brother, who fought them and loved them and stood up for them and taught them and learned from them. Now the family circle, though severely challenged today, must bond ever closer to ensure that Albert will never be forgotten."

Dr. Riley peered across the sanctuary. Young men and women were in private reveries. Stolid men and women dressed in black mourned another fallen soldier in the long war for Southern white survival. Standing in the back, two familiar Negroes, dressed respectably, visibly grief-stricken, were looking to the ceiling and saying quietly but audibly, "Yeah Lawd, yeah Lawd." Dr. Riley closed his eyes and bowed his head.

"Oh, Lord, let us call to mind that You test the faith of Your dearly beloved, that You ordered Abraham to sacrifice his beloved Isaac; that You reduced the great Job, a perfect man in his piety, to poverty and ill health; and that You sent your only Son to the Cross. As You reminded us each time, mortals will never know Your mind, but we must have faith in Your infinite mercy even as we try to employ Your gifts of reason and compassion to further justice on earth."

"Amen," Mabel Cobb Allison murmured, and an echo reverberated pew to pew. The father took his wife's hand.

"Yea, Lord," Dr Riley continued, "the young men who sacrificed in wars for our just liberty, in wars for our just dignity, in wars for our just independence, have the imprint of justice on their immortal souls and forever in the hearts of a grateful nation. But what about the young men who die simply in the cause of just plain making it through the day, who are cut down by an unspeakable evil, an evil only You, Lord, can comprehend? What is the imprint on their souls, how are they to be remembered? Well, if they didn't die on the battlefield in pursuit of justice, maybe it's our job to pursue justice on their behalf, I mean the justice for which You would be proud—justice through Your law, Lord. Amen.

"Now let us open our hymnals to page 246."

Two hours from sundown, heat searing the landscape, only family and close friends gathered for final rites at Oakwood Cemetery. The ritual was short and to the point; people needed to go home, undress, and drink cool lemonade. The nineteen-year-old associate preacher, a classmate of Son's, made brief remarks about fond memories and good times before he bid the Lord to take his friend into His loving arms. Albert lingered at the newly dug grave until only family remained.

As Albert pulled the Buick in front of their house, Ken exclaimed, "Uncle John! Uncle John!" Albert was not surprised to see the old man sitting on the porch, but he was not happy. His uncle and his cousin Herbert, Uncle John's youngest son, were here for a momentous occasion; and, out of respect for the ancient hero, the family would have to pay homage. 'Maybe he's tired,' Albert thought. 'Not likely. He has the stamina of a man forty years younger. Not even that large goiter slows him down.' Worse still, he was dressed in his formal Confederate uniform—the one he had made long after the war to wear to reunions and rallies.

Little Ken ran to the old man and grabbed his hand, "Howdy, Uncle. Son's been killed."

'A few years before,' thought Albert, 'Son had sat on his great-uncle's lap and helped him kill Yankees in 'Virginny' and Gettysburg.'

"We fired and fired," the old man would say. "My gun barrel was so hot it dang near melted, then we fired some more…we charged that Little Round Top and got into the wildest fight of the war right there in the Devil's Den. That's where they got your grandpappy, boy—shot him in the leg; and before we could get him out, they snatched him."

Albert gently shooed his youngest son away, "Evening, Uncle John. Evening, Herbert. We appreciate y'all coming all this way." Albert and Herbert had not been friendly since Herbert's Klan days, but Albert did appreciate his cousin for bringing Uncle John the forty miles from Marquez.

"Yes," Mabel added, "thank you, sir. You are too thoughtful. If I may, I will tend to the kitchen. Please excuse me."

Uncle John nodded to her and made sufficient effort to stand to satisfy the code of chivalry. He had an unmistakable tear in his eye.

The ladies followed Mabel to the kitchen, and the men settled into chairs on the porch. The temperature was abating a bit; lightning bugs were sparkling in the dusk; cicadas were steadily humming; and mosquitoes were taking appetizers.

Uncle John's little red eyes beamed from deep dark sockets and locked on Albert.

"Herbert," Uncle John ordered while holding his gaze, "why don't you pass that lemonade? I reckon everybody could use its relief."

Herbert dutifully unscrewed the lid of a fruit jar and handed it to Uncle John. The old man took a sip, made a face, exhaled a loud breath, and stretched out the jar in both hands to his stricken nephew. Albert took the jar, followed suit, and passed the jar to his sons-in-law. 'Well,' he thought, 'Bill graduated from Colorado University with honors in gin martini. But that smooth liquid warming its way into his veins right now is strictly for a PhD. And Ed M. is not much of a student to begin with." On any other occasion, Albert would have seen the lighter side of his sons-in-laws' learning limitations.

"Albert, I'm so sorry for you and Mabel…All y'all," Uncle John was looking at Lod, who was sitting on the step.

"Thank you, Uncle. He was one of the lights of our lives. Mabel'll never get over it."

Uncle John's red eyes began to glow, "Killed by a negrah. Goddamned Allison curse. Another Allison boy lost."

Uncle John thus signaled that he was demanding attention for one of his stories or school lessons. Albert settled comfortably, and the others respectfully turned to the old man. Uncle John had stuck it out with Lee for almost four years, all the way to Appomattox, one of the honored few to "stack his rifle." Albert's father had admonished him and his siblings never to show disrespect to their Uncle John. "He stacked arms," Arthur Allison had often said. "God knows, he stacked arms and saved the family's pride."

The old man started with a cough, then proceeded quietly, sometimes hardly audible, but distinctly enough to be understood. Some of the men lit cigarettes. Herbert lit Uncle John's cheroot for him.

"For thousands of years no Allison—or Cobb for that matter—ever even laid eyes on a black man. We might of heard of the Moors from Shakespeare or somebody; but none of us ever saw one until 1623, when our Scotch ancestor got off the ship in Jamestown and saw a few darkies working in the tobacco fields. Course, we knew about slavery. Wouldn't surprise me if we ourselves weren't slaves at some time or another. In most of human history, slavery was considered as natural a human state as childhood or kingship or priesthood. So when that Scotchman John Allison bought blacks to help at his new plantation, he was only doing what was natural. And that's the way it was for ten generations of Allisons from Virginny through South Carolina, Tennessee, and Mississippi. When we moved to Leon County from Mississippi, Daddy and Mama brought four or five darkies that Grandpa Cartwright gave them. That was 1853. Just about every family in the wagon train had one or two slaves. For us young folks, having them in the family was like having brothers and sisters. And Daddy treated them fairly. Hell's fire, they ate what we ate, slept the way we slept, and worked the way we worked. Never saw Daddy take a whip to any of them, except the young ones; he whupped them just like his own children. They were happy to be taken care of so well.

"Not long after we settled in Leon County, we heard that slaves were escaping to Mexico. Worse, we heard that slaves were revolting and killing whites. The news from the North was not helping either. I tell you, we were scared. I mean the folks that had come from the South were scared, because most had more money tied up in slaves than anything else, including land. We were scared of losing our capital and scared of our slaves. And all the talk around the country was that Texas ought to leave the Union and become a republic again.

"When the time came in 1861, we and almost everybody else in Leon County voted to secede. The Union was nothing to us except self-righteous abolitionists. We figured they elected Lincoln just to declare war against the South and take us over; and we couldn't stand by, surrender our way of life, and forfeit our property without a fight. Besides, the darkies could not survive on their own; they needed us as much as we needed them. Maybe slavery somehow became wrong; but we were right about the problems sudden emancipation would cause, you know.

"In June 1861, the men of Leon County mustered at the county courthouse in Centerville. A hundred and thirty-five men and boys signed up. I was teaching school, twenty-five-years-old; Albert, your daddy, was eighteen, still working on the family farm; our brother Andrew Jackson was newly married and working his own land. In those days, we figured one of us could whup ten Yankees—well, the Yankees weren't as easy as we thought, but we were dang near right."

Uncle John paused and looked at Lod, "Just remember that we stuck it out. Our poor brother Andrew Jackson got so badly hurt in training down near Houston that he died after a few months. Lod, your granddaddy got nabbed at Gettysburg. I got wounded twice in other scrapes, but kept going until I stacked arms at Appomattox with the ten raw-boned, limping, hungry men left in the Leon Hunters."

Albert had heard the stories all his life, but he was glad that the young people could hear. Juliet's new husband didn't seem offended by the meanderings of the old Confederate. "We stuck it out," that's how Albert's father had put it, too. "I damn near starved to death in that Fort Delaware," he had said. "Ate rats and snakes. Tunneled out one time and was swimming the Delaware River when they caught me."

Uncle John went on, "When we got back about the middle of '65, the country had changed something terrible. Our brother Andrew Jackson was dead. Our younger brothers Julius Caesar and Columbus Calhoun had gone off to fight in Louisiana. Lum was only fourteen or fifteen. Both had been captured, and they weren't back yet. Daddy was fifty-four, but he looked eighty. The fields were a mess. Cattle and hogs were running wild. Everybody suddenly seemed to be poor, hungry, and sick. Like all other veterans, we Allisons had to go to work; and we had to start from scratch."

Albert's mind raced fifty years back to the days he picked cotton in the searing sun alongside his parents and brothers and sisters and a couple of Negro hired hands. 'Deep, coarse wrinkles came early in life to Allison men and women of the Reconstruction era,' he thought.

Uncle John continued, "I don't know how the Negro problem would've turned out if we'd been left alone. East-central Texas was full of them. They were wandering everywhere. No doubt some would be trouble because they didn't have the least idea how to support themselves. Daddy gave forty acres to each of the four families that we used to own, and three of them continued to work Mama's cotton until she died. They even called themselves 'Allison.' I'm certain we would've figured out a lot better solution to the problem than the Yankees imposed. Those bastards caused a lot of people to get killed—black and white."

Uncle John's voice choked, "Still happening."

He waved a bony hand at Herbert, who unscrewed the lid of the jar and handed it to Uncle John.

After the old man took a small sip, he coughed and continued, "The occupation force showed up a few months after we got back and then the State Police and then that damned Freedman's Bureau. They made our lives hell; the first thing they did was to try to confiscate our guns. Well, we wouldn't give them up. We needed our rifles to eat; more importantly, we needed them for self-defense, especially against those colored troops and the State Police, which itself was mostly colored. In 1868 they ordered all the men in Leon County to go to Centerville to vote—they lined us up, told us we were going to vote Republican; and they jailed a bunch of us for refusing. Then, just as we were becoming able to feed our families, the Yankee soldiers started marauding. They called themselves 'foragers.' Said they were collecting a 'military tax' to pay for the occupation; and they'd take our chickens and pigs, our produce, anything else they could find, including ladies clothes right off the lines. Just like prison. For eight long years we had to pay for our own imprisonment.

"At first we didn't fight back at all. But the soldiers and police, especially the colored ones, started being insolent to our women and picking fights with our young men. They'd have on their uniforms and badges and hang out in our saloons. Imagine those ex-slaves, armed to the teeth, getting liquored up in a white man's saloon. If we were going to survive, we had to take a stand. We were too weak to fight them in daylight, so we started night riding. It worked."

Albert noticed that Bill Tarver had arrived and taken a position on the rail. He was smoking a cigarette and seemed enthralled. When Albert caught Bill's eye, Bill gave a gesture that he wanted to talk. Just as Albert was about to excuse himself, Uncle John said, "Now, here's what you don't know, Albert. Nobody but us brothers has known. I'm the only one left, and out of respect for my Mama I have never talked about your Uncle Columbus until tonight. You must remember him some, Albert. He died when you were a little boy. He was only twenty-eight."

Albert had a vague memory of his young Uncle "Lum," as his daddy referred to Columbus Calhoun Allison. He did remember when Lum died, however. Albert's older brother John, age nine, had died from a fever that summer, and Albert recalled being overwhelmed by the mystery of death. Then, soon after, he was told that Uncle Lum died; but no one talked about him, except for his service to the Cause. Only just now did Albert realize how little he knew about the Allison family.

Uncle John stopped his monologue again. Pointing from the darkened porch to no one in particular, he rasped, "Boy, my throat's getting dry from all this talking."

Herbert handed the quarter-empty jar to his father. Following Uncle John's reinforcement, the jar dutifully passed from lip to lip. The draws were a little deeper this time. So was Uncle John's draw on his cheroot.

His voice became raspier, "Columbus was only seventeen when he came back from the war. More than any of us he was bitter and high-spirited. He'd seen things in that Louisiana prison camp no boy his age should see—men dying from every known malady; boys his own age without arms and legs. But the insults from the Yankee guards ate at him more than anything else. Then he comes home and finds that his Pappy's grown old and that everything he loved and fought for is now a near-as-dammit Yankee prison. He was too young to marry or have own his farm, so he lived with Daddy and Mama. But he spent his time in the saloon drinking and raising hell. When Yankee soldiers or a state policeman would come in for a drink, he and Buck Winn and the Weaver boys would sing 'Oh, I'm a Good Old Rebel.' You know it?"

The old man paused, held his head back and closed his eyes, hummed a phrase and put the defiant words to a crackly tune:

> "Oh, I'm a good ol' rebel, now that's just what I am,
> For this fair land of Freedom, I do not give a damn,
> I'm glad I fit against it, I only wish we'd won,
> And I don't want no pardon for anything I've done"

Uncle John's right foot was tapping, as the men on the porch broke out in appreciative grins.

> "I don't want no pardon for what I was and am,
> I won't be reconstructed and I don't care a damn."

Breathing a little heavily from the singing, Uncle John grinned wryly, shook his head, and continued, "Lum and his friends were attracting unnecessary attention. He'd brought a Colt .44 back from the War—said an officer from Alabama gave it to him before dying from fever—and he spent idle hours practicing with that pistol, taught himself all kinds of tricks. Of course, he had to hide it from the Yankees.

"Daddy died in 1886; he was fifty-seven. The Yankee occupation broke his spirit, but what happened after his funeral would have broken his heart. When we came out of the church, seven or eight mounted policemen, including a couple of darkies, were out there just sitting astride their horses. One of the Negro police was smiling like he was glad. I could see that it was old Jeremiah's boy Shad. Jeremiah and his family had been our slaves. Daddy had given them their land. When they were little, Shad, his two brothers, and your uncle Julius Caesar and Lum used to fish together on the Navasota River. I suspect that the seeds of this tragedy were planted when these boys were allowed to know each other. When buddies turn to enemies, the hatred is fiercest.

"Well, Shad was obviously mocking us, maybe showing off to the other policemen. It was like he was celebrating Daddy's comedown and flaunting his own sudden good luck. He was also carrying his rifle at ready and sporting a big side arm. We used to fear the consequences of armed ex-slaves, and now we had them. Only it was worse than we feared, because we were disarmed, leastways in the open. Well, Lum walked right up to Shad, looked at him hard for a long minute, said nothing, and then walked on. Everybody saw it. When they found Shad's riddled body on the Marquez to Rogers Prairie road a few weeks later, Lum was the prime suspect.

"Albert, your uncle Julius Caesar, and Arthur, your daddy, had started a business with a little one-stand steam gin and a farmer's merchant store. If the Yankee soldiers decided to get mean, they could have snuffed out their business without a second thought. So Arthur and Julius had a serious talk with Lum, and Lum disappeared. I remember not too many days went by before we heard about a lone gunman killing a colored state policeman in a bar in Springfield. Believe me, no white man grieved; but our family worried about Lum. We heard about all kinds of killings, about gunfighters roaming the country helping folks fight Yankees and coloreds. That was John Wesley Hardin's heyday, you know; but we never saw him. Well, a few years went by; and then one evening in seventy-five, or thereabouts, out of nowhere Columbus rides up to Mama's house. The Yankees and state police had been gone a year or so, and things were getting back to normal. Lum had been leading a hard life on the run, and he just wanted to come home."

"We were happy to have Lum home, but by then we all had families of our own; and the last thing we wanted was trouble from the hard, wild man Columbus had become. He had worked on farms, had hung out in saloons, had lived off gambling, had been out to Indian country, had been chased by soldiers and the law, and had served time in jail. He even bragged that fancy women supported him from time to time. He had been in fights, but we didn't know if he was ever involved in any killings. We never asked. He still claimed that he had nothing to do with Shad's murder. That was his story, but it wasn't convincing. There was still a reward for him; but with the Yankees gone, no bounty hunter would try to collect on it. Anyhow, he stayed with Mama and worked for her. She even got him to start going to church and tried to introduce him to young ladies. But, of course, nobody could keep him away from the saloon; and soon everybody in Leon County knew he was back. I guess we thought we had tamed the Negroes enough by then that they wouldn't do anything. That's why we talked him into turning himself in and getting tried. With the Yankees gone, no Leon County jury would convict him.

"So that's what he did, but he never made it to trial. Lum was soon out on bail, and he went back to spending his afternoons at Copeland's saloon over in Centerville. One late afternoon in August, Shad's older brother Meshach, who worked at Dawson's stable in Centerville, stood outside with a pitchfork waiting for Lum to come out. No one knows if Lum saw Meshach or even knew what hit him. Meshach drove the pitchfork through Columbus so hard he was pinned to the wall of the saloon.

"About ten people saw it happen. A few grabbed the Negro and held him for the sheriff (damn, getting old, can't recollect his name). Anyhow, that sheriff took Meshach to the jailhouse and waited for us to get there."

Uncle John stopped talking. He licked his old cracked lips, took out a handkerchief, and removed the broad brimmed hat with the CSA medallion. "Whew," he whispered, as he placed the hat on the seat beside him. He held out his hand to Herbert, who obliged. Following a short swig, the old man shut his eyes. No one talked. Albert's head hung. Images of young men ran through his mind, one moment alive and smiling, the next moment their life was spewing over the ground 'Uncle Lum, then Andrew...now, Son. Uncle Lum, Andrew, Son. Yes,' he thought, 'the "Allison curse."'

Uncle John's voice became steely; his eyes turned redder. "My brother Julius Caesar got there first. The undertaker had already taken over poor Lum's body. It tore Julius up something awful because he and Lum were close growing up. Also, he and Meshach had played together as little boys. After he saw Columbus, Julius went from the undertaker to the jail. Word had spread through the county; by sundown hundreds of people were crowding in the square. Julius had his gun, and neither the mob nor the Sheriff would've stopped him from shooting Meshach then and there. But Julius wasn't about to do anything without Arthur and me.

"When I got there, Julius was sitting in the jail, just looking at Meshach, who was standing in his cell just looking back. I don't know what got into me; my first words were to ask Meshach what happened.

"He said that he saw Mister Lum come into that saloon day after day, the same saloon Meshach and Shad drank in during Yankee times. After the troops left, Meshach said that the saloonkeeper wouldn't allow Meshach or any other 'nigger' anywhere near the place. All he could do was work in Watson's stable and go on home at night. A few days before, according to Meshach, Shad's haint wearing a police tunic with four bullet holes in it had appeared to Meshach on the road and walked silently by him. The next night Shad's haint was there again, but this time he moaned, 'Kill Mister Lum.'"

"Hell," Uncle John whispered, "Julius and I were so stunned, we just listened."

"Meshach told us that the next night Shad's haint threatened that if Meshach didn't kill Mister Lum that day, Shad would haunt Meshach and his family to their dying days. He said he was terrified. He said, 'I knows I'm going to be swinging, boss, but Shad's in peace and my family's going to be all right.'"

"I said, 'You're wrong about that, boy. You people were better off living with ghosts than even thinking about killing a white.'

"If Columbus did kill Shad," Uncle John concluded, "he did it to honor Daddy's memory, to defend Daddy and his beliefs from being mocked by Yankees and savage Africans. The day Lum was killed, we, his brothers, had to take a stand, too. As men of honor, we owed justice to Columbus, Daddy, and our country. Meshach swung for three days on the old Tree of Justice in front of the courthouse. Julius, Arthur, and I made a pact never to speak of it to our families; and nobody in the family went to Centerville for a week. We buried Columbus at Brushy Creek, close to Daddy, and nobody ever spoke of him again. Mama never recovered and passed within the year. Hard to imagine having your little child killed that way."

Uncle John's speech had been slurring a little. He started to nod. Albert instructed Herbert to help the old man upstairs, first room on the left. "You can have Lod's room, Herbert. Also, there's plenty of food in the dining room. Folks have been too kind, more than we can eat in a week."

Then to his son Lod, "After you eat, get some blankets and sleep on the porch."

Albert then signaled to Bill Tarver to follow him into his private reading room.

It was not yet 8 PM, but Albert was having a hard time keeping his eyes open. However, when Tarver described his conversations with Governor Sterling (who had called Tarver again after the funeral), his senses sharpened. The governor had told Tarver that bonfires were alight in front of the Travis county courthouse and that the singing had started. Tarver said that singing was a certain danger sign: the old songs bonded the crowd, and *Onward Christian Soldiers* justified their purpose. Worse, people were arriving from as far as Dallas and Houston. Henry Brooks and Ranger Captain Hamer had tried to address them, but they would not listen. The governor needed Albert down there as soon as possible.

Albert looked at his old friend sardonically, "Bill, you heard what my old Uncle thinks."

Tarver nodded, "Yep, he'd be pleased if you went down there and led the mob to crash the county jail."

"Family honor," Albert sighed.

"Albert, you know what Judge Cobb would say."

Albert's lips tightened, "Yes, I know. Can you drive again?"

Mabel was sitting with her sister Bunny and daughter Eloise at the dining room table. Ed M. and Evelyn had left while Uncle John was talking, taking Bill and Juliet Wright with them. Albert went to Mabel and took her hand.

"What was that old man going on about, Albert?"

"Just a family story, Mabel. Something I didn't know. I'll tell you later. I think Uncle John was trying to comfort me."

Albert's quiet chortle drew curious glances, but he just shook his head.

"Honey, I have to go Austin tonight—right now. It seems I'm required to stop a lynching."

After Lod's father left for Austin with Mr. Tarver, instead of going to bed, the sixteen-year old paced alone on the porch. Alone; he was alone; his mind swirled with agonizing questions he could pose to no one without invoking contempt or laughter. He was alone, and this was no to time to be alone. Friends his age would understand. He needed his friends. He went to the kitchen and told his mother that he was taking the Ford to town. She just nodded and returned to her conversation with Aunt Bun.

The night waitress at the City Café told Lod that she heard that some friends of Albert, Jr., were gathering at the old camp spot at Richland Creek. Albert, Jr., had told Lod about this secret place, where Albert and his clique had spent night-time hours singing, telling stories, learning to drink, and wondering about the opposite sex. 'Tonight I'll stand in for Albert,' Lod thought, 'Tonight I'll stand in for my brother.'

When Lod arrived at the clearing beside the creek, he saw Frank Cheney and Frank Caldwell leaning on their cars. Hands in pockets, he sauntered over to the older boys, and for the first time in his life they did not immediately treat him like a little brother. Without a word, Frank Caldwell handed Lod the jar.

"What the hell happened, Lod?" tall, lanky Frank Caldwell asked.

Other cars full of young people were creeping into the campsite. To hide his grief, Lod turned his head away.

Frank Cheney quietly said, "Sonny Mayes called me before the funeral and sends you his condolences, Lod. He said he had to stay in Austin for the grand jury, but he told me what happened."

Both Caldwell and Cheney looked at Lod as if seeking his approval. Lod understood. He nodded his head, and said, "What did Sonny say, Frank?"

For a moment Cheney stared into the clear liquid in the quart jar he was holding, "Sonny said they was only heading for one of those hootchie-kootchies to get beer, not really night-riding like the old days. But you know old 'Satan,' he was driving like a maniac and the boys were doing some 'yeehawin.'"

Albert's old nickname, one of several, jarred Lod. He never had seen the humor in it, and wondered if Albert's old comrades really did think Albert was evil. Then he berated himself for being sacrilegious or disloyal or both.

In the few minutes that Cheney had everyone's attention, he related details of the incident as Sonny Mayes had related them to him.

"Who's this Wofford guy, Frank?" It was Billy Stamps, an old classmate of Albert's, who was on summer break from college. When Lod looked up to wave to Stamps, he noticed that the clearing was full of cars, and that he, Cheney, and Caldwell were surrounded by a dozen or so old friends, most of whom were Class of '30, Corsicana High School. Cheney took a swig from the jar and passed it around.

"Surprised you ain't heard of him, Billy," Frank Cheney said. "He was an all-state pitcher at Austin High last year; threw a no-hitter against San Antonio. When Satan and them went over to the field to see a ballgame Friday night, old Harry Granberry introduced them to Wofford, who was pitching that night. Naturally, old Satan wanted Wofford to show them to the beer. And that's when they headed to the hootchie-kootchie bar."

"Damn, Frank, don't call him 'Satan' no more," admonished a pretty young woman who was hanging onto Billy Stamps's arm.

"Sorry, it's an old habit. But he sure as hell did lead us all into temptation at one time or another." Cheney's voice had become louder and he held up his jar in a mock toast.

Nervous guffaws and cries of "Yeah, brother."

"Anyway, young lady," interjected Frank Caldwell, "his real nickname was 'Coon' and everybody knows it—old Coonalee Allison."

Lod's memory flashed back almost ten years when he had sat next to his delighted parents in the school auditorium while his irrepressible brother was on the stage at Robert E. Lee Elementary. Albert's black and white minstrel song and dance sent kids, teachers, and adults into gales of laughter. Forever after, he would be old Coonalee, the famous song and dance man.

"Hey, Cheney, you know how it happened?" cried a new arrival who had just taken a couple of sips from a jar.

"He's been telling us, if you'd just open your damned ears," snapped an irritated Frank Caldwell.

Lod felt a familiar sting and slapped his arm. A girl still recovering from convulsive whimpering, said, "Why don't you boys build a fire to get up smoke. These 'skeeters are getting bad."

Soon, in spite of the hot July evening, a fire was burning on the creek bank. The smoke seemed to work.

"I guess they panicked," Frank Cheney repeated. His voice broke a little. "Coon's Dallas cousin Bob Cobb and Harry Granberry and Sonny jumped out of the car and ran behind the power station. Sonny thought Coon and Wofford did, too."

He paused.

"Then he heard the shot. Sonny ran back to the car where he saw Wofford throwing a rock at the Model T as it was driving away."

He paused and drew a breath. The tears were welling up; they were contagious.

"I guess Albert was slumped over the wheel. He never had a damn chance. That old nigger just drove by Albert's car and fired point blank."

For a few moments the gathering was quiet as the weight of tragedy sank in.

Lod knew that word of Albert had spread quickly Saturday morning. He knew that Son's friends had been reflecting for quite a few hours on the friend, on the nature of death, on heaven and hell. That night they were reminded about the war into which they were born, the never-ending, ceaseless war that killed their ancestors and was now killing them. 'Too much to bear, too much to bear,' Lod thought.

In any event, Lod knew that Albert would have appreciated Louise Barth Swenson being there, even if she was married. His brother had more than once talked of her beauty in near breathless whispers. But on that night, the face of the recent bride was so contorted in misery the young men who noticed only shook their heads. Reputedly she was a teetotaler; but when a bottle of "pre-war" arrived, she took a deep swig before her husband gently took the bottle for himself. She pulled herself from the young man's arms, stood, steadied herself, and began to sing "Dixie."

Whether it was the only song she could remember that night or whether she was honoring her friend with his theme song (from his "Coonalee" act), Lod could not tell. But mixed with alcohol, with the deep-seated commitments to the South, with youth and rage, the song was combustible. Her sweet power filled the hearts of Albert's old friends, and she became radiantly beautiful again as they joined in, "Look away, look away Dixieland." When the song came to its slow, plaintive end, she exclaimed bitterly, "I can't stand the thought that dear, dear Coon was killed by a...a...coon. Damn those murderous niggers!" The vehemence was shocking, especially from this sweet girl.

"She's right!" Billy Stamps shouted. "It's a disgrace for the darkies to be strutting around so damned prissy while old Satan is dead. They'll kill us all if we give them half a chance."

"Don't call him that no more, Billy."

Darkness was now complete. The fire was roaring in the eighty-five-degree heat. Young bodies swayed in their grief-stricken stupor. Louise Barth's "Dixie," a song once sung in jest, tonight mournfully recalled images of boys in gray. The young ladies moved from the boys, joined hands in a circle, and started swaying in a counterclockwise direction. The message was clear. "We are the symbols of Southern unity and virtue. You protect it." The boys started shouting threats to unseen black specters, taking large swigs, daring one of another to make the move. Then one ran for his open top car, others joined him, and the car roared north with two boys standing on sideboards. Two more cars followed.

Lod was astonished at the ferocity and the suddenness with which his young friends had turned from sensible melancholy into rage. For the briefest instant he thought he should say something to stop them; but before he could organize his thoughts, the cars had revved up and moved out. The best he could do was to refuse to join in. Instead he lingered for a while with a few of the girls, sharing the last of the pre-war and indulging in as much of the girls' comforting as convention would permit. At least their attentions numbed the pain for a while, and once numbed he longed for sleep.

When Lod returned to the house, he went to his makeshift bed on the sleeping porch. As he slipped from consciousness, he wondered if he was looking at the twinkling soul of his brother in the rich tapestry of stars that stretched across of the big night sky.

12

Dilemma

Hiyah Pop. Son was sitting in his open top Chevrolet.

Ain't the car swell? Uncle Andrew thinks so, too. A young man in his mid-twenties came into focus, grinning from under a wide-brimmed black hat with a high peak.

A light brown Negro drove up, gun in hand, and an old Negro with a shotgun appeared behind Andrew. Black faces looming large, gunshots…then the figures faded.

Son had blood pouring from his left shoulder. Andrew's jaw was missing. From somewhere, Albert's father, in his Confederate uniform, said, Lookee over yonder, boy.

On the horizon a Negro chained to a tree suddenly burst into flame, and the Confederate's old eyes burning red drilled into Albert's, See what you have to do, boy.

Yes, just like they had to do for me and for your granddaddy, there, spoke an unfamiliar young man (Uncle Lum?). He was pointing to a slight, gray-bearded, deep-wrinkled man in old farmer's clothing, standing on a far-off horizon. But even from a distance, Granddad John Allison's voice was clear: We cut through forests and drowned in rivers. We fought the French, the Redcoats, the Mexicans, the Indians, the Yankees, and the outlaws. We gave our wives to childbirth and our babies to cholera. We poured all our sweat and blood into the soil and gave what was left to y'all for the glory of our God, the faith of our forefathers, and a better life. Negroes and Yankees kill us because we are honest, because we work hard and love God. Our mission from the Lord is to stop them with all our ferocity.

Albert tossed awake in the moving car, soaked in sweat. Bill was concentrating on the road. Out of the car window, Albert saw the stars in a thick layer over the massive Texas night; and his mind turned to what his younger brother Leon had told him about Andrew's death.

Albert had been away at Sam Houston Normal Institute that afternoon, but Leon had been working at their father's store and was one of the first on the scene. From Leon's description, Albert learned enough to realize that something important happened in his own life that day. For one thing, if Leon's tale was only close to the truth, Judge Lodowick Cobb was one of the greatest heroes in Limestone County history.

'The judge must have thought that at least justice had a chance,' thought Albert. 'But he was not aware that Arthur Allison and the sheriff had been friends since their pioneer families first settled in the area. Yes, Arthur did his duty, and so did the judge. And I am caught between them.'

Albert knew that Tarver had made a special point to remind him of the judge, but he had no need to. Albert's upbringing had bathed him in the imperatives of the Southern story—virtue, property, family, and community. And he was immensely proud of that story, but when the judge introduced him to the imperative of the law, something in Albert clicked. The judge's law was grounded in reason, the Creator's fundament of the universe. The judge's law did not derive from the way people were raised or the way they lived. But at times during the past two days Albert had wanted to scream that the law of reason had to give way to the ancient commands of blood, that family honor trumped civility. Thanks to Bill Tarver, the judge's memory prevailed; and Albert held his tongue.

Tarver continued to drive without speaking. They had passed through Waco and were on Highway 81, destined for a midnight arrival in Austin. Albert again leaned back and shut his eyes. 'The judge,' he thought. 'The judge and his magnificent mind.'

The first time he had sat on that straight-back wooden chair in the Cobb living room, he seemed to be in a witness box, with Judge Cobb scrutinizing him from the big leather chair.

'The judge must have had his doubts about Arthur Allison's son. But he was doing a superb job of rising above his feelings.'

"Mabel tells me you have just returned from a trip east, all the way to Massachusetts. That right, young man?" Thus the judge had opened Albert's opportunity to describe his recent trip to Harvard University to receive the George Peabody medal for mathematics.

"I guess I have a knack, sir."

"Well, that knack sure helped you get that county surveyor's job. I liked ciphers myself, but I don't think they liked me much, especially algebra and geometry. I guess that's why I write wills for a living."

"To me, mathematics is a clear path to truth," Albert responded, "It shows us that immutable laws govern the relationships of the physical world. It shows that they are logical, constant, consistent, and predictable. All we have to do is figure them out. What's more, I'm in awe of the fact that my mind can comprehend these laws; it seems that the human mind and the universe are a match so perfect only Perfection Himself could have arranged it. But I sometimes wonder if we don't superimpose on nature the laws formed by our minds."

Albert caught himself; he was rambling like a schoolboy, speculating uninvited in wild philosophy with the most respected, sensible man in Limestone County. Even Albert's father begrudgingly admitted this was so.

"That sounds like the old Sophist maxim: 'Man is the measure of all things,'" was the judge's surprising response. To Albert's delight and relief, the judge had picked up on his little rant and had joined the fray.

"As I see it," the judge went on, "truth can't emanate from any man, only something outside man, like God and nature. But I agree that our job is to discover it, like old Pythagoras discovered his theorem…." The judge scratched his chin, "How's that go?"

"The square of the hypotenuse of a right triangle equals the sum of the squares of the two other sides."

"That's it. Now is there ever an exception? Is there ever any kind of right triangle where it won't work?"

"No sir, not that anyone could know about."

'Where is Mabel?' the young man had wondered.

"You know, Mr. Allison, I believe the same thing about the law. Just like old Pythagoras's hypotenuse, the law applies every time, without exception. 'Thou shalt not kill' came right from the Lord to all mankind for all time. And the Constitution, I would argue, was surely written by men inspired by the same God. You know what that means?"

"I guess it means we'd be as foolish going against the Constitution as trying to prove that one plus one is three."

"You figured it right, young man. The Constitution hasn't always sat well with Southerners. Lots of people around here even think our customs should hold sway. But that's just saying we should make up the rules as we go along. Well, it seems to me that the God who made the eternal law about that right triangle would also make the eternal laws about human governance. When we discover those laws we'd be fools not to follow them."

Mabel had been lingering in the hallway out of sight. She later told Albert that ordinarily she would never have interrupted men's conversation; but this conversation had been getting too deep, so she had swished into the room. After her magical entry, Albert's thoughts turned immediately from the ponderous and immutable to the fascinating beauty flooding the room. He jumped up and offered his arm to escort her to his rented surrey.

Driving through the night to confront the judge's greatest enemy—the mob—Albert again saw the judge in his mind's eye shaking his head, smiling, as if wondering to himself why he had been surprised at Mabel's good sense in marrying her young mathematician. In that instant Albert also imagined the judge pondering the Negro who had killed Son, his own grandson—the Negro schoolteacher, the man, the man with whom under most circumstances the judge could have had a sensible conversation, the killer.

'My divergence from the beliefs of my ancestors had begun before I met the judge,' thought Albert. But his journey was private, unarticulated, through amorphous passages. Albert was too respectful of his heritage to allow his intellect to make him insolent.

Harvard had made a big impression on Albert. 'Ah, this is what it's about,' he had thought as he strolled through the Yard. He never forgot the feeling that he knew the place, that he was at home. Over the years he often recalled the pleasant, cultured people with whom he visited at the reception in his honor at Memorial Hall. There and then, amidst Harvard's powerful tribute to its Union dead, Albert knew why the South had had to lose the War. Industrialization, the Constitution, and slavery provided good explanations or moral imperatives; but the real reason was education—too few of the South's resources had been committed to education. And, as if called to a Godly enterprise, right there he had resolved to deliver Texas from its cycle of self-imposed ignorance.

'Yet,' Albert thought, as his consciousness returned him to the speeding car, 'I was raised with Southern mores, and I am comfortable in the role of the Southern gentleman and landowner.' He loved the formality, the gentility, the rules, and the mutual respect. But the South had to break out of the strange, untenable conceptual commitment to both the Modern and the Middle Ages—the former grounded on first principles of property and equality under the law; the latter based on tradition, community, religion, status, and fealty. The former guided by reason; the latter enchained by superstition.

That is why Albert saw the judge as the model transitional Southerner, a man whose life represented the best of Southern virtue, and who, at the same time, was dedicated to the rule of reason over the tyranny of tradition. At the judge's funeral ten years before, community leaders, jurists, and lawyers of all stripes praised his even-handedness in the application of the law to white and black alike.

"If mathematical truths are eternal, so are legal truths," the judge had stated. "Moreover," he had said, "just as we cannot tamper with mathematical truth, we should not tamper with legal truth. The rub is that God gave us no choice but to obey His mathematical truths, but He did confound us with a will to choose whether we will obey His law for man."

'So there it is,' thought Albert. 'The law of the people, the law by which my Allisons had lived, versus Judge Cobb's laws of God. Thus far, in the South, the people held sway; the frenzied mob ruled.'

'But,' thought Albert, 'the South needs the law. The law's time has come.'

As the lights of the capital dome signaled their approach to Austin, Albert made the only choice his reasoning would allow: That night the mob would not decide Charlie Johnson's fate. In time, the Judge's law would.

Bill Tarver told Albert that he would drive straight to the courthouse. "You better start gathering your thoughts," he said.

13

Judgment at the Courthouse Door

After Raymond Brooks had filed his story for the Saturday morning *Austin American,* he had lingered at the courthouse off and on throughout Saturday. "Cousin" Henry Brooks, the district attorney, had kept him abreast of developments on the search for the killer. Then, after the arrest, Henry had made sure that Raymond had the confession in time for the afternoon *Austin Statesman.* Raymond was in the press conference when the sheriff had nervously assured reporters that he had no plans to move the prisoner to a safer venue. At the time, Raymond thought that the officials had puffed a little too much bravado.

Brooks had returned Sunday morning to find a larger crowd, the grounds in a mess, and more people arriving. He had headed straight for the courthouse; the sheriff's deputy tipped his hat and let him in. In the district attorney's office Sheriff White and Henry Brooks were looking out the window. Henry had just visited the governor, alerting him to the possible need for the National Guard. The governor had already ordered Captain Hamer to mobilize all available Rangers. Henry told Raymond that the governor was trying to track down Bill Tarver. He figured Tarver might be able to get the father to help them. Raymond Brooks frowned. It might work. But putting a landlord in front of that mob could be like pouring gasoline on a fire, especially if he was defending a Negro killer.

By Sunday evening, the reporter realized that the crowd had become more like a mob: It had grown by several thousand; its impatience was evident; some folks were on their feet and beginning to gravitate toward a core. Occasionally a shout: "Send the nigger on out here," or "Let's get this over with." But the crowd did not yet seethe; Brooks sensed no bond, no eyes searching for leadership. 'The crowd's on the brink, but only on the brink.' Brooks thought. 'Anything could happen. Damn, look at these people. Look at this mess.'

The evening air was breezeless, stifling. Hundreds of old cars and rusted trucks jammed the center of Austin. The men and women who drove them were gaunt, burnt, unsmiling. From small groups, Brooks heard bitter laughter, drunken singing, and even a little preaching. Humanity, barbecue, and campfires emitted an unfamiliar, noxious smell across the city streets. 'All that's missing here,' Brooks mused, 'was old Jim Ferguson making a speech or two.'

Looking for human interest or a special angle, Brooks circulated through the crowd. He introduced himself, shook hands, took names and hometowns, and recorded comments. Then, there they were, at first only vaguely familiar. They recognized him immediately, and waved. As he walked toward their little campsite, Tucker and Ellie Childs came into focus. Tuck was steel hard, burnt to a crisp, almost old. Ellie (at what? thirty-five?) was brittle, burnt, and—as always—pregnant. Neither could manage a smile. Apparently the past ten years toiling behind mules and picking cotton in the blistering sun had sealed their smiles and sapped their sentiments. 'What little remained,' Brooks opined, 'was reserved for Jesus on Sundays, blood pride, and occasional lust for each other.'"

Brooks took a seat on the ground. Ellie's eyes fixed on him, and again he felt her enormous pull. Remembering Waco, he realized that the mob had the catalyst it needed to mobilize and attack. When Ellie stood in front of the courthouse, all hell would break loose. Envisioning the scene, Brooks gratefully accepted the jar of the oily, clear corn and took a long, fiery swig.

"Y'all have come a long way," Brooks said to open the conversation.

Ellie quietly puffed on her pipe and fixed those steel blue eyes on him.

Tucker grunted. "Duty," he said. "Can't let the niggers do these things, even in tea sip town."

Then, in response to Brooks's questioning, Tucker said, "Yep, I heard about the killin' Saturday mornin' at the coffee shop before I went to work at the Gulf station in Bell Mead. All day folks stoppin' for gas talked about nothin' else, expressin' horror, but as usual too gutless to do anything. On the way home, I had my Saturday drink with the boys, and we made plans."

Ellie laughed, took the pipe from her mouth, and said, "Boy howdy. Did he ever get snockered! I was rocking on the porch when Tuck's truck wove up the road. The kids was already in from the fields. I'd fed 'em, and had helped our oldest gal dress for her beau. We got seven now, Mister Newspaper. Anyhow, Tuck come onto the porch; and the first thing he said was that the niggers kilt a white boy down in Austin."

Ellie looked at Brooks with inviting familiarity. Whispering low, as if confessing, she said, "When I heard that, I wanted to throw up. I could not help but imagine my own son lying dead, spewing blood from a nigger's knife. Ain't nothing more horrible than niggers killing our kids—not even molesting our women—even if it is a landlord's kid."

A fierce edge had crept into her voice.

"Mister Newspaper, you heard about that nigger gang on a raping spree over in Alabama? About them riots in Washington? About banks and landlords using niggers to force poor whites out of their jobs?"

Brooks held his tongue, but nodded his head sympathetically.

Tuck, looking at Ellie, said, "Well, when the niggers start killing white boys not a hundred miles from our very doorstep, we're going to do something about it."

"Yep," Ellie said, "That's what Tuck said after he come home. He said the boys might be getting up a posse to help. I just thought of daddy and told Tuck that the oldest kids could handle things 'til we got back.

Brooks could feel the crowd compressing. Ellie's demeanor had begun to change, and he began to see the face that had doomed the Negro Jesse Thomas ten years before. Explaining that he had work to do, Brooks stood, thanked Tuck and Ellie for their hospitality, and merged into the crowd that continued to gravitate to the core. 'When all hell breaks loose, Tuck and Ellie will be in the middle,' he thought.

Brooks ran into a number of familiar Austin faces, but most of the folks were from the country. The singing was becoming louder, the dancing more energetic, and the shouts more frequent. The moonshine continued to do its work. Brooks saw Captain Hamer himself guarding the courthouse door with a few Rangers. Sheriff's deputies and city police formed a visible cordon in front. But the crowd was not yet a mob.

Brooks worked his way closer to the courthouse door, where again a deputy waved him inside. "Cousin" Henry and Sheriff White were clearly edgy.

Henry said, "It's too late to move him. They'd trap us on the road. The governor's talked to Tarver, and he's bringing Mr. Allison back from Corsicana. We thought they'd be here by now."

Raymond shook his head at the image of hate burning in Ellie Childs's hard, blue eyes. "Mr. Allison's a powerful speaker, but can he overcome that?" he asked himself.

Henry seemed not to notice Raymond's frown, "What do you think, Cousin Ray?"

Raymond described what he had seen the last few hours. He told them that he didn't sense that this was the same kind of mob that strung up Jesse Thomas in Waco. Instead, he was afraid it was more like the mob that almost destroyed Sherman a couple of years back.

"They're here for war," Raymond said. "They're not talking about justice, or even vengeance. They're talking about fighting against an invasion. God help us if they turn on East Austin."

Men helpless to do anything said nothing. Mr. Allison would be here soon; that was their only way out. Raymond Brooks shook his head and walked back outside. As he surveyed the crowd, he noted that the torches and automobile headlamps—complementing the moonlight—gave the midnight gloom an eerie half-light.

Albert was stunned at the cars jammed into downtown Austin. Bill had to park two blocks from the courthouse.

"Damn, Bill, this is a real lynch mob!" Albert exclaimed.

Recalling Luther Johnson's courageous confrontation with the Streetman mob a decade before, Albert silently said, "Luther Johnson, I could use your help now."

As Albert and Bill approached the courthouse, the stench, the heat, the temper of thousands of people enveloped them. Albert and Bill pushed their way close to the courthouse door, where one of the deputies recognized them. He strode into the crowd and escorted the two men into the building. Few people noticed.

District Attorney Brooks wasted no time. After abbreviated courtesies, he said, "Mr. Allison, we know you are accustomed to addressing large crowds, but this mob is different. They may have reached the danger point. Captain Hamer and I have both tried to talk to them, but things just get worse. We hope they'll listen to you; but if you don't feel like risking it, we understand."

The father assured the district attorney that he wanted to try.

Raymond Brooks stood on the courthouse steps surveying the mob from a slightly raised vantage point. He made out familiar faces holding torches over their heads, looking as if they were waiting for a speech, or a signal. Then Brooks saw Tuck and Ellie Childs where he knew they would be—not twenty feet away from the courthouse door. Ellie stood as if in a trance, focusing on the door just a few feet from Brooks with that relentless, steely stare. As in Waco ten years ago, she held her corncob pipe in her right hand, arms folded over her protruding stomach. Next to Ellie, keeping one eye on her, Tucker cocked his head to talk to the huge man Tuck had previously pointed out to Raymond. Others in their vicinity were also keeping an eye on Ellie, but she was oblivious. Suddenly the singing and preaching died down, and the crowd moved closer. Brooks saw Ellie start to sway side-to-side. As her movement became more pronounced, Tuck picked it up, then five more people. Within minutes Brooks saw the movement spread through the mob; the torchlight began to flicker eerily side-to-side. He could see the swaying mob becoming the monster; he could feel the heat of the monster, the breath of the monster. Soon the monster would rage with a singular, persistent roar, like no other monster on earth. He knew he should be alarmed at the mounting disaster, yet he could not contain his excitement. At any moment, the woman Ellie would whisper to those around her, "Okay. Now!"

At that moment, the courthouse door opened and Albert Allison emerged accompanied by Bill Tarver and Henry Brooks. With a bullhorn in hand, Allison stood on a table and faced the mob.

Raymond Brooks noticed that when the father raised his hand, the swaying became less pronounced; and the roar abated.

"I am the boy's father. Please hear me out!"

'Such a booming voice from such a small man,' Raymond Brooks thought. Despite the rustling, coughing, and one angry outburst from a woman's shrill voice, Brooks was able to hear most of Allison's words.

"Ladies and gentlemen! Please hear me out," he began. "I am Albert Allison, the murdered boy's father. I want you to know how much Mrs. Allison and I appreciate that so many of our son's fellow Texans are determined that his murderer be given the full measure of justice demanded by the laws of God and man."

Some men around Brooks quietly said "Amen, brother."

"You who have children," Allison continued, "know our deep pain and anger. You know the searing ache ripping away at the boy's anguished mother. You understand why, since the moment we were told about our boy, we prayed to the great God Almighty that the Negro be delivered to the hounds of hell."

Brooks heard a few shouts from the front of the crowd, "Amen, Brother Allison, let's send him to hell!"

Allison held up his hand.

"He's earned their respect," Brooks said to himself.

"My friends," Brooks heard Allison's words clearly, "my son did not see nineteen birthdays. Yet, the story of his short life is still a Texas story, a story of a boy proud of his country, proud of its history—and proud of the laws that made this country and its history possible."

Silence.

'The eye of the storm,' thought Brooks.

"Mrs. Allison and I appeal to you to respect the story of Albert's life by allowing its final chapter to be a testimony to that country he loved, that history he loved, and those laws he respected. Let us allow the judges and the fine officers of the State of Texas and the County of Travis to do their jobs."

Suddenly a shrill scream blasted from the core. Ellie's clear voice full of rage erupted into the silence.

"The landlord's saying we got to let a murdering nigger have a white man's trial! The landlord wants to save the nigger! *No! No! No!* Not here! Not now! Not never! Let's do it. Let's do it now!"

Then she was swaying again, and the people around her were swaying again. A roar returned, and the core surged a few feet. 'Allison has failed,' thought Raymond Brooks. He saw Henry leave the steps and duck inside the door. 'To call the governor,' Brooks suspected. 'Time for the Guard.'

But Allison shouted, "Wait! Don't move! *Don't move!*"

The crowd stopped its movement for a critical moment. It quieted just enough.

Allison's voice carried the authority of a father, "Lady, you know what I know, and what Captain Frank Hamer over there knows and the sheriff knows, and all you folks know. When that Negro pulled the trigger, he was not aiming just to kill my boy; he was aiming at every white man, woman, and child in Texas. That's why for the sake of justice—for my boy, and all of us—I ask you to let the chosen representatives of every man, woman, and child in Texas do their job. That job is to make sure that every Negro who thinks about murder or violence against us sees that the law of the State is a more terrible avenger than the righteous vengeance of the people."

The swaying had stopped. Brooks found Ellie Childs. Her eyes fixed hard on the father, she puffed her pipe in short, furious bursts. But she remained still and silent, and moment by moment the rage began to drain from the monster. Tuck, standing beside Ellie, seemed transfixed on the men standing in front of the courthouse door. Then he pointed at Bill Tarver and said something to the large man standing beside him.

Allison then stood as erect as his short stature would allow, "My son respected the almighty vengeance of the law, and I am asking y'all to let him have a say in this matter. Giving the Negro to civil justice would have been his fervent wish."

Silence. The father's voice, so strong and steady at the beginning, had audibly cracked as he closed.

Finally, even with Ellie and Tuck starting again to sway side-to-side again, the edges of the crowd began to break up, and Brooks heard a man's voice, "Well, folks, if that's what the daddy wants, that's it. I'm going home."

Torches began to go out, and the mob started crumbling. People in fives and tens, and finally hundreds, returned to their rusty cars and broken-down trucks. Soon Ellie, Tuck, and their friends were the only ones standing before the courthouse. At last, she looked at Tuck, turned, and walked away. The men around her followed.

Raymond Brooks rushed to the newsroom to file his story.

As Albert stepped down from the table, Bill Tarver felt giddy and nauseated at the same time. For a long moment after that woman had screamed, he was certain that he, Albert, and the lawmen would be trampled. That woman! And beside her was the Bell Mead gas station attendant whose face had haunted Tarver the past twenty-four hours. When the man pointed at him, Tarver's stomach had knotted. Knowing how important it was to hide his fear, he had to remind himself to look secure, solid, and determined. He hoped he had.

District Attorney Henry Brooks whacked Tarver on the back and grabbed Albert's hand. Albert seemed a bit overwhelmed at first, and Tarver thought he saw a tear trickle from his friend's eye. In fact, for an instant Tarver thought that Albert might break down, and who could have blamed him?

"Well, Mr. Allison, you sure turned this mob." It was Frank Hamer. "You've done us all a great service, sir. The governor's on the telephone and wants to have a word."

While Governor Sterling congratulated Albert, Captain Hamer, Henry Brooks, and Bill Tarver went outside and walked around the courthouse to survey the devastation: dying campfires, newspaper wrappings, smashed glass, bottles, scorched poles used as torches, and the inevitable stench of feces and urine.

Before Captain Hamer left to dismiss his men, he remarked to Bill, "The prisoners will have a big job tomorrow. Seems like the least that Charlie Johnson can do."

When Tarver and Henry Brooks came inside, Albert asked the district attorney for a rundown on the sequence of events from that point forward.

"I mean with regards to the prisoner," he said.

"Well, the grand jury will meet this morning," Brooks responded, "I'm sure they'll return an indictment for first-degree murder. Judge Moore will assign a trial judge, most likely Judge Charles Wheeler, and Wheeler will set a trial date. Wheeler's got another murder trial scheduled later this month, so I reckon we're looking at late August, early September. I doubt that the Negro will see the outside again."

"Has he got representation?" Bill Tarver asked.

Brooks shrugged. "Not that I know of, sir. Judge Wheeler'll appoint one of the new university graduates, I imagine," he said quietly.

'Or one of the courthouse drunks,' Tarver thought wryly.

Charlie Johnson had spent the day praying. Convinced that at any moment he would be led to glory, he was determined to be at peace with himself and die like a man. As the day went on and into the evening, the crowd noise outside the courthouse had picked up—louder and louder shouts, louder laughter, louder singing. Charlie knew drunken voices, and he knew that with drunken mobs a thirst for blood often mixed with the 'shine. He knew that sheriff's deputies and Rangers were out there with rifles and shotguns; but that was not real comfort, not until the young deputy called Homer came to his cell.

"You notice something, Charlie? You notice that the crowd is gone?"

Charlie listened intently—no voices, no general commotion—only a few cars driving by.

"They're gone, Charlie, like I told you. You know what happened? That Mr. Allison come down here from Corsicana tonight. He asked them to let you alone. They couldn't go against the boy's daddy. What do you think of that, Charlie?"

Charlie's head felt light, "Praise be the Lord, Sheriff. Thank you. I guess the other side'll have to wait for old Charlie a mite longer."

14

Mabel and Emma

"Thank goodness the house is finally quiet," Mabel sighed. Well-wishers and mourners had quietly disappeared. Lod had returned from visiting his friends and had taken his blankets to the summer porch to join Eloise and Ken. Uncle John and Cousin Herbert had taken the twin beds in Lod's room. Since Juliet and her husband Bill were returning to Chicago by an early train the next morning, they were staying with Ed M. and Evelyn. After a long good-bye hug, Juliet promised to return soon with their new baby, whom they had left with Bill's parents. Except for Mabel's sister Bunny, Mabel was alone. While Bunny finished cleaning up the kitchen, Mabel looked for solace in the reading room.

To most people, Mabel presented a disciplined, constant stoicism that gave little evidence of delight or depression, but not to Bunny. Still, that night she could not burden even Bunny with too much of her grief. So, as Mabel had done that morning, she turned inward to "Worms."

> You were too young to slip away
> Into that unknown land
> Where I could no more see your face,
> Could hear your voice or touch your hand.
> Will you still be my gay young son?
> When I am come to that far place?
> And will you know me—
> Old and gray—
> When we meet face-to-face?

'Dear, dear Bunny,' Mabel mused after putting down her pen, 'Son's favorite Aunt. The two just sparked.'

Albert had approved Son's taking the job with the gas company in Dallas because Bunny and her husband Stanley had moved there a couple of years before. Son would stay with Mabel's somewhat serious unmarried sisters, but would have Bunny close by for wit and comfort.

'Yes, Son and Bunny shared a secret understanding of a happy world designed by God to give us cause to smile easily. A world now shattered by a Negro's bullet,' Mabel cried to herself.

Earlier that evening, when Bunny's rage and weeping was spent, she had clung limply to Mabel and would not detach herself. Stanley and the Kerr children had needed to return to Dallas soon after the funeral, but she had stayed. And Mabel wanted her to stay. Both needed a sister's comfort.

Bunny was comfort, but Mabel longed for Albert. She needed his arms around her, needed to have one more cry with him. He had been so tired after returning from Austin. Then at the governor's behest, back to Austin—two late-night trips to Austin in three days…he was no longer a young man.

But she knew that he would not call until morning.

Despite Bunny, Mabel would fret through another night.

Since Albert was away and the other beds were taken, Bunny was to sleep with Mabel that night; so when Mabel told Bunny she was ready for bed, Bunny quietly tagged along up the stairs. They changed into bedclothes, and Bunny suggested a prayer. Like their nights as little girls when they dutifully prayed, "Now I lay me down to sleep…" the sisters silently knelt by the bed side by side.

After a moment, Mabel prayed aloud, "Please, oh Lord, please take my beautiful boy to your bosom, and help us, dear Lord, to cleanse our hearts of the bitterness ever-threatening to consume us. Please let Son know that he will be forever a part of our hearts…never to be forgotten." She choked, "Amen."

Bunny whispered, "Amen."

When Mabel awoke, the other side of the bed was empty. Apparently, Bunny had risen at daybreak without a sound. No sounds.; When Mabel woke, all was quiet. Except for bird chatter, quiet. A house full of people and no sounds—no raucous laughter from a tow-headed boy, no taunting or teasing or delighted shrieks from the boy's little sister. The tears began to form, and the unbearable ache returned. But Mabel wiped her face and reminded herself that she must not surrender, that the ache would be with her always, and that…hungry guests would soon want breakfast.

Bunny had been busy in the kitchen. The aroma of coffee and baking biscuits wafted through the house. Uncle John and Herbert sat patiently at the breakfast table talking to Lod, Eloise, and little Ken. Mabel looked for Emma to help serve them, but Emma was not there. Chester, their handyman, was missing, too.

"Unlike them to be this late," she said to Bunny.

"I saw them at the service yesterday evening," Bunny said. "I'm sure they'll turn up soon."

With Eloise and Lod helping, Bunny and Mabel served an ample breakfast. After they had eaten, Uncle John and Herbert gave their final condolences and left just as Stanley Kerr arrived back from Dallas to take Bunny home.

Soon after the Kerrs said their good-byes, Albert called. He told Mabel about the mob, how they had listened to him, and, thank God, that they had gone home. He had stayed with the Tarvers overnight, and would come home later in the day. Albert then gave instructions for Lod not to go to the farm, but to stay at home and make himself useful. Mabel told Albert that everyone, including Bunny, had left after breakfast; but she did not mention Emma and Chester. Just as she was about to say good-bye, Bill Tarver got on the telephone.

"Mabel," he said, "Albert stood tall for everything your father worked so hard for."

Bill's voice sounded so respectful that it made Mabel feel better.

Evelyn and Ed M. had arrived while Mabel was on the telephone with Albert. They told Mabel that after taking Juliet and Bill Wright to the train, they had stopped by the City Cafe for their routine morning coffee and gossip.

"Folks were talking about a bunch of kids making trouble on the east side the night before," Ed M. said.

"Apparently," he added almost sheepishly, "they were shouting Albert, Jr.'s, name, and set fire to some old tires."

After a brief pause, he went on, "Apparently a lot of maids and yardmen stayed home this morning, afraid because a Negro killed Albert Allison's boy."

Mabel turned to Lod and frowned, "Your friends?"

The teenager blanched. Quietly he said, "I guess so, Mama. I found Frank Caldwell with a bunch of kids at Richland Creek last night; they were drinking and getting pretty steamed. But I didn't go with them. I even…"

Mabel put up her hand and stopped the boy before he said something foolish like "I even tried to stop them."

"Is this what boys do these days? Isn't this what Albert said that boys in Austin were rumored to have been doing this summer? Are responsible people going to stop this nonsense before we have another tragedy? These boys have disgraced themselves and us, too. If Albert were here, he would be on the phone doing something…and poor old Emma and Chester. They must be scared out of their wits."

And then an idea formed; within minutes the idea spurred her to pick up the telephone.

"My name is Mabel Allison. May I speak to Mr. Caldwell, please?"

After Mabel thanked Frank Caldwell, Sr., for his condolences, she told him what she had heard; and, as she expected, he was upset—at first disbelieving, but on reflection, upset. Frank, Jr., had come home late the night before and had been a little drunk.

"Frank, before you get after your boy, I have an idea that might teach him and the others a lesson and maybe make peace with the Negroes as well. Also, it might bring me some consolation. Bring young Frank and as many boys who were with him last night as you can muster to Fifth and Gray streets on the east side. They have some cleaning up to do. Lod and I will meet you there in two hours."

After she put down the receiver, Mabel caught Evelyn's incredulous look. Holding her hand up to suppress the inevitable protest, Mabel told Evelyn that she could help by taking Eloise and Ken to the country club.

Mabel was dressed in mourning attire. But as she and Lod approached the east side she began to feel like a schoolteacher, and she pushed back her sleeves. Lod pulled the Ford in behind two other cars already parked on the dirt roads. As he assisted Mabel from the car, six-foot-six-inch Frank Caldwell, Sr., strode to them. He removed his Stetson, and, waving at a group of large young men, said, "Well, Mabel, here they are. Some of the boys were at work, but I talked to their employers."

"Go stand with your friends, Lod," she said.

Then, looking up at Caldwell (as she was only five-foot-two), "Frank, thank you. The boys don't look too happy; but every one was a Cub Scout with Albert, Jr., and I was their den mother. I can take them from here. Feel free to leave, if you wish."

Without waiting for an answer, Mabel strode to the group of boys. 'How these boys have grown,' she thought, as she approached the tall, muscular young men she and her husband had once taken on their first overnight camping trip.

"Billy Stamps, is that you?"

The boy had always had a mean look, and he was about as tough as these boys came; but she knew him as an obedient, serious boy with a good heart. Mabel knew that when boys like these do terrible things, they have to be cut down to size.

"Yes, Ma'am."

"What did they teach up there at SMU, Billy? Did they teach the football team to bully and raise Cain?"

"They killed Albert, Mrs. Allison." It was Frank Cheney.

"*They* did no such thing, Frank. But *you* committed an incivility and disgraced yourself—*and* Albert," her voice was quiet and crisp. "You know better, young man. You all know better."

Then she told the shame-faced, shuffling young men what Cub Scout Pack No. 119, Robert E. Lee Elementary, was going to do. First, Frank Caldwell, Jr., was to take Lod and four other boys to clean up the burnt tires and any other messes they made. Frank's father, who had stayed to support Mabel, would deal with their employers, she said.

The tall man nodded, "Yep, no going back to work until the job's done. Your pay's going to be docked one way or the other."

Frank, Jr., spoke up, "Mrs. Allison, Lod had nothing to do with this. It ain't fair to make him do this."

"Lod was with y'all when you were working yourselves up to this disgrace, and he did not stop you. That makes him responsible. Now go on; there's no quitting until these streets are twice as clean as when you made your mess."

As the work party trudged off, she turned to the two remaining boys—Billy Stamps and Frank Cheney.

"Now, you follow me," she said. "We're going to make some face-to-face apologies."

Stamps pouted his lips and shook his head, "Me and Frank ain't apologizing to no niggers, Mrs. A. It ain't becoming; it ain't natural..."

She turned to face them squarely, "Young man, what would your parents think if they just heard you? Not only is your grammar bad, you're talking like the Klan. I know your father and mother too well, Billy—and yours, too, Frank. I know they raised you both to be gentlemen, and that means using civilized language and that means being kind to those who are less fortunate. Do you understand me?"

Mabel had surprised herself. She knew neither the Stamps nor the Cheneys that well, and from what little she did know, both couples might easily have been in the Klan. But, if the boys knew this to be the case, they could never admit it to Mabel.

"Yes Ma'am, but—"

"*But,* nothing! You are coming with me. We are going door to door together, and you two are going to tell these people you're sorry." After a slight pause, she added, "And never, ever use the word *nigger* in front of me, again!"

The young men did not respond, but their downcast faces spoke volumes to Mabel. 'Nobody calls football players to account,' she mused. 'They're expected to drink, curse, crash cars, despoil girls, fail classes, harass Negroes, and mangle the King's English. In fact, many in Corsicana would say that it was their duty. Folks need their heroes to be a little special, a little above the law. Folks need to overlook their misdeeds. Folks need to forgive them with a wink, a pat on the back, and good luck wishes for the next season—but not their den mother. Their den mother expects them to stand up for virtuous manhood. And they dare not disobey their den mother.'

With Stamps and Cheney ambling behind, Mabel walked quickly to the little house across the street, and rapped on the door. She had noticed someone drawing the window shade back and heard movement from inside. Yellowish goo clung to stanchions holding up the porch roof.

"Who's there?"

"I'm Mrs. Allison. Is that you, Estelle?"

Silence.

"Estelle, I've come about last night. Please open the door."

"We ain't done nothing, Mrs. Allison," Estelle's voice was a plea. "We's most sorry about your boy. It be horrible. Please, Mrs. Allison, we never want to see him hurt."

"Thank you, Estelle. I know you and Alvin would never hurt my son. And that's what I wanted to talk to you about. Last night some white boys did a bad thing over here. These boys here were with them, and they want to say they're sorry."

Silence.

Slowly the door creaked open. A tall, well dressed Negro with short gray hair stood erect, clearly confused, but with a look of trust. Mabel could see Estelle's head beside his shoulder.

"Alvin, this is Billy Stamps and Frank Cheney."

"I knows them, ma'am. They been at Mr. and Mrs. Fortson's house many times."

She stood aside, waved the reluctant young men to step forward, and looked at them expectantly.

Frank Cheney would not make eye contact, but he said the words that had a semblance of an apology.

Mabel said, "Alvin, I personally want to assure you that nothing is going to happen to you or anybody on the east side because of what happened to my son. I know the Fortsons are missing y'all today, so please go over there as soon as you can. One more thing, Alvin: Did these boys do any damage to you or your property?"

"No ma'am. They just make noise and yell bad words."

"Well, I think I see some damage," she said, pointing at a spot where an egg had smashed against their house. "If you'll bring us a pan of warm water and soap and a couple of rags, I know that these boys will want to clean up the mess they made."

Billy laughed, "What?"

"That's right, young man, you volunteered."

Within minutes, Estelle, obviously trying to hide her delight, appeared with a large pan of hot water, soap, and a pile of washrags. Mabel told the boys she saw three egg splotches on the house and one on the Model T parked in the rutted driveway.

To Estelle she said, "Y'all go about your business. We'll clean this up and leave these by your door."

Mabel knew Billy Stamps and Frank Cheney would stand only so much humiliation. It was bad enough to have to clean up their mess—best not to press the point with two gloating Negroes observing.

When the boys finished, the unlikely trio marched to the next house, and repeated the process. Again the residents were frightened, again they had to be reassured and coaxed, again Stamps and Cheney had to clean off the eggs. And so it went. By the time they made half-a-dozen apologies, they noticed that there was less reticence, even some anticipation, as they approached the affected houses.

A half hour later they came to a small house familiar to Mabel. The only egg mess was smattered on an old wooden rocking chair. The front door was partially ajar behind the firmly shut screen door.

"Chester? Y'all there?"

"Yes ma'am, yes ma'am," Chester's voice came from within the house.

Chester opened the door, "Oh, Mrs. A., I cain't think what I do, poor little child, I be crying and praying. Old Emma, too."

"Thank you, Chester. I know. I know y'all were at services yesterday," she said. "We're all crushed. Is Emma here?"

"Why, yes ma'am. She here 'cause she let that ol' screech owl kill poor Son, and she scared you be mad."

Sometimes Mabel felt that she understood these folks, but instances like this made her realize that much ran deep and unrevealed.

"Chester, please ask her to come on out here."

Another small black figure appeared at the screen door, but did not come out. She wore a small round hat with a dried flower stuck in the brim, and her matchstick legs rose out of old unlaced men's shoes.

Whatever irritation Mabel may have felt vanished, "Emma, Chester, we want you to know how much we appreciate your joining us at the service yesterday. We know you loved Son. Now I need y'all. Please come on, and Lod'll drive y'all to the house."

"Oh Mrs. A.," Chester said hesitantly, "we can't go there. White folks want to kill us 'cause a colored killed Mister Albert."

"No, Chester, we want you to come. Nobody would dare hurt you."

Chester looked quizzical, "Missus not mad at old Emma?"

"Why, of course not." She turned to the little woman, still shrinking behind the door, "Whatever gave you that idea, Emma?"

The old black lady pondered a moment, "I told you I choke that ol' owl. I thought he be dead, but he must've gulped twice and get back in the yard."

The owl again.

"Emma, Albert died in Austin—a long way away from that owl."

"Yes ma'am."

"Now tell me what happened here last night."

"The white boys done ride last night," Emma responded in a low terse voice. "They throw rocks and eggs at folks on the porches; they scream bad words and say they coming with ol' Judge Lynch. They holler 'Remember Albert,' 'Remember Coon.' They hit ol' Chester with a egg as he sit right here."

Mabel looked at Chester. She saw no damage, but she knew that this old man, to whom dignity was everything, must have been deeply hurt.

"Chester, I'm going to put a stop to this nonsense; and I want everybody to know it. Before we go, please go tell your neighbors they have nothing to worry about. I'm sorry the boys did these bad things, and," turning to look at Billy Stamps and Frank Cheney as she spoke, "I am offended mightily that they used Son's name. Now you go tell them, please."

Mabel felt eyes, many eyes focused on the porch from behind the corners and curtains. She knew the word was spreading and could hear their thoughts: "Mrs. Allison's knocking on doors with two big white boys, and they ain't got no guns and ain't got no riders with them. Those boys has mops and buckets and is cleaning the egg messes. Look at poor Emma and poor old Chester; it's like that Austin man killed they own boy."

Chester looked sternly at the boys, too. "Yes ma'am," he said, with a slight emphasis on the "Yes." The old man straightened his posture and strode purposefully over the sun-baked ground to speak to his neighbors. 'Chester feels those eyes, too,' Mabel thought.

Emma then said, "We be scared you gonna' kill everybody over here."

"Oh, Emma, I hope you will come with me. Nobody is going to hurt y'all. Believe me."

Emma, her face cast in an unfamiliar sadness, disappeared into the house and returned with a large, bulging handbag. When Chester returned, Mabel told them where the car was parked and asked them to go there and wait.

After another half hour and three more apologies, the Cub Scouts gathered where they had parked the cars. The boys, now covered in dirt and sweat, acted appropriately subdued, and even managed respectful—if half-hearted—gestures toward Emma and Chester, who were standing near the Allison's Ford.

Finally, young Frank Caldwell walked up to Mabel, "Mrs. Allison, we acted like a bunch of idiots. Even if we wanted to disgrace ourselves, we had no right to drag Albert down with us."

After the other boys mumbled various forms of agreement, Billy Stamps came to her and looked her squarely in the eye, "I'll always remember this day, ma'am. I'll always remember Albert, too."

Back at the Allison house, Mabel gave brief instructions on household chores to Emma and Chester; and she told Lod to clean himself up and go to the country club. He was to be back with Eloise and Ken by suppertime. Feeling grimy herself, she too went upstairs to clean up. While in the bath, as surprised as anyone at her audaciousness, she began to chuckle. Lod was aghast, she could tell; but he was also proud. 'Evelyn will be mortified when she hears,' she thought with a smile.

Two hours later, Sheriff Pevehouse called. At first, Mabel's heart beat faster with a tinge of apprehension. Maybe one of the boys or his parents complained about being forced into involuntary servitude. But if anything, the sheriff was overly solicitous. He said that a lot of folks were talking about what she had done that morning.

Before she could respond, he continued, "The Negroes have been mighty jittery ever since we arrested Alice Stewart's boy for killing that Austin Negro. I think folks over there figure Alice was involved in that killing somehow, and maybe somehow involved with your boy. You know, some connection with Austin."

"Well Sheriff, I don't know what Alice Stewart is telling people, but from what I heard this morning they are a lot more afraid of our rabble-rousing boys."

When Mabel mentioned Alice Stewart's name, a loud gasp came from the living room. Mabel turned and saw Emma dusting the piano.

"Yes, Ma'am," the sheriff responded. "What you did calmed things down. It's a shame that somebody didn't do something like this in Austin before things got out of hand down there. Me and Mrs. Pevehouse was real sorry about Albert, Jr. We're praying for y'all."

Mabel returned to her kitchen to lose herself in mindless drudge. Minutes later, as she was kneading flour, Emma's little figure edged beside her.

That small black face was strangely contorted; her voice choked, "Honey, I's so sad, I cried all the whole time and I can't seem to stop it."

"It's just terrible, Emma," Mabel replied quietly.

"It's that ol' owl. I try to choke him but it don't work and now that poor Son be dead—" As she said the final words, she broke into sobs. Mabel also began weeping, and turned and took Emma in her arms.

After a moment, Mabel gently pulled away and said softly, "Emma, please do not speak to me of the owl again."

Then she returned to her piecrust, and Emma went back to her housework.

But Mabel knew that Emma had news she had to report, and she knew that Emma knew Mabel's ways better than any person alive, except Albert. Emma knew that her lady did not like to talk in the kitchen, that the best time to talk was when Mabel was in the reading room, at her desk, writing with the pen she dipped in the ink bottle. Mabel knew that Emma would choose that time to dust the reading room.

Even knowing Emma this well, when Mabel finally went to the little room for her afternoon solitude, she became so lost in "Worms" that she did not notice Emma ease imperceptibly into the room.

"Honey child," Emma gently broke into Mabel's reverie, "you remember ol' Mister Kessner over on the eastside?"

Mabel looked up and nodded. She had recorded Emma's tale of Mister Kessner's buried treasure.

"Why yes, Emma. He spoke to you through a black cat and told you where the treasure was buried."

"Yes'm. That's the one. Well, last night I's over to the eastside for church after Son's funeral and before those nightriders come. When I come out of the church I hear this voice. It say, "Emma," kinda soft-like. Then I sees perched on a ol' fence post a big, black ol' crow; the biggest and blackest I ever did see.

"The crow, he say, 'Emma come over here 'cause I got something to say.' So I say, 'Who you be and what you doin' coming round here after church on a sad,

sad day like this?' Then he say, 'Emma, I'm the Rhambo man from Austin. I be a screech owl some of the time, but I be a crow when I've got to talk to folks. Now don't be scared 'cause you kin see that I'm not no screech owl now.' Well, I say, 'I don't know no Rhambo man from Austin.' And he say, 'Sure you do. I be the man killed by that boy of Stewart Allison.' And I say 'I don't know no Stewart Allison.' And he say, 'Sure you do. I seen you at the Allison house trying to choke me.' And I say, 'Them's not no Stewart Allisons. Them's my white folks Allisons.' And he asked, 'Don't they have the colored funeral home?' And I say you fool ol' crow, 'My Allisons ain't got no funeral home. They be politicks and they be white.' 'Well,' he say, 'Who be the funeral home?' And then I see he mean Missus Alice Stewart, who be at the colored funeral home two years back. Her son Carl done be arrested for killing a' Austin man.'"

Emma paused and took Mabel's hand, as if preparing Mabel for the crushing news she had to bear.

Clearly confused, Mabel said, "I think Mister Allison mentioned something about a murder in Dawson a few weeks ago—as I recall a prominent colored man from Austin. Sheriff Pevehouse mentioned it, too."

"That's right, honey. Sheriff Peeveehouse hisself catched Carl Stewart, Missus Alice Stewart's boy. But that ol' dead Rhambo got mixed up. And when I sets him right, he flapped his wings and jump and squawk, and then he bawl and say his screech owl self go to de wrong yard.

"So I say to the crow, 'You come in good white folks yard and make all that trouble and sorrow?'"

"And then he say he almost gets his revenge when that Stewart be driving his car with his dead body, because his screech owl self rose up in the back seat, and flapped, and when Stewart saw him, Stewart wrecked that car and almost killed hisself. But the car be hurt and not Stewart, aleast very much. The sheriff bring Mr. Rhambo's car from Dawson to Corsicana. That car carried his dead body and his owl and crow spirits. The crow figured that when the sheriff say 'Alice,' Rhambo's spirit think he hear 'Allison.' Stewart Allison. So to get his revenge he head for the Allison yard."

Emma paused again. Tears formed in her old eyes as she suddenly took Mabel in a strong embrace and broke into sobs. A moment went by as Mabel tried to comfort her.

Emma backed away and composed herself. Then she said, "Honey, that ol' crow say straight to my face, 'When I got into the Allison yard Friday night and screech three times, the next Allison be in Austin be taken by my curse and be killed. And it happen that night; so I got my revenge and stop my screech.'"

"Emma!" cried Mabel, "Stop this nonsense. Nothing of the kind happened."

"Oh, honey, when that ol' Rhambo see my face, he say he mighty sorry, dread sorry; and he want me to ask you if he can haint some peoples for you or something."

Mabel knew it was useless to gainsay Emma again. The only way to end this matter was to be agreeable, "No, Emma, if you see him again, just ask him to protect my other children."

"Yes ma'am," Emma almost whispered, obviously relieved that she had finally got the whole episode off her chest, "I'll tell him that. Be easy for him after he finish with ol' Alice Stewart's boy."

15

Charles Johnson and Carl Stewart

For a moment Charlie did not realize that the clamor in the cellblock was not his dream. "Everybody wake up and get ready for a day's work," a deputy was shouting. Hazily, Charlie and about twenty-five of his fellow prisoners rolled out of their cots, put on their shoes and uniform tops, and walked single file to the small dining hall, where they lined up for biscuits, hash, and coffee. Ten minutes later, a deputy had them fasten ball and chains to their ankles, and marched them outside to clear up the mess covering the courthouse grounds.

Later in the morning, while Johnson was clearing a campfire site, the deputy standing near him pointed to a group of white men entering the courthouse door. He said they were the members of the Travis County grand jury who would charge him and Carl Stewart with murder. Since Charlie had no lawyer, the deputy said, Charlie might be called to answer questions sometime today or tomorrow.

An hour or so later Johnson saw the deputy take a young white man in a dark suit to where Carl Stewart was working. With Stewart carrying his ball, the three walked off together. When the inmates returned to the jail after completing the clean up, Stewart was already in his cell, looking frightened and dazed.

Just after lunch, much to Charlie's relief, Louis Lyons and Reverend Adam Black arrived. The reverend carried a newspaper and a wooden chair. Louis sat on the bed beside Charlie, inclined his head and said, "Charlie, Charlie what you doing in here? Did you shoot that white boy, Charlie?"

The reverend wordlessly handed Charlie the newspaper.

Charlie shook his head. "Thank y'all for coming. I can't tell you how much I appreciate it."

Then he looked at the two men steadily—first at Louis, next the reverend—and shook his head again, "Well, I did fire a gun at a car some white men

139

was riding in. They ran into a ditch in front of me on Chicon; and I stopped to help them; and they threw the rocks at me. One hit me here," Johnson said, pointing to his head. "So I drove off; but they followed me, passed me, and stopped at that substation on Seventh. I had to drive by, and then I heard a crack like a rifle. I thought about old Rhambo; and the next thing I know, I'm firing at the car. Then I go on home. I didn't think anything be wrong until the sheriffs came."

"So you thought those boys might be working for the same people that killed Nathan?" Louis asked.

Charlie nodded and put his finger to his lips. In a whisper, "That Carl Stewart be in this very jail."

Louis and the reverend frowned and put their own fingers to their lips. Reverend Black then said, "We's praying for you, Charlie, the whole church, most all day yesterday."

Charlie nodded gratefully, "I scared I'd be on the rope last night, Reverend. You know it. But your praying got the Lord to send me an angel. The sheriff told me that the boy's daddy hisself came down here last night and asked that mob to leave me alone. They can't go against the boy's own daddy."

Reverend Black suddenly fell to his knees.

He then raised his hands, "Oh great God Almighty," the booming preacher's voice reverberated through the jail. After exchanging startled glances, Charlie and Louis reflexively fell to their knees.

"Thank You Lord for hearing the prayers of these poor sinners. Thank You for filling the daddy with Your spirit. Thank You for sending him here on a mission of Your most eternal mercy. Thank You for sparing our brother Charlie Johnson. Thank You for the breath of life You give us each new day."

After Louis and Charlie had said their "Amens" and returned to their seats on the bed, Louis said, "Mighty nice words, Reverend." Then, as the reverend returned to his wooden chair, Louis turned to Charlie, "Old Perry's a mite worried about the policy business. We all are."

Charlie nodded.

Louis continued, "On Saturday he call me, Dr. Everett Givens and Mr. Will Fuller to come to his farm." Then, as Reverend Black and Johnson quietly listened, Louis told of their meeting on Saturday and of Will Fuller's devastating announcement that he was backing out of the deal.

Charlie shook his head, "Colonel, I've thought about how I can keep the business going. Just have young Everett Rhambo come see me everyday. I think I can train him enough to make Mr. Fuller happy, but Mr. Fuller's right not to count on me. The Lord may have sent the boy's daddy to save me last night. But that same daddy come here Saturday and just look at me; and when I tell him I's sorry, he just nod…Whatever he do with that crowd, Colonel, he still want to kill me. I know it."

"And he be a big shot, too," Louis added. "The papers say he's rich. All the big shot politicians came to the hospital to meet him Saturday morning when he come down from Corsicana.

"Speaking of politics," Louis went on, "we can only stay a short time this morning, because I got to drive the reverend back to East Austin and then get back to downtown. Me and Dr. Givens is going to meet with the headman of the Democrats, Mr. John Patterson, to try to get us the vote in the election that's coming."

Louis then leaned his mouth toward Charlie's ear and in a whisper, "This afternoon Lester Armand's going to try for an absentee voting paper."

The three men stood, and after Louis embraced Charlie, Louis said, "Don't worry none about your house. I'll check on it once in a while. And we'll be coming to see you again, soon."

When they left, Charlie was suddenly very much alone. This afternoon or tomorrow those white men on that jury would hear how he killed one of their children. And when they heard it, they would vote to put his neck in their hangman's noose.

Just after lunch that day, from another part of the courthouse, a young *Statesman* reporter telephoned Raymond Brooks to say that he had been lingering in the courthouse hallway when an old Negro named Lester Armand, dressed in his Sunday suit, came through the courthouse door ("shuffled" was the word the reporter used), removed his hat, and proceeded up the stairs to the County Clerk's office. Sensing a story, the reporter told Brooks he had followed the old Negro, and that he had heard the county clerk himself explain that he could not issue Lester an absentee ballot. The reporter told Brooks that the old man simply smiled, thanked the official for his trouble, and walked away.

Brooks immediately called Democratic Chairman John Patterson for a statement.

"Ray, the first thing this morning I told a couple of these darkies that I would see them later this afternoon. Call me later and I will give you a complete reaction.

At 2 PM, Louis Lyons sat with Dr. Everett Givens in the imposing anteroom of the law firm Hart, Patterson, and Hart. Louis knew that this was the room where Nathan Rhambo waited to talk to Chairman Patterson about allowing East Austin to vote in his primary last May. Based on what Nathan had told them, Louis and Everett knew they would be kept waiting a long time; and they were not at all bothered by the secretary who made a point of ignoring them.

When the chairman finally did invite the two men into his office, Dr. Givens, in his deep, booming voice, got directly to the point, "Mr. Patterson, we are here on behalf of all the people of the east side to petition to vote in the Democratic election a week from next Saturday."

'If the dentist is nervous,' Louis thought, 'his voice don't betray him.'

Patterson narrowed his eyes at the two men and sighed. Finally, he said, "Everett, you and Louis here are good leaders for your people; and I understand that you have to be here today to keep your firebrands happy. But y'all and I both know the Travis County Democratic Party is an association of white people. The State Executive Committee controls this; and I can't change it, even if I want to. But I'll send the chairman of the Committee a letter asking for a ruling."

At that Mr. Patterson stood, clearly indicating that the meeting was over. Louis and the big dentist also stood and thanked Mr. Patterson for his time. Givens extended his huge hand, which Mr. Patterson instinctively took. As the two men walked out of Mr. Patterson's office, Louis glanced back to see the white man wiping his hand with a handkerchief.

When Raymond Brooks called Patterson for his reaction, he heard a riled man on the phone.

"These darkies are taking big risks to get the vote, Ray. What happened to that uppity Rhambo made no difference to them—and you know why? Ray, the payoff is huge. Look what the darkies do in city elections right now. That Rhambo was squeezing city council candidates for payoffs and projects; and in close elections, the politicians had to go along. If the darkies get in the primary, that east side bloc vote will be too tempting for some of our candidates. They'll be running over there to kiss black backsides. That means deals at the County Commission, and even pandering in some state races."

Brooks asked the chairman for the names of the Negroes who visited him.

"An old grocer, name of Louis Lyons, and a young dentist named Givens. That boy's a big'un. These fellows could get rich living off campaign promises that'll hardly ever get filled. God knows, if some stupid politician ever did fulfill a promise to a black, white voters would send him packing. Hell, Givens wouldn't want the promises filled anyhow—he and Lyons need problems, not solutions. They need white politicians to make promises, and then break them. Then every two years the white candidates would have to go running over to make more promises, and to pay them more for East Austin votes. Well, not if I can help it." Patterson's voice was strident.

For the next few minutes Brooks worked with Patterson to outline the story that would appear in the next day's paper. Patterson wanted to assure the white community that the Party was safe from the Negro. People were nervous enough after that killing Friday night and the near-riot on Sunday.

16

Judge Cobb's Justice

West Austin

Bill Tarver had risen at sunup that Monday to a still house. He had thrown on old clothes and tiptoed outdoors to survey his sunburned lawn and garden. 'Judge Cobb would have been so proud of Albert,' he thought again.

Bill had always marveled how such a voice could come from Albert's small body. 'And before that rowdy, inebriated mob, that voice proved itself again. It gave the mob what it needed to have to contain its hate and go home. And, by God, that is just what they did. Yet, Albert assumes the system will hang Johnson; and, given the system's record with blacks, Albert has good reason. But what would Judge Cobb think about that?'

Bill then rehearsed the old mantra for civilized criminal justice to which the judge had committed his life: writ of habeas corpus, bail, competent counsel, due process, jury of peers.

'Would Albert really be satisfied to see Johnson tried by a system that routinely disregarded these matters with black defendants?' Reluctantly, Bill had come to terms with the dilemma swirling through his mind—after making a show of due process, Austin courts would hang Johnson regardless. Yet, that show would taint the judge's legacy and be forever associated with his grandson.

'My God,' Tarver realized, 'poor Albert. Only he can make possible the trial that the judge would almost certainly have demanded. And I'm the man who needs to help Albert come to terms with his responsibility. This morning Albert and I will talk."

Albert was pleased when he had heard Bill praising him to Mabel; but when Bill repeated the same words directly to him, he felt a deep elation. The judge's approval was a prized honor to those who had loved him, even when it was posthumous and delivered through Bill. "Well, Bill ought to know," Albert thought. 'Bill had been the judge's protégé.' Then, with words that Albert could tell were

144

carefully chosen, Bill reminded Albert that the judge had called any punishment imposed by society without the full benefit of due process "lynching." Albert recognized that Bill's statement was a sort of *non sequitur,* signaling that Tarver was looking for a way to make a point.

"Judge Cobb," said Bill, "was concerned that Negroes and poor whites had all the protection due them as citizens. That means, as a minimum, bail privileges and quality representation. Otherwise, according to the judge, the accused would be lynched just as sure as if a mob strung him up."

Getting his friend's message, Albert asked, "What about Austin?"

The tall man squared his eyes on Albert, "Look at the story in this morning's *Statesman,* Albert. They are sympathetic to your loss and pay lip service to the law, but the story clearly suggests that you thwarted the people's justice. Look at this."

Tarver handed Albert the paper, pointed to a passage in a small story under the headline "Citizen's Rally to Protest Negro Murder of White Boy," and sub-headline "Bereaved Father Speaks." The final paragraph said that the "concerned citizens departed confident that the courts of the Travis County will defend the lives of our youth through a fierce assertion of the prerogatives of Anglo-Saxon justice."

After a moment, Bill continued, "There are no Judge Cobbs in Austin, Albert. The paper almost says that maybe the boy's daddy can defend the darky from the people, but in this town the people's courts serve the people's justice. That means that Johnson will stay in that jail without benefit of *habeas corpus* until the court sends him to the hangman, helped along by whatever college kid or incompetent drunk they find to defend him."

Bill said nothing more. Nor did Albert. It was time to leave. Bill had a speech to make, and Albert had things to do before returning to Corsicana.

When Albert departed the Tarvers' house, he drove to the courthouse to check on the grand jury proceedings and to meet Mabel's brother, Delmore, who, despite the circumstances, was in an improved mood—resigned, at any rate. Rather than return to Dallas, Delmore, his son Robert, and Sonny Mayes had stayed at the Stephen F. Austin. They had heard about the commotion at the courthouse, but had stayed away. Delmore said that he had read the piece in the morning paper about Albert's remarks to the crowd, and that he imagined that Albert was tempted to let the mob get the Negro.

"But you know you did what was right, Albert," he said. "You know that many of your neighbors are going to wonder about a father who protects his son's Negro killer. But you can live with that better than if you had stood by and the mob had lynched the Negro. Still, I imagine folks in Corsicana'll be a mite uneasy about where you and Mabel stand, especially with your anti-Klan reputation."

'Spoken like Judge Cobb's son,' thought Albert. Albert had hoped he could spend a little time with Delmore that morning to get his understanding of the judge's attitude toward justice for Negroes. But before he could raise the subject, Robert and Sonny walked out of the courtroom. Delmore was anxious to get on the road, so the opportunity was lost.

With Tarver's and Delmore's words swimming through his mind, Albert waited in the hall until proceedings were completed. After a short time, District Attorney Henry Brooks emerged from the grand jury room, greeted Albert warmly, and informed him that the Jury would indict Johnson for murder in the first degree. Everyone had testified, Brooks said, and the grand jury had Johnson's confession. Then Albert asked if Johnson had a lawyer. Brooks replied, "Nobody's been assigned yet, Mr. Allison. But he doesn't need one for the grand jury. No lawyer could do anything with that confession. We'll let you know as soon as the judge sets the trial date, Mr. Allison. Thanks again, for all you did last night. Have safe strip home."

A week passed; and Albert's pain had not abated. He knew, of course, that it never would. That evening, after Albert had put away business letters, invoices, and purchase orders for the weekend, he and Mabel sat on the summer porch watching Ken chase lightning bugs. Mabel was reading by the evening light. A Schubert serenade came from the Victrola in the living room. Albert diffidently stared at the pages of on old book of Milton's poems that he hoped would bring him solace, but his mind went back to that Sunday night.

'Thank God the mob dispersed,' he thought. For an instant, the furious face of that woman flashed in front of him. It was bad enough that a Negro murdered Son. It was bad enough that the murder happened in the wrong part of Austin at the wrong time of night. But for his son's murderer, for Mabel's son's murderer, for the judge's grandson's murderer, for the murderer of *this* boy to be lynched would have been too much for the family to bear.

'The judge's grandson,' the phrase rolled over in Albert's mind. The more he thought about it, the more it mattered. The judge's legacy was imposing a weighty responsibility on Albert.

'What was Bill Tarver really getting at? What would the judge do?' Albert looked over at Mabel, who was rocking, eyes focused on her book. 'How far would the judge go to defend the Negro who murdered his grandson?'

In 1932, most leading families were not as strident about Negroes as their Reconstruction forebears had been. People like Albert and Bill Tarver were beginning to realize that social harmony would not occur through Jim Crow, that only universal access to all the institutions of society could secure peace and guarantee prosperity. Nonetheless, Albert had to admit, he and Mabel were ambivalent about the practicalities of living day to day with Negroes. On the one hand, the Negro's simple, often wise outlook on life and the Negro's ability to attain a deep spirituality through music and faith brought a rich, unique dimension to white lives. On the other hand, Negro sexual vulgarity and the Negro's attitude toward work, family responsibility, personal achievement, learning, hygiene, and living standards was alien to whites. Albert was sympathetic to arguments that the differences between the races were due to three centuries of the Negro's unnatural degradation. He thought it plausible that once white society had done its duty to nurture the Negro into civil society, the differences would hardly be noticed. In fact, many of those traits he found objectionable were also extant among some classes of whites. Still, he could not shake the disturbing feeling that lower-class white children and grandchildren would be educated into acceptable behavior ('we Allisons are an example,' he thought); while something about the Negro portended that even when the problems of color, language, and behavior were overcome, deep, mysterious differences would still cleave black from white.

Albert had had enough conversations on the subject with Judge Cobb to be reasonably certain that the judge, too, reluctantly harbored these suspicions. Notwithstanding, to be sure, especially when in office, the judge had put those suspicions aside and obeyed his allegiance to the supremacy of the law.

'But what would the judge do in the case of the Negro who murdered his own grandson?'

Chester brought a fresh pitcher of lemonade, refreshed Albert and Mabel's glasses, and then said that if they had nothing more for him he would be leaving for the evening. Albert broke from his train of thought and realized that Chester had stayed much later than usual. He told Chester to bring the Buick around, that he would take him home.

After a few blocks, in a voice packed with admiration, Chester said "My, my, Mr. A., with you off stopping a lynching, that Missus A. takes those boys by they ears and sure make them pay for being mean. Son be in heaven, I know; and he be so proud he be y'alls child."

"I hope so, Chester. Mrs. Allison has never done anything like that, that I know of. But when something irritates her, she can be fierce."

When Albert's familiar Buick appeared on Chester's street, people rocking on their porches or talking in small groups in front yards beamed brightly and waved. "Another thing, Mr. A, don't be too mad at ol' Emma gotta leave town. She just can't be in that house no more, not after she can't choke that ol' screech owl."

As Chester got out of the car, he straightened to his full height, eyes glistening, and walked strongly to his door. At his porch, he stopped to tip his hat to his neighborhood.

'Well,' thought Albert as he noticed the smiles and Chester's demeanor, 'at least we are appreciated somewhere. And I suppose Chester is right about Emma; I hope she finds peace somewhere.'

Mabel had mentioned that Emma had disappeared; but she was accustomed to the vagaries of Negro help and seemed not to be too concerned. Mabel had liked Emma, nonetheless, and seemed taken with the old woman's strange superstitions. Albert had not commented when Chester mentioned the screech owl, but he did recall that Mabel had remarked on Emma's screech owl concerns a week or so before. He was not about to engage either Mabel or Chester in a conversation about such nonsense.

'However,' Albert's thought shifted, 'Mabel's brother was right about our neighbors suspecting our racial loyalties.' Within seventy-two hours of Son's murder, in the throes of almost unbearable grief, Albert and Mabel had dampened the Ranger's vengeance, had stood before the mob, and had humiliated the bullies. Many in Corsicana would wonder if the Allisons were dangerously close to being "nigger-lovers," traitors to their kind. 'Mabel and I are established in this community,' Albert said to himself, 'and the community will be looking for reassurance.'

Mabel had been reluctant to tell Albert about the East Side incident—Lod had been punished enough and the boys' families had been humiliated enough. But Lod could not contain himself, and the newspaper publisher, whose son had been on the clean-up crew with Lod, could not resist mentioning the episode in the paper.

The newspaper had also run a small article about Albert's "visit" with the outraged citizens of Austin. But if anyone noticed, they had said nothing. At least they had said nothing to Albert or Mabel.

After Albert returned from taking Chester home, he joined Mabel in the reading room. Mabel watched Albert fidget a little, and then he related what Bill Tarver had told him about Austin's courts and her father's attitudes about courts like that. Mabel recalled the judge's rants about "legal lynching." But, like Albert, until that moment, she had not realized that her father equated mob lynching and corrupt courtroom procedure.

"What would the judge do in our place, Mabel?" her husband asked

"Why do you think the judge would do anything?" she replied. "Why would the judge want to interfere with Austin's courts, especially if they were certain to give us satisfaction?"

"Maybe the judge would not want the final chapter in his grandson's story to mock his heritage. Son died senselessly; but the resolution of his death need not be senseless or vengeful—or vulgar."

Mabel often wondered if she had fallen in love with Albert because he had revered her father, with whom he shared a rare intellectual camaraderie. It was as if Albert latched onto the judge to rescue himself from the bitter climate of post-Reconstruction Limestone County. The judge's crusade for fairness for black as well as white became Albert's hope. 'And this hope has served my love well,' she mused. 'Me, too.'

"There's another thing, Mabel," Albert's voice broke the momentary silence. "I went to Johnson's cell. I wanted to see this man face-to-face."

She had expected as much. Albert was that kind of man.

"He isn't an animal, Mabel. He isn't a rough-looking field hand, chip on his shoulder, mean, bitter. He's my height, slightly balding, light skinned. He faced me squarely, not insolently, nor fearfully, but sadly. He faced me squarely, and he told me with a tear in his eye that he was sorry."

"Would the judge try to get his grandson's killer freed, Mabel?" Albert asked.

Mabel felt a tinge of the rage rise again. 'What does it matter? Why the attention to form?

'But Albert was right,' she thought, 'Son's only chance for redemption, for a glorious final chapter, is for his killer to be tried and executed without a hint of corruption or vengeance.'

'Don't ask what the judge would do,' she reflected. 'What would his daughter and son-in-law do? What would Son's parents do?'

Mabel then heard herself speak from the judge's heart: "If Johnson is railroaded, his punishment will mean nothing. He'll be just another hanged Negro, and Son will be just another dead white boy in the never-ending war. If Son's death, and also his life, is to have meaning, Johnson must be convicted the way the judge would convict him."

After a pause, she said, "You'll need to go to Austin again, Albert."

17

Perry's Plan

Louis Lyons was watching fireflies from Perry Rhambo's porch that evening. With him, in addition to Perry, were Dr. Everett Givens and Mr. Will Fuller. Perry had summoned Louis and Everett because he thought it time they report the latest news. After the usual small talk, Perry asked Louis to tell them about Charlie.

"Charlie's okay, gentlemen. He had a scare last Sunday; that's for sure. But he's okay, now."

Louis told his colleagues that just that afternoon he had visited Charlie. Charlie said that, as Perry had instructed, Perry's nephew Everett Rhambo had been to the jail, and the two had worked out a way Charlie could teach Everett how to get policy up and running again. Everett was to come to Charlie's cell everyday before supper, take instructions for the next day, and do them. Charlie also told Louis that Judge Wheeler had set his trial for the second Monday in September. He still had no lawyer.

Perry drew on his cigar and looked at Mr. Fuller for a reaction. Louis did the same and saw nothing.

"Well," Perry said, "we ain't here to talk about old Charlie's health. Right, Will? Especially since the dead boy's daddy kept Charlie from being strung up. When that happened I got to thinking on this whole problem, and it so happens that what my nephew and Charlie is doing fits what I be thinking. But first I want to go over some things. Dr. Givens, I knows you have lots to say; but I want to ask you a question. Since you the political brain now that we don't have Nathan, I want to know what you think about this governor's race."

Louis saw Givens try to act casual after Perry's comment, but the dentist's eyes danced a little too much. Perry had just elevated the large man's status, and Givens wanted to make the most of it. He held out an empty glass that Ferris took in a flash.

"Most folks think Governor Sterling's way ahead of Ma Ferguson, but things might be changing. Old Jim's heaping this Depression on Sterling so much that people are starting to think the Governor is Hoover's brother. Also, the 'wets' have taken over the Democrats and that's helping Jim and Ma, though it's not too good for you, Perry. The Fergusons get lots of money from the whiskey makers to oppose Prohibition."

"How much power will these friends of Mister Allison have if Ma is governor again, Doctor?" Perry asked, looking at Fuller.

Clasping his refreshed glass in both hands, Givens stated the obvious. "If she won, Mr. Allison's friends couldn't get anybody hung."

"In fact," he opined, "coloreds might even have a little more power. Think about Ma's term back in '25 when she pardoned that group of Negro convicts on Juneteenth for half-price."

Then Givens looked at Perry and smiled. "Of course, the Fergusons will pardon just about anybody for the right price."

"What about a black man who murdered a white boy?" Perry asked.

"Hell, Perry, it would be expensive; but he could be freed. The Fergusons are open to us. My San Antonio contacts say that old Jim Ferguson is helping them get the vote in a few south Texas primaries this year, maybe even San Antonio."

Perry looked at Louis, "I guess Dr. Givens and you'll do everything you can to have us vote in Travis County, too."

Louis nodded. He was careful not to wince.

The pre-war was cutting through the oppressive heat, and the conversation waned. Louis watched Perry light another cigar, lean back, and turn toward the sun setting over the cornfield. He seemed to be tuning in to the cicadas just beginning to sing. Two crows were perched together on the lower branch of the sprawling live oak tree. Perry smiled and raised his glass in their direction. As the sun approached the western horizon, Louis noticed that the crows were joined by a screech owl. Perry then stood, walked to the porch railing, turned and faced his three colleagues.

"Brothers," he said, "I have a plan."

Since Perry held the key to a substantial portion of their income, Louis and the other men listened with astonished respect—astonished because, like everyone else in East Austin, they had assumed that Nathan had been the Rhambo family schemer. No one credited Perry with strategic ability. Even Mr. Will Fuller paid close attention. 'If Perry can make some crazy-ass scheme work, Fuller will be a rich man,' Louis thought.

Perry began by stipulating that Charlie Johnson was critical to the ongoing success of Mr. Fuller's insurance business and policy. Without Charlie, both businesses would collapse; and that was a fact. But Mr. Fuller would not be the only one to suffer. Senior policy agents like Louis and Dr. Givens would lose a lot of income. And a lot of lesser agents would lose badly needed commissions. Perry said that he would not even mention the excitement that policy brings to the drab lives of East Austin and the wonderful changes it represents to the lucky few. Therefore, keeping Johnson alive and out of jail was worth a lot of money not only to the men on this porch, but to many deserving folks in East Austin, and even around the state.

Mr. Will Fuller raised his eyebrows and shook his head.

"Brother Fuller," Perry said, "If Charlie stay in jail, you don't lose. If he get out, you win big."

Perry then asserted that to get Johnson off, they needed a good white lawyer and a Ma Ferguson victory. The lawyer might be able to get Charlie out of jail on bail and keep him from being hung until Ma became governor. In the meantime, Charlie could keep getting the businesses back on their feet through Perry's nephew Everett.

"Who knows, Will," Perry laughed, "Everett might get so good that you won't need old Charlie."

To Lyons and Dr. Givens, Perry said, "If old Jim Ferguson thinks we're doing everything we can to help Ma, we can buy Charlie's pardon if they do get elected."

Perry was emphatically confident of it.

"If we can't do anything practical-like to help the Fergusons in the Primary, we have to let them know we tried. Lester Armand's trip to the courthouse to get the absentee ballot is the kind of thing I'm talking about."

Turning to look in the direction of the live oak, Perry said, "I got a feeling this election will make us all smile."

Seeing that the men were not objecting, Perry said, "Will, please just hold on before you make up your mind about Nathan's business. You just might want to do this deal."

Fuller put on his Stetson, stood up, and extended his hand to Perry. "I'll do that, Perry. Let's go, Dr. Givens."

When walking down the porch steps, Mr. Fuller turned back to Perry, "By the way, who gets the lawyer?"

Perry pointed at himself. Charlie's lawyer was Perry's end of the bargain.

Louis also had to leave. He walked with the other men to Givens's car, and then turned to wave good-bye to Perry. But Perry was sauntering to the ancient live oak tree, glass and cigar in hand. To Louis's amazement, Perry seemed to engage in a rollicking conversation with those two crows, while a screech owl watched them from a branch high up in the tree. Perry's laughter made Louis smile, too; and he drove home strangely confident about this peculiar plan.

Less than two weeks to July twenty-third, Election Day; and, as in campaigns past, an amazed George Nalle watched his father-in-law's metamorphosis into the "Politician"—with a capital *P*. Even though in 1917 the Texas Legislature had impeached and convicted Jim Ferguson and had barred him from ever seeking statewide office, he was still the most feared and respected vote-getter in the history of Texas. In seven tempestuous campaigns, whether successful or not, whether running for himself or for his wife, Miriam, this phase of the campaign was always his time to shine. This was the time when days and nights merged, when the road and the crowds blurred in the sweat and heat, when hyperbole, accusations, and counter-accusations forgot the truth. This was the time when Jim dispatched young Nalle to East Texas to embrace the courthouse boys, to South Texas to negotiate with political barons, and to the cotton counties with cash for poll tax receipts for the "boys at the forks of the creeks." This was the time that Jim leaned hard on contractors, bootleggers, textbook publishers, and Austin lawyers to dig deep for that extra hundred dollars. This was the time for which Jim Ferguson lived, the time that he was at his best; the time when being his son-in-law was joyous hell.

Just before lunch Jim stormed into Nalle's office at his lumberyard, threw the morning's *Austin American* onto his desk, and asked Nalle what he thought. A large red circle enclosed a small story about the father who had talked the mob into leaving alone the Negro who had killed his boy. Nalle was long accustomed to his father-in-law's unique political insights; he knew this bit of news had raised the former governor's antenna.

Before Nalle could comment, Jim said, "George, get us a rally going in Navarro County. This time we're going to put that landlord Allison in his place."

Nalle looked at Ferguson quizzically. Landlords had been Ferguson targets for years; and, because of Albert Allison's fierce opposition to Ferguson in campaigns past, this Navarro County landlord was high on the Ferguson's hit list. But Allison's boy had just been killed, and Allison had thwarted an Austin mob intent on lynching the boy's Negro killer. 'How could Jim put that man in his place?' Nalle silently wondered.

"Look," Jim declared as if reading Nalle's mind, "In '26 and again in '30 Allison hurt us bad in Navarro and surrounding counties; and, if it wasn't for his boy, he'd be after us again."

Then, with that wicked wink, Jim said, "But this time he's a little tainted by that fool cotton moratorium he had the governor ram through last year; and now, with a little help from Ma and me, his well known so-called progressive views on Negroes are going to haunt him. His hard-scrapple tenants may sympathize with him for the loss of his boy; but, if I handle this right, they'll suspect that this is punishment for his being a traitor to his race."

On Ferguson's way out of Nalle's office, he said, "When you get the rally set up, drop by Gabriel Hawthorne's office. He's got a $1,000 for us from the wholesale liquor people."

Nalle spent the afternoon on the telephone. By 6 PM Ferguson's man in Navarro County had arranged for the Fergusons to have the town park in Emhouse, about fifteen miles from Corsicana. In May, Ma and Jim had kicked off their campaign in that park. They would have another enormous turnout; Nalle was sure of it.

After Nalle finalized the Emhouse arrangements, he walked to the third floor of the Norwood Building and through the door that read "Gabriel Hawthorne, Attorney at Law." As on many occasions that summer, after a few minutes bantering with the garrulous lobbyist, he left with an envelope containing ten one-hundred-dollar bills.

18

Judge Wheeler's Court

Everett Rhambo did not miss a day visiting Charlie. He had been nervous and little surly at first, and he had panicked slightly when he learned that Carl Stewart was in the same cellblock. But when Charlie told him that Stewart "seem a might upset by a screech owl that sing to us from the park by the jail," Everett's attitude lightened. He even remarked that he might enjoy this work. On every visit afterward, Everett made at least one, usually bad, attempt to screech; but Stewart never gave him the satisfaction of a response.

After a few sessions, Charlie could see real progress. Within two weeks policy receipts measurably increased, and the drawings and prize distribution system was working again.

No lawyer came, but Charlie was not concerned. A few days after the mob had left him alone, a deputy had told him that his trial had been set for early September, just after Stewart's trial. He assumed that when the time was right, the court would send someone like the young man who had visited Carl Stewart the day the grand jury met.

Louis Lyons came every few days. On one occasion, Louis entertained Charlie with "adventures in the vote," as Louis called it. He had told Charlie how old Lester Armand braved his way into the courthouse, spotted the young newspaperman and motioned to him, "You follow me." That way he got the newspaperman to witness when the county clerk himself turned old Lester away.

"This time they don't ask why Lester wanted to vote absentee," Louis had said. "Too bad, because Lester was ready to say that he thought he should vote absentee since they don't allow no 'negrahs' in no voting places."

Louis described how he and Everett Givens had waited for an hour in John Patterson's office, and how Mr. Patterson neatly said he would ask for a ruling from the State Committee. Louis showed Charlie a newspaper clipping dated July seventeenth, almost a week after the Patterson meeting. The paper reported that the Democratic state chairman had issued a ruling that prohibited Negro participation in the primary, except where a county executive committee had voted otherwise. However, the Travis County Democratic Executive Committee had not considered the matter and would not meet until after the primary. Louis chuckled that the chairman had a funny way of getting somebody else to say what he wanted said all along."

The last Sunday in July, Louis Lyons and Everett Givens came to see Charlie with "good news." As a result of the election the day before, Ma Ferguson and Governor Sterling were going to be in a run-off in late August.

"Ma's got a good chance of upsetting the governor," Givens said.

Charlie was not sure why these results or Ma Ferguson's chances were "good news," but if the big dentist thought so, that was good enough.

"Sheriff White lost," Louis then said. "That's not good news."

Charlie was shocked. The Sheriff had been a fair man—and there was a certain comfort knowing that Mrs. White had his ear.

"True," Lyons added, "ten years ago the new sheriff became famous for fighting the Klan up in Williamson County; but he also promised to clean up Austin's vice. He might not be as lenient with East Austin's ways as Coley White."

However, Givens thought that White lost because he had been too hard on white bootleggers and small-time beer producers; and the county just got tired of seeing good people in jail just because they provided folks a little relief from a hard life.

He added that the new sheriff had better be careful about fooling with people's fun.

Then with a big smile, Lyons handed Charlie the Saturday afternoon *Statesman*. Right there on the front page was another "good news" story; at least Louis thought so. He said that he and Dr. Givens had had a big week.

The *Austin Statesman,* July 23, 1932, front page

"NEGROES PETITION TO GET VOTES
JUDGES REFUSE PRIVILEGE TO COUPLE

Denied the privilege of voting by election judges at two Austin polling places Saturday morning, a group of Austin negroes was preparing Saturday afternoon a mandamus action to force County Chmn. J. M. Patterson to permit them to vote in the democratic primary.

The group of negroes lead by Louis Lyons, negro grocer, appeared at the Precinct 5 A box at Wellmer's store and the sixth ward box at the Labor temple shortly before noon, the elections officials said.

Courteous Request

Len Mueller, election judge at the 5 A box, said Lyons and another negro "named Frazier," presented poll tax receipts, declared they were willing to take the democratic party pledge and asked the right to cast ballots. Other negroes were also in the group but did not present poll tax receipts, Mueller said.

Mr. Mueller said he refused them the ballot privilege with the declaration he was following the instructions issued by County Chmn. Patterson. The negroes were courteous in their request, Mueller said.

Sent to Patterson

Tom Walling, judge at the ninth ward box, also said a group of negroes headed by Lyons appeared there with a similar request and were also denied ballots.

"The negroes were rather insistent, but I turned them down and told them to see County Chmn. John Patterson," Mr. Welling said.

Lyons said his and the other negroes vote request was the predicate for a court action to be filed in federal court in San Antonio to force Chmn. Patterson to permit negroes the balloting privilege. Lyons said he was in touch with a San Antonio lawyer and expected the injunction papers to reach him sometime this afternoon."

After Charlie put the paper down, he looked thoughtfully at Lyons, "Well, Colonel, what you is doing is wonderful. Did that injunction come? Did we get the vote?"

Lyons shook his head, "Naw, but we don't care. What we wanted was this newspaper article for those San Antonio lawyers, so they can get the judges to make these Democrats let us in."

"Who's that Frazier?"

"Oh, that's Everett. That white newspaperman can't hear so good."

Charlie smiled. 'Those whites,' he thought, 'always so danged smart, always get so much so wrong.'

"You ever wonder what the difference between a privilege and a right, Colonel?" Charlie asked. "The paper says that voting is a privilege, but who gives that privilege—Mr. Patterson? No, Colonel, it ain't Mr. Patterson like the paper says. It's the State Committee—that's what Mr. Patterson told you. But it ain't the State Committee, because only the counties can allow us the vote. But it's ain't the county chairman. It's the county committee, which don't meet to decide nothing. The Constitution say voting's our right, so Chairman Patterson and his committees don't need to bother about no privilege. That's what I think, anyhow."

Dr. Givens winked at Lyons, "Lordy, Colonel, Charlie must be feeling good, again. Been a long time since he give one of his schoolteacher talks."

Without responding, Louis smirked and remarked to Charlie, "If the judge give us the vote, we're all going to line up and vote for Ma. Ma lets our people out of jail."

Albert Allison was unable to meet with Bill Tarver until Wednesday following the primary. Bill had just spent a sleepless weekend in Dallas at the Texas Election Bureau monitoring the returns for Governor Sterling. He then had to attend a series of urgent meetings to plan the campaign for the run-off election a month hence. Albert could not help noticing that the long hours and constant travel had taken their toll on his friend. But, even though the governor had trailed by almost 100,000 votes, Bill seemed confident enough. Two years before, Bill reminded Albert, Ma led the first Primary by 80,000 votes; but the anti-Ferguson forces united for the run-off to hand Sterling a handsome victory. Still, Bill was troubled by lopsided results from Ferguson strongholds in east and south Texas.

"Old Jim's courthouse cronies are notorious for pilfering votes," he said, "but this year the pilfering has become grand larceny."

He muttered something about sending Rangers to run the elections or fighting fire with fire, then shrugged and dropped the matter.

Albert silently thanked Bill for not mentioning the Navarro County results. Albert's inattention to his campaign duties, though excusable, showed. Ferguson's sudden campaign appearance in Emhouse had made a serious impact. In fact, Albert was astonished and little confused at how effective Ferguson's personal attacks had been. People in Corsicana were beginning to think of Albert as something different from a well-intentioned, high-minded spokesman for fairness. Ferguson had painted Albert as a threat to their way of life; and folks had listened. But Albert had persuaded Navarro county voters to his viewpoint before, and he would do so again. He was relieved, nevertheless, that Tarver did not make him pledge a Navarro County victory then and there. Besides, he had not come on political business.

Albert did not want his personal affairs to become a nuisance to his old friend, especially in these critical times; but he needed Bill's help. So Albert went straight to the point: he and Mabel wanted to ensure that Charles Johnson received a fair trial, Judge Cobb's kind of trial, with a proper lawyer.

Bill brightened immediately.

"Our Corsicana friends are not likely to understand, Bill," Albert said. "For both our sakes, I hope we can do this discreetly."

Albert told Tarver that he had visited District Attorney Henry Brooks that morning, and that Brooks had informed him that Judge Charles Wheeler had set the trial for September twelfth. Assistant District Attorney Jim Hart, who had been elected to replace Brooks beginning in January, would be prosecuting. As far as Brooks knew, Johnson still had no lawyer; but, Brooks had said, this time of year all the judges had a hard time finding *pro bono* defenders.

Bill nodded thoughtfully. He wrote on a pad and handed Albert a slip with the names of three lawyers. "I've personally heard both Bill Yelderman and Tass Waterston voice disgust at the treatment of those Scottsboro boys in the Alabama courts. One of them might be looking for a cause—if you know what I mean. I doubt Warren Moore has ever represented a Negro, and I doubt he would now. But he is the best criminal defense attorney in central Texas, and he might have a suggestion."

The newspapers had been reporting on the nine Negro boys who were nearly lynched near Scottsboro, Alabama, for gang-raping two white girls. Albert had also read that Northern papers were stirred up because rigged courts had condemned the boys to death. Albert did not ask Bill to elaborate. He said his thanks and moved to leave, but Bill motioned for him to stay seated.

Bill lit a cigarette and exhaled.

"Couple of more things, old friend," he said. "First, Warren Moore represents the way most lawyers in this town think. I've heard him say more than once that because Anglo-Saxon courts represent Anglo-Saxon culture and tradition, they ought to serve only Anglo-Saxons. He believes that in black-on-black crime situations, Negroes should administer their own punishments and discipline. He once told me that when Negroes transgress against whites, they are not committing crimes, but acts of war; and that's why the vigilante code is right for them and why Negroes ought not to be served by the courts. He thinks by affording Negroes the protection of our courts we are providing them cover to wage their war against us without receiving just retribution."

Bill paused, sighed, and blew smoke in the direction of his framed diploma from Southwestern University. Albert said nothing.

"Next thing, Albert. Judge Wheeler is no Judge Cobb. In fact, about fifteen years ago, while attending one of the Judge's seminars, Wheeler got after Judge Cobb for putting so much emphasis on the 'immutable, rational construction' of the law under the Constitution. Wheeler threw up Oliver Wendell Holmes's argument that the Constitution is not a logical construction but a living guide that evolves to bring order according to prevailing mores."

Bill smiled, "I'll always remember Judge Cobb thanking Wheeler and Oliver Wendell Holmes for bringing back 'frontier justice.'"

Albert got the gist of Bill's concerns about Wheeler; but, again, he did not ask Bill to elaborate.

Bill Yelderman and his wife and partner, Mae, listened respectfully. Albert sensed a little disbelief at first, especially from Mae; but Bill seemed genuinely impressed. Nonetheless, Yelderman told him that Tass Waterston and he had recently agreed to defend Carl Stewart, the Corsicana Negro accused of murdering Nathan Rhambo, "a prominent Austin Negro." Judge Wheeler, Yelderman added, had just moved the trial from August to October; and it would occupy them both fully. With a knowing glance at his wife, Yelderman suggested that Albert see Gabriel Hawthorne, a lawyer/lobbyist who was known to represent Negro business groups.

Warren Moore's reception room reflected the southern decor and southern sophistication of a successful Southern lawyer. When Albert walked in, a gracious lady beamed and told him that Mr. Moore was expecting him. She invited him to sit, offered him lemonade, and made polite small talk until a tall man in a white suit complemented by flowing white hair appeared from his office. Moore and Allison exchanged greetings, and Moore invited Albert into his office.

"Mr. Allison," began Moore, "I've just talked to Henry Brooks. He told me how you took on that mob. This city owes you a great deal, sir. Also, I want to say how sorry I am about your son. How painful these days must be for you and your family."

"Thank you, Mr. Moore. I appreciate your giving me this time. It's because of my son that I'm here. Mrs. Allison and I want the final chapter of the boy's life to be remembered as the finest expression of good faith to his heritage. He was just beginning to appreciate the value of that heritage, especially that which his grandfather Judge L. B. Cobb passed on to him and all of us."

Albert's voice faltered briefly, but he continued. He wanted to get this out. "My wife and I want to see the Negro convicted and punished to the limit of the law, make no mistake. But we want him to be convicted in a truly fair trial. That's why it's important to us that the Negro has competent representation."

"Well, I guess I understand, Mr. Allison," Moore responded, "but I'm simply not a *pro bono* defense lawyer, if that's what you're getting at. Austin does have a few experienced lawyers who are concerned about these matters—I mean they talk about equal justice for the darkies and so on. Bill Tarver can introduce you to these fellows. Gabriel Hawthorne is a lobbyist who also represents a few

Negroes; he might have some ideas. I can introduce you to Hawthorne if you like. For my part, I'm involved in several cases that are consuming all my time, but I do confess to some interest in your concern."

Moore's expression when he mentioned Hawthorne bespoke disapproval, so Albert did not jump at the chance to meet the man.

"Thank you for that, Mr. Moore," he responded. "I wasn't expecting a lawyer of your caliber to work *pro bono*. If I had to pay your fee myself, it would be worth it to me to ensure that the trial be conducted between knowledgeable gentlemen searching for justice. I must say I would still be cheering for the district attorney."

Albert smiled ruefully at his own remark. Moore looked the father in the eye, nodded and smiled back, but said nothing. Taking the cue, Albert stood, thanked Moore for his time and consideration, and said he would let Moore know if he wanted an introduction to Mr. Hawthorne.

In a telephone conversation that evening, Bill Tarver told Albert that Gabriel Hawthorne was not someone Albert should see. He said Hawthorne hung around with the likes of Archie Parr, the boss of the South Texas machine that gave Ferguson thousands of suspect votes. Bill said that Moore and the Yeldermans probably mentioned Hawthorne because he was rumored to represent Negro criminal elements.

Albert sighed and mentioned that since they seemed to have run out of ideas, he thought he would call on Judge Wheeler to voice his concerns and get his thoughts.

"Damn, Albert, be careful," Bill warned. "Don't even hint that the judge doesn't run a fair court. As a matter of fact, since you're an interested party in a trial he's adjudicating, I doubt the judge will even see you."

Bill paused.

Before Albert could raise a mild protest, Bill said with a voice of resignation, "On the other hand, I can't give you any better ideas; and Johnson does need the lawyer."

Judge Charles Wheeler made an exception. The fate of the Allison boy's murderer was sealed anyway; and the father deserved every possible courtesy, especially since he saved Austin a major embarrassment by stopping that mob. Anyhow, it would be reasonable that such a man would want to know how the law is dealing with his son's murderer, and no reasonable person could accuse either of them of collaborating on such a cut and dried matter.

However, the judge was curious about Henry Brooks's report that Allison had talked to Warren Moore and Bill Yelderman—defense lawyers.

Allison arrived at 11 AM. He thanked the judge for his courtesy, and extended greetings from the Texas Agriculture Commissioner, whom Allison had just left. Then, Allison got straight to the point.

"Judge, my wife and I are concerned that Charles Johnson have competent legal representation, and I wanted to visit with you to see if you could give me suggestions."

Wheeler at first was not sure he had heard properly. Trying not to show his irritation at Allison's ham-fisted implications, he said, "Mr. Allison, I assure you that the lawyers—I mean both the prosecutor and myself have a great deal of experience on these matters. We are not a bunch of Alabama bumpkins who will be so sloppy that Johnson's conviction will be overturned."

Allison shook his head and said he was sorry to convey the wrong impression. He did not intend to impugn the competence of the court; he only wanted to ensure that Johnson have first-class counsel.

'Well, this explains why the man met with Warren Moore and Bill Yelderman,' the judge thought.

For a moment the judge wanted to smile when he thought about Warren Moore's reaction, which would have been much the same as his own. The judge had always believed that, as an official, his first duty was to the Southern way of life; then second, as a judge, to be a lynchpin for law and order. He hoped the two roles were congruent most of the time. Allison's visit, however, disturbed this congruence.

"Well," Judge Wheeler told Allison, "first, there's a matter of money. Your most qualified criminal defense attorneys are expensive, as they have every right to be. That's why we have public defenders—fellows willing to work on public pay to get experience. Frankly, with a confession like the one we have from Johnson, I imagine the young man I have in mind will give Johnson about as good a defense as he can get."

Allison just shook his head, "Judge, I'm relying on your complete discretion. The lawyer would be fully compensated, I assure you."

Wheeler tried to hide his incredulity. 'Would the trial be compromised if the father of a white victim paid a darky's attorney's fees? Of course not. Would the father be called a...? Well, lots of folks would come up with a few names.'

The judge wanted to reply that even if the Negro had the money, after Bill Yelderman and Tass Waterston, there was no one else who took Negro cases. But he affected a nod intended to show understanding, "I'll think about it, Mr. Allison. But may I ask how you feel about helping a killer? Your own son's killer, no less."

"Judge, my late father-in-law, Judge L. B. Cobb, taught me to have faith that the process at its best will render justice, that less than the best would be nothing but a lynching without a mob."

Allison leaned forward; his voice started to quiver.

"Judge Wheeler," the father was looking straight into the judge's eyes, "that Negro fired point blank at my unarmed boy and killed him. If there is justice, he will hang. But for my family's sake and the sake of my boy's legacy, the Negro must not be lynched—in or out of court."

The judge leaned back and his chair and folded his arms. 'Now, I guess he thinks he's a lynching expert. Well, let's just see how he likes expertise.'

Feeling an edge creeping into his voice, Wheeler said, "I said I'd think about it. No defense lawyers of that caliber come to mind now. But, as long as we're talking about not 'lynching' this darky, we might as well consider a couple of things.

"First, Johnson's a sixty-year-old school teacher; taught here more than twenty years. I imagine some of East Austin's finest citizens would guarantee his bail if somebody would file a writ of *habeas corpus.* If he skipped, there are a few folks in East Austin that would run him down and hang him for us, especially if their houses were on the line. If we set bail at twenty-five hundred, more than likely Johnson will be out a while before the trial. How does that strike you, sir?"

Allison nodded, "Sounds fair, sir."

"Second thing," the judge continued, "I set the trial date for early September, but a competent defense attorney will immediately petition to have the trial rescheduled to give him time to prepare."

Allison again agreed, "No doubt, it's the right thing to do."

"And a hell of lot more expense to the taxpayers just to kill a killer, Mr. Allison. But out of respect for you and Mrs. Allison, I'll set a new trial date right now; that way there's time to find competent counsel."

The judge picked up his calendar and walked out his office door. When he returned, he said, "All right, November fourteenth. Now, Mr. Allison, I want you to understand that I run a solid, fair court. I seldom relax my rules for anyone, but I reckon you deserve some consideration. Now, I think you see you have had that consideration. Please don't try to tamper with the wheels of justice any more."

"Thank you, judge. I know you're making special concessions. I'd be obliged if you could let me know about a possible defense attorney, when you hear of one."

After Judge Wheeler closed the door behind Allison, he peered desultorily over the papers on his desk, then suddenly put on his suit jacket, and walked into the secretary's anteroom.

"Tell anybody who needs to see me that I'm at the Austin Club."

As Albert walked from the courthouse to the hotel, he wondered why the judge admonished him for "tampering with the wheels of justice." The judge had brought up *habeas corpus* and a new trial date with no prompting. Did even the suggestion of bringing a competent lawyer into the equation pose a threat? And there's the bail question. Could Johnson's friends raise twenty-five hundred dollars?

When the young deputy called Homer handed Charlie Johnson an official document declaring that the trial date had been changed from September until November, he prayed quietly, "Lord, You must be looking after Your Charlie; two more months here, two more months before the hangman. Maybe there's an angel with that old screech owl."

The following Sunday afternoon Louis Lyons and Reverend Adam Black brought Johnson fried chicken from the church ladies and some newspapers. Louis had heard the news of the trial delay from Everett Rhambo. He said he had never heard of a Negro being given this much help. Charlie nodded and said that when he first heard about the delay, he suspected that Perry had figured out how to bribe the judge.

"Well," Lyons replied, "when I gave Perry the news, he laughed and slapped his thigh and said, 'Goddamn, Colonel, how'd you do it?'"

Louis Lyons had not expected to see any white politicians during this campaign. Austin's politicians usually hankered after East Austin's vote only during city elections. But the Saturday following the primary, George Nalle, a man very familiar to Louis, sauntered into Lyon's grocery store holding a week-old *Statesman*. Suspecting what Nalle wanted, Lyons turned away pretending to be busy. He knew he must not appear to be too pleased.

"How'd this go, Louis?" the white voice asked. Nalle was pointing at the article about Louis's attempt to vote.

Louis wiped his apron and looked up, "Why, Mister George, how you be? Long time since we see you over here."

Nalle responded that he was fine, that he was a family man now. Louis smiled knowingly. He knew that Mr. George had married Jim and Ma Ferguson's oldest daughter. Despite Mr. George's high place in the world, East Austin was at ease with him; and he was at ease with East Austin. Nalle's lumberyard had been the largest business on East Sixth Street. But when East Austin was officially designated the "Negro District," Mr. George's father was forced to relocate to the West Side. East Austin had regarded Joseph Nalle to be a good and caring boss and a generous community benefactor. Mr. George had grown up in the lumberyard, working comfortably with East Austin folk, according to their ways. They knew him as a man never quick to judge, and for this reason he was one of the few whites who fit into the east side.

But when Mr. George walked into Lyon's Store that day, he was not dropping by on a friendly visit. And, for Louis, "dealing in votes" with any politician was strictly business.

When *"dealing in votes,"* Nathan Rhambo had taught Louis, *always demand something big.* The white politicians were so greedy for power, he had asserted, a good vote boss could always get both "pay and a promise."

"You have to get both," Nathan had said. "First, there's cash for the Poll Tax. The dollar-and-a-half tax for a voting license is the white man's way of keeping poor niggers from voting, but we just collect the cash from the white politicians and buy them in bulk. Cash for the poll tax, for the churches, and the walking around money—total, four dollars a vote. And the promise to give the east side something like paved roads, sewers, electricity, or a library. If they say no, come election day East Austin go fishing, and why not? But one of them always want our vote bad enough, if only to keep the other man from getting it."

Another time Nathan had said, "Colonel, I never can figure what's so damned holy about the vote. Hell, it's just like anything else you gather up and sell—just like hogs or ears of corn. Folks sell you their votes wholesale, and you turn around and sell them to the politicians retail. The politicians buy the votes with money taken in tax or gouged from the businessmen they help. It's the sucker that can't harvest votes or can't collect taxes that gets robbed. We can't collect taxes, Colonel, so we harvest."

"Well, Louis," George Nalle said, "it looks like you've kind of taken charge since poor old Rhambo's gone—God bless his soul—so I guess you're the man I need to see. You know I'm campaigning for my mother-in-law. Pure and simple, if the court goes your way, we want East Austin's vote. I don't have to tell you what Ma and Jim have done for your people. A dang sight more'n the present 'Encumbrance,' as Jim calls him, that's for sure; and they will do a lot more."

Louis couldn't help but join in Mr. George's chuckle at Ferguson's wit. He told Mr. George that nothing had come of the lawsuits, yet; but the San Antonio lawyers were working hard; and East Austin was ready.

"By the way," Nalle asked, "who is this 'Frazier' the paper mentioned?"

"Oh, that Everett Givens, the young dentist. The paper got mixed-up. Everett helped me try to do what Nathan would have done. And sure he'll be talking to you if we get the vote. But right now East Austin don't care too much."

Nalle smiled, "I'll see you soon, then, Colonel. Good luck. By the way, friend, don't be too eager to get your name in the paper. Some people aren't happy about y'all killing that white boy a few weeks back and then going after the vote."

Louis let his smile fade. He knew that Mr. George Nalle was talking as a friend, but he did not like that not-so-hidden message.

19

Bail

Mabel Cobb Allison's husband seldom bothered her with business or political worries, but in his morning telephone call he admitted that he had slept fitfully the night before. His strong, deep voice had quavered just enough to indicate that he was unsure about what to do. Bill Tarver had encouraged him to get Johnson a lawyer, but the two fellows Bill had suggested either could not or would not help.

Much to Mabel's relief, Albert also told her that the judge had moved the trial to November fourteenth. She wanted to get the trial over, but she had trepidations about facing the killer and about having to relive the final moments of Son's life. Besides, she thought, the early September heat would have made the courtroom pure hell.

Albert said that Judge Wheeler had not been helpful about a lawyer. As yet, he had not even appointed a public defender. Also, from what Albert could tell, Austin had only two high caliber lawyers willing to represent Negroes; and they were already engaged defending Alice Stewart's boy for killing that Negro undertaker. But, Albert observed, at least now there was time for Son's killer to try to find someone.

Then there was the bail question.

"How is a Negro teacher going to come up with that kind of money?" he asked rhetorically. "Judge Wheeler would have been happy to forget Johnson's bail privilege and let him sit in jail until the trial, or until a lawyer got him out. When I said I wanted Johnson to have a fair trial, the judge rubbed my nose in the law a little. He told me that bail was part of a just process, at least for white folks. Since I wanted Johnson to have white treatment, he set the bail at twenty-five hundred."

After a pause, Albert continued, "Mabel, you know as well as I that no bondsman will help Johnson, and Johnson won't be able to raise the money. Unless he gets help, he is stuck; and Bill says that is wrong."

As Albert talked, Mabel watched through the front window as Chester strug-gled with the lawn mower. Old adages began tripping through her consciousness. "Be sure you're right, then go ahead." Albert peppered his speeches with that one. Or "to thine own self be true." Albert wrote that in the Bible they gave to Son the day he left for Marion Military Institute.

'He's not talking to me like a husband,' she thought. 'He sounds a little at sea, like a lost boy who wants the wisdom of the Big Sister. Should I feed him old say-ings that he could feed himself? Did adages satisfy her siblings when they came to Big Sister? No. Neither adages, nor old saws, nor the Bible, nor Shakespeare. Her siblings had needed Big Sister to carry the burden, to relieve them of the agony of uncertainty. So Big Sister had once had to say to Delmore, "Do it. Marry the girl and be happy."'

"Albert," she said to the man who at that moment was little brother, "do it. Or, I should say, let's do it. I'll get Lod to drive me to the bank right now, and I'll wire you the money."

There. For the second time in a week she had assumed the responsibility. And, yes, she surprised herself, Albert, too, most likely. But he was looking for direc-tion, and she knew which direction was right for them both.

Albert's voice suddenly became stronger. "Have the bank call me at the Stephen F. Austin when the money's on its way. I'll see what I can do."

Little brother became Mabel's confident, strong husband again.

Albert ended the call by describing the meeting he had had with the Agricul-ture Commissioner before he had seen Judge Wheeler. The Commissioner had told him that because of the failure of Texas's cotton moratorium law, the cotton brokers were shocked at Albert's success in selling his national cotton moratorium proposal to the Democratic Platform Committee at the national convention. The brokers were seeking allies with Roosevelt's people to fight him again. But the Commissioner said that he believed that the New Yorkers were suspicious of the brokers and that their ideology dovetailed more with Albert's program. When Mabel had asked Albert what the Commissioner meant by that statement, he thought for a moment and said he wasn't quite sure, except that the Commis-sioner was optimistic that the cotton moratorium would become national law.

"Speaking of politics," Albert concluded, "I could hardly face old Bill Tarver over the sorry results for the governor in Navarro County. I have to get back soon and concentrate on the run-off."

Without asking for an explanation, Henry Brooks gave Albert the names of Louis Lyons and Reverend Adam Black, as two prominent East Austin residents who might vouch for Charles Johnson. Brooks said that Lyons was a grocer active in east side politics; and that, according to the jail log, both he and the Reverend had visited Johnson several times.

Despite Albert's misgivings about bothering Bill Tarver, after leaving the district attorney, he returned to Bill's office and asked him to prepare the bail paperwork. Tarver was happy to do so. Understandably, he asked for complete discretion.

"You can imagine the field day old Jim will have if I'm caught arranging bail for a Negro who murdered a white boy," Bill said. "That goes for both of us, Albert. He'll crucify you in Navarro County if he learns of this. I understand he blistered you pretty good for stopping the lynching."

Albert just shrugged. He didn't want to dwell on that. Instead he outlined a plan for keeping both of them out of it. Tarver nodded and told Albert to come by his office for the documents the next morning.

The Rising Star Baptist Church was little more than a small meeting hall with a podium backed by a few religious pictures, facing about forty wooden chairs. A large lady in a sweaty bandana standing by the front door, broom in hand, told Albert that he could find the Reverend in the next-door grocery store.

Using his Stetson to fan at houseflies attacking vegetables disintegrating in the afternoon heat, Albert walked just inside the door of the small store and yelled "Hello!" Immediately a lanky, graying black man wearing a soiled grocer's apron emerged from the rear and asked, "May I help you, mister?"

"I'm Mister Allison, and I'd like a word with Reverend Black."

Adam Black was visibly startled; but he identified himself, and removed his apron, "Follow me over to the church, Mr. Allison. As you can see, I'm the preacher and the grocery man for the neighborhood."

In a voice tinged with sympathy, the Reverend said, "I know you, Mr. Allison. You the last man I ever hope to see. Me and everybody over here is so sorry about your boy."

Then after a little hesitation, the reverend looked down at Albert as if he were suddenly pronouncing from on high, "But surely heaven smiling on your boy and you after you come to Austin to save old Charlie."

Albert nodded his appreciation and tried to smile, "Thank You, Reverend."

After Black had led Albert to a small room that appeared to serve as an office, Albert got to the point. He told the Reverend that certain important people in Austin had told him that the reverend was a community leader and a man with an honest reputation. He said he was sure that the reverend would understand why everything that was said today must be forever secret. Black got up, went to an adjacent room, spoke to someone, returned, and shut the door behind him.

"I have reason to believe that you are a friend of Charles Johnson. Am I right?"

"Yes sir. Charlie's my friend."

"Well, I don't want to mislead you, Reverend Black. Despite what I said to stop that mob, I want your friend to hang for what he did."

Albert concentrated on maintaining eye contact. The reverend's face froze; but he did not show anger or disappointment.

Albert continued, "But it's important to my boy's mother and me that Johnson be given all the protection due to him under the law. That means he cannot be held in jail without being convicted. We figure that if you and someone like Louis Lyons sign surety for Johnson to get him released on bail, he won't leave town."

The reverend was sitting stone still, but his eyes registered incredulity.

"For that reason," Albert went on, "we're offering to help with the bail. A lawyer is preparing a writ of *habeas corpus* right now, and we'll help with the money."

Black's eyes widened to the bursting point. "Praise God. You stop the mob…now this? Who have you talked to about this, Mr. Allison?"

"Only Mrs. Allison, the lawyer, and you, Reverend Black. I'm sure you appreciate why we can't post the bail ourselves. Too many of my friends and relations would never understand, and I simply don't want to explain it to them. Also, if something happens to Johnson while he's out, people will think I put up the bail just to get to him. I assure you; I don't want anything to happen to your friend. I want him tried and hanged properly."

Black was thoughtful for a moment. "When you puts up that bail money, you gets it back, right?"

"That's right, when Johnson shows up for the trial."

"So you're offering a loan like. When Charlie goes back to the trial, you get your money."

Albert said, "That's it. If you take the money to the court with the writ and sign the surety, when Johnson comes to the trial, they will return the money to you and then you give it back to me. It will be a lot of money; that's why I'll only entrust it to somebody with your reputation."

Albert was greatly overstating his knowledge of Black's reputation. Indeed, he was really counting on Black's fear of his own reputation to ensure the safety of the funds. While Albert did not intend to hand over the cash until the reverend was on his way to the courthouse—the next day, he thought—he was very aware of the risks entailed in this scheme.

Black pondered for a moment, then politely put Albert off. Clearly, Albert saw, Reverend Black took the offer seriously. Albert guessed that Black just wanted to be sure of his footing. 'Well,' Albert thought, 'I did not expect an immediate decision.' The reverend agreed to call Albert at the Stephen F. Austin before the end of the week.

"One last thing, Reverend Black," Albert said. "Johnson was driving with a loaded pistol late at night. People tell me that white outsiders had been making a lot of trouble in East Austin, and it occurs to me that maybe Johnson was patrolling to stop the riders. Were y'all organized to have men patrolling the streets?"

Black looked a little surprised, "Why, yes sir, there's been trouble this year; and people are getting a mite nervous. But, naw sir, we ain't patrolling like that. Old Charlie was just coming home from leaving off Annie Davis after Bible study. Anyhow, if we ever do get patrollers, we won't ask a peaceable old man like Charlie Johnson."

Well, Albert thought as he drove away, 'I've done my duty. I wonder if I'll hear from him.'

By the time Louis Lyons had arrived at Perry's farmhouse, Dr. Everett Givens, Mr. Will Fuller, and Perry were already on the porch. As Lyons walked up, he heard them talking about Charlie's success in training Everett Rhambo. Will was saying that real money was starting to show. Givens said that young Rhambo had already worked with his agents, and that this week—for the first time since Charlie had been arrested—Dr. Givens had made money. Louis was happy to interject that he, too, had made money.

Fuller remarked that he wished he could credit Everett, but he was sure that Charlie was pulling all the strings from jail.

Everett Givens said, "Well, Brother Fuller, everything seems to be happening according to Perry's plan. Ma's in the run-off with the governor, and she looks strong. The Colonel and I have made a big stink about the vote; and Mr. George Nalle himself has paid the Colonel a visit, right Colonel?"

"That's not all, brother Givens," Louis said. "The judge change Charlie's trial to November; that means we have time to find that lawyer. Most important—and this big news—there's a secret lawyer who do the papers to get Charlie bail if we got the money. Old Charlie ain't got it, but maybe somebody does. That mean that old Charlie could soon be out selling insurance and running policy for Mr. Will Fuller, at least for a few months."

Fuller laughed, "Yes, yes Colonel. So you can put old Charlie on the street until November—that's good. But then what? Ain't no lawyers gonna help Charlie with the trial, not even the judge's lawyer."

But Louis could see the wheels turning in Mr. Fuller's mind: If Charlie could be out working with Everett until November, the future of policy would be secure.

Louis figured Perry could see Mr. Fuller thinking, too.

With one of his broadest, whitest grins, Perry said, "Yes, Will Fuller, ain't no lawyer yet. But if Ma win the runoff, lawyers'll be looking for pardon money. Maybe they'll listen to a way to get some from Charlie. And look here, Will, old Charlie'll be working with Everett for nigh on three months before the trial. Maybe young Everett'll be ready to run the insurance and policy by hisself. Another thing you got to think about. Maybe he'll figure he likes it so much that he won't let his old Uncle Perry sell the business."

Louis Lyons nodded. 'Interesting idea,' he thought. 'My extra income from policy is too important to me and my family. I need to keep it, and keep it growing. Charlie's the key, but Will Fuller and Everett Rhambo have to do their parts. If Will can't or won't, maybe young Rhambo can—with Charlie's help, of course.'

"Well, one way or the other," Louis said to his colleagues, "I hope that Charlie'll be out soon. But that bail might be more than a thousand dollars, Perry. You put it up?"

Perry looked at Louis directly. He would raise the money if Will Fuller does the deal, he stated matter-of-factly. That meant that Mr. Fuller would have to take a chance that in November he might lose Johnson to the hangman.

Louis could not contain himself any longer, and this seemed the right point in the conversation to give the men even more news.

"A man come to Reverend Black today offering the cash for the bail, if me and the reverend agree to be responsible for Charlie showing up for the trial. Reverend Black was sworn never to say who it was, not even to Charlie. But the reverend is sure about the money; he just ain't too sure about why the man wants to do this. Maybe the man wants Charlie out of jail to kill him. Maybe he wants to buy the business with Charlie's help. Anyhow, the man told the reverend that he would get his bail money back because me and the reverend would guarantee that Charlie showed for the trial." Louis added the unlikely possibility of the man's interest in the business to give Mr. Fuller more than Everett Rhambo to worry about.

Perry said nothing. He just rolled his cigar around in his mouth and looked disinterested. Mr. Fuller's eyes narrowed. Louis knew he was calculating the odds.

"Does Charlie know, Louis?" Fuller asked quietly.

"I told him just before I came here. He don't think he'll be in danger. If the money's there, he says get him out."

Mr. Fuller said, "Well, Perry, I'll go with Louis to talk to Charlie tomorrow and get back to you in two days. Thank y'all. I never thought the deal would get this far."

As the men started to depart, Louis lingered to have a private word with Perry. When Perry heard that the offer was from the Allison boy's father—the same man who saved Charlie from the lynch mob—he yowled. Then put his finger to his mouth, and instructed Louis to tell no one. Perry said only that he would see Louis again in two days, when Fuller came back with his decision.

As Louis headed for his car, Perry added with a grin, "Louis, that little bit about Charlie buying the business with this stranger's help might just earn you a tidy bonus. You one smart cat."

As Louis drove off, he looked over his shoulder to see Perry stumbling in the direction of two big yellow eyes beaming high up in the live oak tree. Rhambo's loud, cackling laughter was filling the country night.

Charlie Johnson had started to feel desperate. He was being weighed down by the hot, restless nights on that lumpy cot; by the constant stirring, snorting, farting, and yammering of the prisoners; and by Carl Stewart's sniveling about his Mama and Nathan Rhambo and the screech owl (which Johnson had not heard in a couple of weeks). In fact, Charlie was becoming testy, and testy was not one of his normal traits. He had to get out of there.

When Charlie thought about it, he realized that the Stewart boy was the main cause for his mounting depression. The boy had murdered Charlie's good friend and benefactor; and that was enough for Charlie to hate Stewart, pure and simple. But Charlie had to admit that the boy had reason for a grudge: Even though Rhambo had nothing to do with Forest Stewart's disappearance, Rhambo did put Alice and Carl out of business; and Charlie did have a hand in that. Not that Charlie had any second thoughts. Truth be told, the boy's whining about all that didn't bother Charlie much, if at all. What was beginning to weigh on Charlie was that damn screech owl business.

About ten days before, Stewart had approached Charlie during exercise period and asked for a cigarette. When Charlie was giving Stewart a light, the boy had blustered a little about why Charlie let that fool Rhambo kid make stupid screech owl noises.

"Is that nigger some kind of idiot?" he asked.

Charlie had smiled back. "Gets to you, don't it?"

Stewart had frowned with that hint of insolence so common to younger men. He started to walk away, but stopped and turned around.

"What he know about old screech owls? If he know what I know, he be careful about messing with them."

Suddenly the image of the stuffed screech owl in Rhambo's office had flashed into Charlie's mind. 'Everett must have grown up looking at that old bird most days of his life,' Charlie had thought.

He looked quizzically at Stewart, "Yeah? What you know?"

Stewart had looked at Charlie in the strangest way, and then the boy just started blubbering out a rush of words. From what Charlie could gather, Stewart was saying that on the night Nathan Rhambo died, a white gang paid Stewart to go by taxi to Rhambo's funeral parlor and, on a ruse, to convince Rhambo to drive him to a prearranged place in Round Rock. There the gang beat up Rhambo bad and then shoved him, bloody and unconscious, into the back seat of Rhambo's Buick. When some men at a gas station across the intersection started shouting at them, the white men took off, leaving Stewart with the Buick. Stewart panicked, jumped into the Buick, and sped off. Not knowing what to do next, he headed for his Mama, who lived just south of Corsicana, a 150 miles away. Somewhere along the way, Rhambo came to and yelled for Stewart to stop the car; then, while attempting to climb into the front, Rhambo tried to grab the steering wheel.

"They give me the .38 before I fetch Rhambo," he had mumbled. "That bloody old man was fighting, and fussing and carrying on. I find the pistol, put it to his face, and pull the trigger."

Rhambo's body slumped back into the rear seat; and Carl, needing his Mama more than ever, continued to drive.

Then, just before midnight, just after Stewart passed through Dawson, he heard rustling behind him, then wings flapping, then a loud screech; and in the rearview mirror he saw a huge pair of yellow eyes looming in the back seat. That was when he ran off the road and wrecked the car.

By the time Stewart had blubbered all this out, he was sweating and his wide eyes were bloodshot, his mouth contorted into a speechless grimace.

Charlie had said nothing. Other prisoners had stopped their own activities to watch, but when Charlie stared at them they had quietly turned away. He, too, turned away. He left Stewart standing, facing where Charlie had been, and had not spoken with the boy since. However, the next day he did admonish Everett Rhambo to stop making the screeches.

Charlie could not put his finger on why he felt so burdened by Stewart's crazy story, but he did recall that he had dreamed about a screech owl the night he killed the white boy. All Charlie knew was that he had to get away from this burden, from this boy.

"Please, Lord," he prayed. "You'll punish me for my sins, I know; but please do it outside of this place."

When Louis first told Charlie about the bail offer, Charlie wanted to cry. He vaguely fathomed the father's good intent, as odd as it seemed, and sensed no harm in it. But whatever the man was up to, Charlie was relieved to know that he could soon be out, even if he had no lawyer.

The next day when Louis arrived with Mr. Will Fuller, he was confident enough to look straight at Mr. Fuller, "Sure, I'll work for you if I get out. I'm sure I can train Everett good enough to run things before the trial. Man, I just need out of here."

The night of August third, Louis Lyons witnessed Mr. Will Fuller agree to Perry Rhambo's terms for buying Nathan's business. Among the terms of sale, Perry committed personally to providing Charlie's bail and to securing Charlie the best white lawyer in Texas. After Ferris recharged the men's glasses, Perry made a show of handing Louis twenty-five hundred-dollar bills for Charlie's bail money. Later, in private, Perry instructed Louis to take the father's money, anyhow. "Just put it in a package and bring it to me, you hear? I want that man to think that he has a lot to lose if something bad happens to Charlie before the trial."

Louis was with Reverend Black at the Rising Star Church the next morning when Mr. Allison arrived. Reverend Black made introductions and told Mr. Allison that he wanted Louis to join him in the transaction so they could be witnesses for each other. The father agreed. He handed the reverend one envelope stuffed with bills and another containing official-looking documents. He told them to go to the courthouse to present the documents and the bail money, and to sign the surety bond; and then their friend would be free until the trial.

At 11 AM Reverend Adam Black and Louis Lyons presented a flawless writ of *habeas corpus* to Judge J. D. Moore, who ordered Sheriff Coley White to accept surety in the amount of twenty-five hundred dollars as bail. Johnson was to report back to the court on October third.

Before walking from the jail, Johnson stopped by Carl Stewart's cell. "So long niggah," he said. "I see you soon where that screech owl take you."

Stewart, sitting on his cot, spat quiet hate in Johnson's direction without looking up.

After dropping Reverend Black at Rising Star Church, Louis drove Johnson straight to Perry's farm. On the way, he told Charlie that Perry put up the bail money instead of Mr. Allison, but that Mr. Allison's lawyer did the paperwork. At the farm Perry greeted Charlie with unexpected severity. He grabbed Charlie tightly on the forearm, led him out of hearing of the others. Louis figured that Perry was taking credit for getting Charlie's bail and warning him not to let everybody down. 'Charlie know Perry; and he know that look,' thought Lyons. Perry was not to be crossed.

After a moment, Perry waved Louis over to join them. He said with his usual smile that he had just told Charlie that if he did not help Mr. Fuller, Perry would personally lead Charlie back to jail and make sure he had a Kluxer for a lawyer.

Then looking Charlie straight in the eye, Perry said, "On the other hand, my friend, if you do a good job, I'll get you the best white lawyer in Texas and save your light-brown ass, so you can spend the rest of your days getting rich. Ain't that right, Colonel?"

Louis nodded. Charlie nodded, too, thanked both men for all they had done; and excused himself to get a drink.

After Charlie left, Louis passed a thick envelope to the smiling Perry.

A friend later told Louis that by mid-afternoon, East Austin had the word that Charlie was out and that Perry wanted everybody to come to the farm to celebrate. The invitation promised barrels of beer, bottles of shine, too much barbecue, and a momentous announcement. By sundown a couple of combos were playing at once, and laughing dancers were prancing around a washtub on which a happy, light-brown sixty-year-old man stood waving a fruit jar slopping with a clear liquid. Sometime after sundown, old Perry stood basking in moonlight on his porch steps and put his arm around Mr. Will Fuller while he announced to several hundred people that Mr. Fuller was now the owner of Nathan Rhambo's funeral parlor and all associated businesses. After the clapping and yelling stopped, Mr. Fuller called Charlie to the porch. Mr. Fuller grasped Charlie's hand, raised his arm, and shouted, "Here's the man that made East Austin safe from the nightriders! He's going to be the next general manager of insurance and policy operations. Let's drink and dance for old Charlie!"

Dr. Everett Givens, feeling the effects of the moonshine, moved his large body next to Louis and was swaying in a slow beat and holding a fruit jar cupped in his large hands. Sweating and huffing slightly, he said, "Colonel, did you see Charlie's look when Mr. Fuller raised his hand like he just won a fight? I tell you Charlie just realized that he's walked out of the white man's jail straight into Perry's prison."

"Yep," replied Louis. "Charlie ain't free. He be as shackled to policy as any man on a chain gang. But, what the hell, I can think of worse things; and I am sure old Charlie can, too."

Louis took a swig from Givens's jar and watched Charlie step down from the porch, remove the clarinet mouthpiece from his pocket, and saunter toward the combo playing under the live oak tree.

Louis also noticed that Perry had stepped off the porch. Perry had edged away from the activity and out to the fence, where he seemed to be engaged in animated conversation. No one was with Perry, but Louis thought he saw two pairs of bird's eyes darting about on the fence.

As Charles Johnson's celebration was getting underway, at a corner table in the dark cocktail lounge of the Austin Club, attorney Will Hart sat with his brother James H. Hart and John Patterson reviewing a single-paged document.

Will nursed a Four Roses and drew on his cigar. As he looked down the page, a tightness gripped his gut. It was a simple profit and loss statement for the law firm of Hart, Patterson, and Hart; and it looked terrible. Fees were drying up; expenses were piling up; and partner distributions were shrinking.

Being a principal of Austin's most prestigious law firm entailed expensive family and community responsibilities to go along with the perquisites and privileges that attended their status.

Will then started to worry that possible rumors of their financial situation could cost them important clients and have even more serious ramifications. His nephew, Jim, the newly elected district attorney might have to resign before he got started. John Patterson might even have to quit being County Chairman.

The voice of Will's older brother, James, who was the senior partner, broke into his thoughts, "We had better start calling in a few chits at the state agencies.

There are plenty of people in important jobs that owe us favors. They might find a sudden need for legal work."

"At least until they're fired in January," Will added dryly. Turning to Patterson, Will asked, "What do you think, John? Is Governor Sterling going to pull this off again?"

"I reckon he will," Patterson replied. "But the Fergusons are running a strong campaign; and folks are half crazy with this Depression. We best not bank on anything."

"Anyhow," Patterson added, "maybe if Ma wins, this time we'll get on the parole gravy train. Last time a lot of our colleagues made good money handling Jim's 'clients.'"

"Damn John, don't make bad jokes," said James Hart.

Will wanted to say something, but held his tongue. Big brother was speaking for him again.

"Well, I imagine you don't have to worry," Patterson said. "I ran into George Nalle in here the other evening, and he said that Ferguson was not happy with me for keeping the darkies out of the primary. He figured to have that vote because of the Juneteenth parole he and Ma pulled off in '25; and Nalle said he needed it."

"Goddamn, those Fergusons are incorrigible, John," said James. "Letting loose twenty-five or thirty nigger murderers and thieves, then bragging they did it half-price just for Juneteenth."

Will finished his drink and stood to leave. "Okay, fellows, I'm due home. Besides, I'm not making us money by hanging around here. Tomorrow I'll nose around the Railroad Commission."

As Will walked from the club, he said to himself, 'Speak for yourself, brother James. If it comes to a choice between kissing old Jim Ferguson's behind and cutting back, I'll kiss. You will, too, if you want to protect your boy's political career. But not at half-price. We'll draw the line there.'

20

White Man's Election

Charlie Johnson tried to keep his mind on business. But the run-off election was on Saturday, and Louis Lyons had said that Perry's lawyer connections were waiting for the election to be over. Even though Louis had insisted that the lawyer matter was under control, Charlie could not keep from worrying. For reasons not entirely clear to him his life hinged on this white man's election.

After Perry had arranged Charlie's bail, Charlie wasted little time losing himself in work. Soon, he was satisfied that Everett Rhambo could manage basic administration and lottery operations without day-to-day supervision, and he began to apply himself to the arduous process of rebuilding the network of agents and runners. Within two weeks Charlie was training a new cadre for Louis Lyons, who was the new senior policy agent for East Austin. Before November, Charlie planned to repeat the process for Everett Givens, who was given the rest of Travis County, and then repeat the process again in half a dozen key central Texas markets. Being busy took Charlie's mind off his problems, but the trial date seemed to be rushing toward him.

In Perry's hotel bar the night before Election Day, just after Friday night Bible study (which Charlie had resumed with special intensity), Everett Givens tried to help Charlie and Annie Davis understand why Charlie should be optimistic that Ma would win.

"Times for many white folks are real hard and keep getting harder," Givens observed. "They're broke; they're scared; they kids've got rickets; their teeth are rotting; their rent's not paid; cotton's getting cheaper; and there's no relief. Now, to some of these folks—white trash, crackers, what old Jim Ferguson calls 'the boys at the forks of the creeks'—everything the high-flown politicians, the newspaper writers, and the big shot businessmen stand for makes things worse. I know this sounds like most black folk, too. But these whites have one thing we don't have, and that's the vote. This year they mean to use it to punish the big shots by putting old Jim and Ma back to work. Doesn't matter if Jim means his nice-sounding promises; nobody believes him anyhow. What the hell, after the last time, everybody knows that if Ma's elected again, old Jim'll turn the governor's office into his own personal retirement plan. I guess poor whites reckon the job ought to benefit somebody."

"I wonder what they'd say if they knew that Ma'd be good for old Charlie Johnson, too?" Givens added with a wink to Annie.

Charlie chuckled. Even though he had suspected as much, this was the first he had heard from somebody in the know that Ma's victory had something to do with his lawyer. He ordered another round of drinks, lit a cigarette, leaned forward, and waved his finger at the large, ebullient dentist. "Hell, white trash love a show, and they love a fighter who 'never say die; just damn, they caught me.'" Charlie chuckled. Givens laughed loud, and Annie Davis laughed, too.

Givens added, "And they love to hear that the big boys are responsible for their rotting food, their sun-wracked bodies, and their kids' worms. Governor Sterling's a big boy—a big, fat, rich boy. Scared folks will blame the man in charge and get behind a crook like old Jim or a dictator like that Mussolini fellow, anyone who promises to hurt the big boys as much as the big boys hurt them."

Bill Tarver certainly thought that Texas could do better than elect a man and his wife who made a mockery of public service. To him, the election had become an historic struggle between good and evil. Given the horrors of past Ferguson administrations, he was convinced that a Ferguson victory this time would damage irretrievably Texas's great standards of public virtue. This concern had motivated Tarver to travel the State ceaselessly during the past month. He had made more than one hundred speeches at breakfasts, luncheons, fairground rallies, and torchlight parades.

On election eve, Tarver dined with the governor, made dozens of last minute telephone calls, and dispatched dozens of telegrams. Just before midnight, he finally went home. All he could do was give Esther a tired hug before he collapsed into bed. The next day would be a long haul. After voting, Tarver would take the train to Dallas, where he would again be the governor's watchdog at the Election Bureau.

Not surprisingly, anxiety prevented sleep; so he climbed out of bed, poured a glass of whiskey, sat on the breeze porch, and let his tired mind run.

In the first primary on July twenty-third, Miriam Ferguson had led Governor Sterling by more than 100,000 votes. But Ma had led by that much in the first primary in 1930, and the Sterling forces were confident that this year the united anti-Ferguson vote would again prevail. However, this time the returns of the first election contained troubling evidence that Ferguson's friends in east Texas courthouses had manufactured thousands of votes from people without poll tax receipts, from cemetery residents, and from citizens of several Louisiana Parishes. Governor Sterling had considered having the Texas Rangers impound the ballots for verification or even take over the administration of the August twenty-seventh run-off in the most egregious counties, but he did not do so for fear of further antagonizing the voters. Instead, he had former Governors Moody and Hobby denounce Ferguson's degradation of the highest public office in Texas.

'Damn,' Tarver mused, 'I've been at the pinnacle of Texas politics for the past seven years. During that time, I've helped Governors Dan Moody and Ross Sterling decimate the Klan, stem the Ferguson tide, and be exemplary executors of the public trust.'

'By now,' Tarver thought, 'I ought to consider myself a hard, practical politician; but, I guess, at bottom I'm an idealist. Maybe, like Albert Allison, I'm an incorrigible idealist. But if it came to it, I guess I would pull out all the stops to beat Ma.'

His wry grin was directed at a mental image of Judge Cobb's sardonic look from the bench when admonishing the young Tarver, fresh out of Southwestern University, at his first trial more than twenty-five years before.

Despite Tarver's youth, he had made enough of an impression that Judge Cobb made a special effort to befriend and mentor him. After Mabel and Albert Allison moved to Corsicana in 1911, the judge—by then retired from the bench—Albert, and Tarver regularly met for drinks on early Friday evenings at the country club, where they conversed for an hour or so about the affairs of the day. By 1916, most of the talk concerned Prohibition or the European War; but Tarver recalled one night in September that year when they focused on the antics of Governor Jim Ferguson. At the time, most people thought that Ferguson's election in 1914 and reelection the previous month were quirks, damaging quirks, to be sure, but quirks that the state would survive and soon forget.

The judge was not so sure.

"You know," the judge had observed, "ever since the beginning, Texas has been a haven for ne'er-do-wells and riff-raff drifting westward day-to-day looking for the shortcuts in life. To them, public officials are enemies occupying fat jobs to do the bidding of plutocrats. Fortunately, for most of Texas history, they were so unconcerned, they seldom voted; and quality folks weren't hindered from giving Texas its great leaders. But the Ferguson-kind has always lurked in our political cesspools, waiting for a chance to get this riff-raff to the polls. What I mean is, that for every General Houston, Judge Reagan, and Governor Hogg, there has been an 'Honest Bob' Wilson or Jim Ferguson."

Then the judge winked, "You both remember 'Honest Bob.'"

Smiling at the blank stares of the younger men, the judge said, "Well, 'Honest Bob' earned his name during his quest for the Texas presidency in 1837 by declaring, 'I'm always as honest as the circumstances of the case and the condition of the country will allow.' He lost, of course; but he received enough votes to show that a certain element enjoys turning government into a game."

Sixteen years after Tarver's first "Honest Bob" lesson, on the night before yet another election, the thought of the judge's grin forced another smile out of Tarver. 'Oh boy,' he thought, 'how many people have since heard me talk about "Honest Bob?"'

As was their Election Day custom, Albert and Mabel Allison voted early. Albert then spent the rest of the day working at Sterling headquarters; and he would be at the Navarro County courthouse most of the night until every box was in, counted, sealed, and reported. Tarver's telegram the day before had asked Albert to camp out in the courthouse to thwart any funny business.

Albert had worked feverishly to stem the support building for Ma on the tenant farms and creek bottoms of north central Texas. The impact of his campaigning had apparently caused tremors in Ferguson headquarters. Ferguson had organized another major rally in Navarro County, this time in Kerens. Ferguson had railed at landlords eager to replace hard-working, faithful white tenants with lazy, subservient coloreds who could live on dirt pie. He also asked if the good Lord had not struck hard with a black hand at one particular landlord who had been faithless to his race.

When the remarks were reported, Albert had responded ferociously; but he had to admit that Ferguson's attacks had struck a chord with some voters. The election in Navarro County would be close.

Most of the Corsicana boxes came in before 10 PM and were counted before eleven; but; as usual, the rural boxes were slow. While waiting, Albert escaped the hubbub in the county clerk's office and wandered out to the courthouse steps for a quiet cup of coffee and a cigarette.

When the renewed Klan arrived in Corsicana in force around 1920, Albert did not clearly grasp its threat. It seemed to differ from the Reconstruction Klan in that its deepest concerns were not Negroes, but the deteriorating moral standards of whites. But Judge Cobb had seen the threat. He warned against confusing public and private virtue—"America doesn't need a moral police," he had said, "especially one that operates outside the law." Heeding the judge, Bill Tarver soon began to argue publicly that no free Republic could tolerate a secret society that meted out extra-legal punishments, no matter how valid the reasons.

Yet, because so many fine people seemed to support the aims of the Klan, Albert had been reticent to go along with Judge Cobb and Tarver. Albert's friends and neighbors voiced concerns that he shared. Rapid changes in social mores and sexual conventions, alien political philosophies, unionism, and other strange influences were creating turmoil in the country. The words *Ku Klux Klan* did bother him, for they conjured up the Klan of the last century that existed only to rectify the excesses of Reconstruction. But he reckoned this new Klan to be more the child of populism than the old namesake, more an assertion of values than a terrorist campaign.

That was why in July 1922, on the Sunday preceding the senatorial run-off election, Albert did not react when the hooded men in white robes assembled in his church at the start of the service. He did nothing when they marched to the altar singing "Onward Christian Soldiers" and appealed for support for their candidate. But just before Thanksgiving that year, hooded thugs burned a cross on the lawn of Sydney Marks, one of the Jewish merchants responsible for turning Corsicana from a railhead oil town into a real community.

Albert may have known too few Texas Catholics and not enough about Texas Negroes, but he did know Texas Jews. Some of his closest business associates were Adolph Harris, Alex Sanger, and Sydney Marks. He was outraged that someone in Corsicana would do such a thing to this wonderful, gentle, cultured person; and he wasted no time in making his views known. His letters pummeled the courthouse and city hall, and were printed in the *Sun* two days running.

Then, a few weeks later, the Streetman lynching jarred Albert into understanding what Bill Tarver and the then-late Judge Cobb had been saying. It was the first time Albert felt the sting of "nigger-lover." It would not be his last.

Over the next two years, Albert emerged alongside Bill Tarver at the vanguard of Corsicana's Klan opposition; and by 1924 they had rallied the community to their side. On election Sunday that year, the Klan was due to appear in hundreds of churches across Texas to support its candidate for governor. Bill was out of town, but he and Albert had prepared for the moment. This time at Corsicana's First Methodist Church, after the hooded men had marched to the altar singing "Onward Christian Soldiers" and had stood facing the congregation, Albert stood up from his pew and motioned to his family, who likewise stood. Then he, Mabel carrying two-year old Ken, the two older daughters, eight-year old Lod, and ten-year old Albert, Jr., holding little Eloise's hand, marched down the aisle and out of the church. The entire congregation followed.

'Even some of those that stood with me that day eight years ago still call me "nigger-lover," he thought as he stood outside the courthouse. 'How ironic,' he was speaking half aloud to the headlights moving toward the courthouse. Albert put out his cigarette and walked out to meet the cars bringing the voting boxes from Dawson.

Raymond Brooks would be up late trying to piece together a coherent story for the morning edition. He had been on the telephone all day to politicians and other newsmen around the state. No one had a feel. Even that old warhorse John Patterson hedged. At the earliest, the first returns would not be reported before 9 PM; so as was Brooks's custom on election nights, he started the story that would never run. 'Well, someday,' thought the reporter, 'if my hunch is right, this story and a few others will be in my book.'

"The Ferguson/Sterling campaign was unquestionably the most ferocious in Texas history—a 'splendid fury,' one Ferguson supporter called it. Aspersions and accusations, hyperbole and outrageous lies had swept across Texas like its rainstorms—thundering, crashing, drenching, flooding, gone, and forgotten. Sterling supporters, whom Ferguson labeled the "bourbons," could not abide the thought of Fergusonism again demeaning every noble standard for public service. Former Governor Dan Moody, Insurance Commission Chairman Bill Tarver and other so-called Moody men made hundreds of speeches. The newspapers pummeled the public with a litany of Ferguson outrages.

"With even more vitriol, Jim Ferguson countered that 'Fat Boy' Sterling was a tool of the oil interests; that Sterling called himself a 'dry,' but was a liquor wholesaler; that the 'present Encumbrance' was a tool of the press barons and Rockefellers. He promised that his 'vest pocket vote'—'the boys living at the forks of the creek'—and his friends in East Texas courthouses would take back the governor's mansion for Ma and Jim.

"Ferguson was not making an idle threat: East Texans had long ago eschewed the politically virtuous for the lovable scoundrels who made public service a practical joke on taxpayers. That's why the denizens of east Texas courthouses recognized 'Pa' as one of their own. He was not some stuffed-shirt philosopher with ridiculous expectations. In 1932 that crowd and the 'boys at the forks of the creeks' would make the difference."

While Raymond Brooks was typing, Bill Tarver paced the corridors of the Texas Election Bureau in Dallas. By 3 AM, 600,000 votes had been tabulated; and Ma led by less than 1,000. With approximately 300,000 votes to be reported, mainly from east and south Texas, an exhausted Tarver reluctantly left an assistant in charge and checked into the Adolphus Hotel.

When Tarver awoke, he ordered room service and a newspaper. The *Dallas Morning News* trumpeted the dead heat, but assured readers that the Sterling camp was confident of victory. 'Well, the "Sterling camp" is right here,' thought Tarver, 'and it's scared stiff.'

After eating a light breakfast, Bill dressed and returned to the Election Bureau. The tallies at 10 AM showed that Sterling had moved ahead by a few thousand votes. An hour later, more returns arrived from east Texas that put Ferguson barely ahead. Bill got on the telephone to campaign chairmen in the counties still to report. That night, Archie Parr's south Texas counties reported; and Sterling leapt ahead. But the next day, more south Texas counties reported and, surprisingly, put Ferguson ahead to stay—by four thousand votes out of a million cast.

21

The Election Mess

Early Monday morning, August twenty-ninth, Louis Lyons answered the telephone to hear Charlie Johnson's giddy voice saying that he wanted to deliver the grocer's policy commission personally. A short time later, Charlie almost danced into the store; and with a big smile he handed Louis a fat envelope.

"It's a small reward for what you do for me, Colonel."

Louis peeked inside the envelope and exclaimed, "Oowhee, Charlie! Do I see a lot of green in there?"

But Louis knew that Charlie had made the special trip because the newspapers said that Ma Ferguson had won the election. Charlie was anxious about the lawyer that was supposed to accompany her victory.

But Louis had bad news. "The newspapers say it look like Jim and Ma won, just like Perry said they would. But it ain't that easy, Charlie, 'cause the newspapers ain't the last word. The last word be by the convention up in Lubbock next Saturday, and Dr. Givens say the governor be mad as stink and ain't going to let nobody in the convention who don't vote for him."

As soon as the Texas Election Bureau had declared the final result, Governor Sterling asked Bill Tarver to lead the effort at the September State Convention in Lubbock to reject Ferguson's stolen votes (estimated at 50,000) and to ratify Sterling's victory. Acting quickly, Tarver ensured Sterling's control of the credentials committee, and then imposed the criteria for certifying delegates. He also had the governor dispatch the Texas Rangers to Lubbock to ensure orderly floor access.

But Jim Ferguson put out a call to his "boys at the forks of the creeks" to go to Lubbock and save their victory. Thousands piled into rickety trucks and rusty cars, streamed out of the piney woods, and creaked over 600 miles to the Panhandle, where they overwhelmed the Rangers, crushed the credentials committee, forced through ratification of Ferguson's victory, and made Bill Tarver the butt of scathing newspaper commentary.

Perry Rhambo had finally started showing up at the hotel at night. "The election must've made old Perry more confident," observed Charlie Johnson to Annie Davis. They were seated at their usual Friday night table.

"And not too soon," Charlie mused. "Especially since his old bartender Johnny ain't around no more. Them white university boys is back, and Perry's best at dealing with what they need."

Perry noticed Charlie and Annie and wandered over. He signaled the new bartender for a round of drinks.

"How is Miss Annie, tonight?" Perry asked as he joined the table. "You be playing some sweet music tonight, Charlie?"

Charlie chuckled, "I think your customers want something more lively than an old man's blues, Perry."

"Well, Charlie, my share of policy says you pretty damned lively; and I bet Annie say so, too."

Annie let out an appreciative squeal.

"I'm glad you like the way I'm lively, Perry," Charlie responded, "and I hope you going to like it in two, three months, after that lawyer keeps me on the job."

Perry's smile turned to pursed lips under narrowed eyes leveled directly at Johnson. He sat in the available chair.

"Two things, Charlie. First, all them white lawyers is working for that Corsicana boy who killed Nathan. That trial's next month. I hope they lose, but I hope they be good because we might need them. Second, Ma ain't won yet, dammit. She ain't won even after the Election Bureau and the Convention say she won. The governor is asking a judge to say that old Jim and Ma stole votes from East Texas. How old Jim do that, I can't figure; but if anybody can do it, he's the one."

Charlie knew not to press the matter. Perry was obviously concerned.

"Hell, Perry, I guess I'm jumpy. I know things'll be all right. Let me buy you a drink for a change."

Perry accepted, waved over the new bartender, and introduced him to Charlie and Annie. While the bartender was pouring their drinks from Perry's stock of pre-war, Charlie asked about Johnny.

"Well, Charlie," Perry's smile became just a hint fierce, "you remember the morning after you done the killing, the paper say a Mexican tell the police where to find you? Well, turns out old Johnny was learning Spanish, so he had to go to where all them good Meskins go."

Perry stood and slapped Charlie on the back. "Annie, tell Charlie not to fret none. We'll get it done. I hear the Ferguson people is moving into town, ready to take over. That's a good sign."

> *Hark, Hark the dogs do bark*
> *The Fergusonites have come to town*
> *Their looks are tough, their necks are rough,*
> *They love their Levi Garret snuff.*

By late September, the *Statesman* was resigned to the Fergusonite invasion and had begun to tweak the bourbons with little limericks. But diehard Sterling men like Bill Tarver soldiered on. Austin was a cauldron of Sterling appointees fighting desperately to hang on, while east Texas courthouse boys invaded state offices to look over their new places of employment. Lobbyists and lawyers jockeyed between the hate.

After the convention debacle, Tarver persuaded Governor Sterling to send the Rangers to questionable east Texas counties to impound the ballots. Then, after a cursory inspection of the evidence, Tarver and former Governor Dan Moody prevailed on Sterling to take Ferguson to court to answer charges about 55,000 stolen votes. The judge agreed to hear the case; but, after process servers were unable to serve subpoenas on the wily Fergusons, the frustrated judge changed his mind, saying that the courts had no business in electoral matters anyway.

Undaunted, the Sterling camp asked the governor to call a special session of the legislature to recount the vote.

At the Austin Club one evening in early October, an ebullient George Nalle ran into the lawyer Gabriel Hawthorne and former State Senator Alvin Wirtz. They were waiting for Senator Archie Parr, who was in town for the special session. These were old friends with whom Nalle could relax. While they waited, Nalle ordered a round and entertained the two men with a description of the Ferguson escape from the process servers, who were trying to get Ma into court to answer vote-stealing charges.

"I got a call from the courthouse that the servers were on their way to the Ferguson house on Windsor Avenue. Miriam and Jim weren't answering their phone; so I jumped in my car, drove over there, hustled them into the back seat, and snuck them over to our house. After about an hour, the deputies drove up and came to our door; but we didn't answer it. So they just sat in their car. Sooner or later they were going to nail us; so after dark, we snuck Jim and Miriam out the back door, down the alley, where we got into a cab we had called. We had him drive us to Bandera. A couple of days later the judge threw the case out for lack of evidence because his evidence was nowhere to be found."

Amid the men's laughter, Alvin Wirtz commented that it sounded like a Hollywood movie. "Hell, Texas needs a little lift, George. That's a story most folks would appreciate."

Senator Parr arrived and gently teased Nalle about the trouble his father-in-law was causing the legislature. The men ordered more drinks, then steaks, and soon the conversation turned to the real reason for the evening get-together: hootchie-kootchie. Even though Nalle was reluctant to be dragged along, he was also loath to be unfriendly to Parr, whose support was essential to thwart Sterling's attempt to get the legislature to do a vote-recount. Besides, as always, Hawthorne would pay. Ouida would just have to understand.

About 11 PM, Nalle and his three companions walked into the smoky haze of Perry's hotel and bar. A smiling bartender greeted Hawthorne and led the men to a table toward the back, next to the dance floor and bandstand. Girls—white, black, and brown—started moving in.

After a short time, drinks arrived; the girls hinted at a penchant for champagne; and Perry Rhambo, whom each man knew, sauntered over. Hawthorne raised his glass and greeted Perry exuberantly. The white men did not stand; no one shook hands; nor was Perry invited to sit. The girls melted away.

"Perry, I've been meaning to write to you," Hawthorne said. "You are now the temporary treasurer of the Texas Negro Undertaker's Association."

Perry smiled wide and thanked the lobbyist, "I be very temporary, Mr. Hawthorne. Mr. Will Fuller'd be the one to take over from Nathan. He permanent."

Hawthorne nodded with a smirk, "I might have known. Well, have him call me, and I'll do the paperwork."

"I'll sure do that, Mr. Hawthorne. But I was hoping you were going to tell me you found the man to defend Charlie Johnson."

Nalle noticed Hawthorne's smile tighten as he shook his head. Perry just nodded. Perry was too smart to say any more, especially in front of Hawthorne's guests.

"Who's Charlie Johnson?" Nalle asked.

Hawthorne said, "Oh, he's the boy that killed that white kid last summer—wounded Derden Wofford with same bullet. It happened just across the street."

Nalle remembered Jim Ferguson storming into his office waving the newspaper, and his frantic effort to set up the rally in Kerens.

"Still no lawyer?" Nalle asked.

"Long story," replied Hawthorne. "The darky was damn near lynched."

Nalle flinched at Hawthorne's crudeness with Perry Rhambo standing in earshot, but Rhambo seemed unbothered. Rhambo smoothly turned his attention to the dapper Archie Parr, seated to Hawthorne's right.

"How are you Senator Parr? Long time. What's brought y'all back to Austin this time of year, sir?"

Senator Parr acknowledged Rhambo with a perfunctory nod and started to look around, obviously searching for the girl who had drifted away from him when Rhambo arrived. Nalle saw Rhambo catch the girl's eye, and she slipped easily beside the Senator.

Without pausing for an answer, the black man turned to the other gentlemen, "And how are you, Senator Wirtz?" If possible, Perry's beaming smile broadened, eerily showing gold and white teeth sparkling like the Cheshire cat's against the dark background. Nalle noticed that Wirtz looked a little sheepish at being recognized. As Rhambo turned in Nalle's direction and asked after him, he felt the same way.

Hawthorne smirked, "Perry, Governor Sterling has called a special session to have the Senate recount the election. Senator Parr here has brought his counting machine."

Parr laughed and said, "Sure thing, Gabe. We're going to find 4,000 votes for Ross Sterling. Here, George Nalle, let's drink to that."

As the men guffawed, Rhambo signaled to the bartender to bring another round of drinks, nodded in the direction of the girls, and sauntered easily away. Soon soft bodies surrounded Nalle and his friends; and the men eased into bawdy jokes and war stories.

During the evening, Alvin Wirtz told Nalle and Hawthorne that on the night of the run-off election, he had been holed up in an Austin hotel with the twenty-three year old, hyper-charged, chain-smoking assistant to Congressman Richard Kleberg:

"The boy—Lyndon Johnson's his name—was completely fascinated as the votes came in, one fraud after another. 'Hell,' I told him, 'no Texas election is over until the last crooks finish changing their votes.'"

Nalle could not help himself, nor could the grinning Wirtz and Hawthorne: all three turned their grins toward Senator Parr, Texas's most accomplished political crook. Unfazed by the dubious recognition, Parr—whose ears had pricked up during Wirtz's story—joined in the laughter.

"Hell, y'all know I always sell to the highest bidder; and that's that. But it's true old Jim has been such a good customer that I've developed a special affection for him and Miriam; and I think they have a small affection for me. Well, before the first primary, Governor Sterling's people made a vague hint of a deal; but Jim wasted no time in laying out hard cash. So I put my votes behind Ma. Then in August, Ross Sterling got serious and beat Ferguson out. So in that election I put my votes behind Ross.

"I got to tell you, George, your father-in-law was a real gentleman about it. But he did ask if the deal with Ross included south Texas counties not under the so-called Parr machine. Well, of course, Ross might have thought so, but it didn't," Parr winked at Nalle.

"So Jim and I did a deal on those counties; and, as you know, it was those counties that finally sealed the election for Ma," Parr concluded with evident satisfaction.

Then, after a taking a sip, Parr added, "Naturally, despite the fact that I delivered the votes to Ross as agreed, his folks are a mite curious about my involvement in those other counties. But now, just like old Jim, they are talking hard cash regarding the legislative recount in this session. I love an election that gives me three opportunities to do business. But, you know fellows, sometimes friendship is more important. Right, George?"

Parr's associates laughed because they knew they were supposed to treat the senator's remarks as a joke (at least Nalle did; and he assumed the others did). But they also knew that the powerful man was signaling the shape of the week to come. And that shape boded well for Ma. George Nalle did not know whether he smiled more at the senator's signal or at the girl seated in Parr's lap when she said, "Honey, I'm looking for three ways to do business with you."

When the judge had rejected Governor Sterling's lawsuit, Bill Tarver and his colleagues had immediately urged the governor to call the legislature into special session to conduct a recount. Even though the legislature faced the practical obstacle of resolving the issue in time for the ballots to be printed for the November general election, the governor still had almost universal support from the press and an outraged public. Bill and others had argued that a legislature that thwarted the governor would commit political suicide.

Bill was lobbying representatives when word came to him that Senator Archie Parr of Duval, arguably the only politician in Texas impervious to public opinion, was filibustering against the recount. Given Senate rules, his opposition would be sufficient to kill it. Bill immediately went to the senate gallery to see for himself. There he ran into Raymond Brooks, who said he had just filed the story.

Brooks appeared to try to suppress a smile when he told Bill that most reporters picked up on Parr's contention that a "recount was just an attempt by Governor Sterling to steal the election." Tongue in cheek, Brooks asked the speechless Tarver for a reaction. But before Tarver could gather his thoughts, Brooks walked away chuckling and shaking his head.

Charlie Johnson nervously walked to the back of Louis Lyons's grocery store. It was October already, and high time something happened about that lawyer.

When Dr. Givens greeted him warmly, Charlie's spirits lifted. Lyons slapped him on the back and handed him a cold bottle of beer. But the dentist just wanted to explain that the governor had ordered the Democrat State Executive Committee not to certify Ma for the November ballot.

"Can't say what it means," the big man said. "Some people allow folks'll just write in Ma's name or the governor's, but others say that they'll forget and that the Republican will be in."

In the recesses of his imagination, Charlie could hear the horses of robed riders pounding; but it was not yet time to seek the tree stump.

As far as Bill Tarver was concerned, the Sterling campaign mission had shifted from reelecting Sterling to stopping Ferguson. At one of his final meetings with the Sterling leadership team, the consensus had been that Texas could survive if the Republican were elected by default (nobody at the meeting had paid enough attention to the Republicans to recall the candidate's name). Not so, they were convinced, if the Fergusons returned. Therefore, if Ross Sterling's name could not be in the Democrat column for governor on the general election ballot, no name should be there. The State Executive Committee—the last bastion of Sterling support—did its duty and approved a ballot with no Democratic nominee for governor.

But this ploy failed, too. In exasperation, the Fergusons sued the Committee. Despite Tarver's arguments before the court, Ferguson's suggestion that the Republican might win by default was enough for the judge to order that Miriam Ferguson's name be placed on the ballot.

For as long as George Nalle had known Jim Ferguson, Nalle had never seen the old man as mad as when they first suspected Sterling was backing the Republican. Sure, Jim Ferguson understood political games; and, sure, Jim admired opponents who played the games hard. But in this game, old Archie Parr had made the last play; and the final whistle had blown. Sterling should have conceded right there. Keeping the State Committee from certifying Ma was silly overplaying, typical of folks who paraded their virtues. But when the judge pissed on those virtues, old Fat Boy sure as hell should have had the grace to concede. But Sterling had not conceded.

"Trying to keep Miriam off the ballot was bad enough," Jim fumed. "Now that we're on the ballot, Fat Boy could throw his support behind the Republican just to beat us."

"Well," Jim continued, his voice quieter, menacing, "maybe the game's not over, George. Maybe we have more work to do."

Two days later, Sterling proved Ferguson to be right. The governor and his allies in the press issued a call to all "loyal Texans" to vote against the Fergusons in the general election. "For the sake of our beloved Texas," the press barons cried, "to be true to its sacred heroes, Texans must transcend party loyalty to stem the evil about to descend on their capital."

Thus, the bourbons launched the fourth—and, George Nalle prayed, final—battle of the long campaign.

Louis Lyons watched Ferris hand Perry a refill, then tend the kerosene lanterns he had placed around the porch to light the approaching evening. Lyons carefully nursed his half-filled glass, as did both Dr. Everett Givens and Mr. Will Fuller.

Perry was frustrated. "How is it," he asked the members of the "weekly meeting," as they had begun to call their regular get together, "how is it that the Corsicana boy who killed poor old Nathan can get two lawyers to defend his black ass, and we ain't got nowhere for old Charlie?

"Well," answering his own question, "right now they be the only lawyers taking colored cases, and somehow that Stewart got to 'em first."

But the Stewart trial was the next week. When it was over, Perry said, he would talk to Bill Yelderman.

Mr. Will Fuller grunted that he hoped the lawyers lost the Stewart case. "Whites ordinarily don't care whether coloreds who kill coloreds get punished, but this time they better care, or East Austin will blow up."

Perry nodded his hard face.

Louis and Perry had had many conversations about help they could get from Jim Ferguson. But the San Antonio legal effort to get the Negro vote into the August run-off had not been successful, and Louis had heard nothing more from Jim's son-in-law George Nalle.

"It's a shame we couldn't vote in that August election," observed Givens, "and I'll bet Jim thinks so, too. Our vote would've given him such a lead Governor Sterling couldn't say nothing except 'good-bye.'"

Perry laughed and said to Louis, "Colonel, there's still another election coming up; and they can't stop us from voting in that one, even though this time Ma don't need any colored help."

Louis had to shake his head. Perry was right. The colored vote in general elections never meant anything. As things stood, Charlie would be lucky to have one of those old courthouse drunks helping him.

22

Carl Stewart's Trial

Monday, October 10, 1932. Texas autumn had brought cooler nights and dry, warm days. But the pleasant climate provided no escape from the Depression that was consuming Albert Allison's assets or from the depressing turn in Texas politics.

Albert stood at the window of his seventh floor room at the Stephen F. Austin Hotel. The traffic on Congress Avenue was thinning; evening shadows were descending. Albert felt alone, like an outsider. Bill Tarver and his other political friends were still too wrapped up in the election fiasco to join him for dinner that night. So he would eat alone and read.

Albert had met with the Agriculture Commissioner that day, and once more strongly defended the cotton moratorium to his old friend. Because of Albert's persuasiveness with the Democratic National Platform Committee, with Roosevelt's election, a national moratorium would likely become federal law under a new Democratic administration. Because of the recent Texas fiasco, the Commissioner was worried. Albert, nonetheless, was still convinced that he would be saved by the national cotton moratorium and was devoting considerable time preparing for action following the imminent election of Franklin Roosevelt.

The commissioner had been reelected by a substantial margin, of course. But he seemed to be intimidated by Jim Ferguson. Albert was not sure that the commissioner was any happier after Albert had taken him step-by-step through the entire rationale one more time.

Albert had also kept in regular touch with Assistant District Attorney Jim Hart and was satisfied that, even though Charlie Johnson still had no lawyer, the trial would be conducted satisfactorily. However, Albert's enthusiasm for aiding Johnson had waned, not least because Albert's commitment to cover the fees would strain his deteriorating finances. It was enough, Albert felt, that he had seen to it that Johnson was freed on bail and was thereby free to find his own lawyer.

Albert had planned to call on young Hart that day, but he was unavailable due to the Carl Stewart trial. With nothing more to do, Albert had decided to stay overnight to observe the prosecutor in action the next day, the second day of the trial.

Judge Charles Wheeler's courtroom was crowded with stony-faced blacks. Only the two front rows were reserved for whites. The night before, Bill Tarver had told Albert that Nathan Rhambo's family and friends wanted the white jury, white judge, and white attorneys to give Carl Stewart justice fit for a white man's killer. But, Bill said, others in East Austin felt strongly that young Stewart was being railroaded; they suspected that he was a patsy for someone with a business grudge against Rhambo. Albert had read in the paper that morning that Judge Wheeler had cleared the courtroom the day before because the two groups had gone at each other.

As soon as the judge called the court to order, Stewart's lawyer, Bill Yelderman, asked for a delay; and the courtroom erupted. Apparently, Yelderman argued, the night before Stewart had cut his wrists while screaming something about a screech owl. Stewart's defenders shouted that the Rangers tried to kill the boy to keep him from revealing his white bosses. Judge Wheeler, looking furious, banged his gavel and announced he would order the bailiffs to make everyone leave if there was one more disturbance. Albert noticed that the well-dressed Rhambo family remained quiet; in fact, they were smiling.

Wheeler denied Yelderman's petition, and the bailiffs brought a dazed-looking Stewart into the room. Both his wrists were bandaged.

'Yelderman said something about a screech owl,' thought Albert. Realizing that Stewart was a Corsicana native, Albert wondered if a strange hoodoo creed had captured the imaginations of Corsicana's east side folk: first Emma, then Chester, now this Stewart boy.

Bill Yelderman's co-counsel, Tass Waterston, then petitioned the judge to have the Rangers who investigated the case, especially Earl McWilliams, removed from the courtroom. The very presence of the Rangers, he argued, intimidated the defense witnesses. Wheeler overruled. Next, Waterston challenged the venue. The prosecution had introduced no evidence to prove that Rhambo was murdered in Travis County. Wheeler overruled. Finally, Waterston objected to Stewart's confession being admitted on the grounds that it was coerced. Before he overruled, Wheeler sent the jury out of the room and heard testimony from the defendant and the Rangers.

'Yelderman and Tass Waterston appear very much at home,' thought Albert. 'They obviously have a cause.'

Being a "cause" man himself, as the day progressed, Albert felt his sympathies lean in their direction.

Bill Yelderman carefully took Stewart through the eight days in June from the time he was arrested until he signed a confession. Albert felt the silent rage behind him when Stewart described being hanged naked on the wall, the water torture, the beating, the sleep deprivation, and the cursing. Even Rhambo's family grimaced. Albert felt the derision when Stewart described Captain Hamer's visit to apologize for the Ranger who had broken his nose.

When the Ranger Earl McWilliams took the stand, Albert felt the courtroom avert its eyes to keep its hate at bay. He felt the courtroom suppress a sardonic laugh when Earl McWilliams said, "I know when they lie. That's why it took eight days....Well, I know he had a right to counsel, but when he made his phone calls he talked to his mother and girlfriend. Yes, eight days might be a little longer than usual....Yep, he did give two, three confessions but they were right smart lies. I don't even recall what he said...Yep, it's true that his mammy, Alice, was in the custody of Corsicana's Sheriff; but that wasn't at our request...And no, we didn't threaten Stewart that Alice would suffer if he didn't confess."

'They arrested Alice Stewart?' Allison thought. 'My God, what kind of sheriff is that drunken fool, Pevehouse?'

Then it dawned on Allison that it was McWilliams who called him the night Son was killed.

'He was also one of the officers who arrested Johnson,' Albert thought, 'and he was a witness to Charles Johnson's confession. Did he use those methods on Johnson? No lawyer was present to prevent it.'

Then it occurred to Albert that whether Judge Wheeler agreed with his assessment of Carl Stewart's confession or not was immaterial. The judge was forced to choose between the word of a white Texas Ranger and the word of a black. Albert found himself pondering how the judge would treat discrepancies between Charles Johnson's version of events and that of the boys in the car with Son.

Then young Jim Hart stood before the jury to make his summation. Judge Wheeler's rulings bothered Albert, and McWilliams's testimony disgusted him. Jim Hart's summation to the jury completely shocked him:

"Carl Stewart is a Negro," Hart declared. "This time he confessed to a crime against one of his own race. Do you have any assurance, if you turn him loose, that the next time he won't go out and kill some white man for money?"

Albert recalled that Judge Cobb once said that when attorneys in his court appealed to race, he would adjust his instructions to the jury to compensate. Not so Judge Wheeler. Judge Wheeler's instructions clearly steered the jury to the death penalty.

When Albert read the jury's verdict in Wednesday's morning paper, he was hardly surprised. However, he was slightly taken aback to read that Ma Ferguson's impending election influenced the jury as much the prosecutor. The paper said that three of the twelve had originally opposed the death penalty on the grounds that a Negro should not die for killing another Negro. However, when their colleagues pointed out that Ma would likely pardon or parole Stewart, they did not want to be responsible for returning a murderous Negro to Texas streets.

After breakfast, with his concerns swirling through his mind, Albert walked from the Stephen F. Austin to the courthouse to see Henry Brooks, young Jim Hart and Judge Wheeler. Brooks said that he had seen Albert at the Stewart trial and had guessed he was educating himself. Albert smiled and nodded, then said he hoped he wasn't too old to learn something. The district attorney told Albert that, as far as he knew, Johnson still had no lawyer; but Johnson did report earlier in the week as required by his bail surety. The judge had extended his bail to November fourteenth. Brooks added that Jim Hart's preparations for prosecuting the case were proceeding well. The father thanked Brooks for his time and left.

From Brooks's office, Albert proceeded to Bill Yelderman's office in the Norwood Building. Yelderman's secretary said that he be would out for a few days, but that he would call Albert in Corsicana as soon as possible, perhaps next week. Mr. Yelderman had just finished a trial, she said, and was under a deadline to file an appeal.

23

Hart, Patterson, and Hart

"George," Jim Ferguson declared to his son-in-law, "I told you that old Fat Boy would do anything to stop us. Asking his supporters to vote Republican sounds crazy, but it might work; and Miriam and I have come too far to take any chances."

Ferguson paused and gave George Nalle a familiar look that said an assignment was coming in the next breath.

"So we're gonna' buy some insurance. We're gonna' help Senator Archie Parr and a few of those East Texas courthouses turn out the vote. And let's not forget the darkies. The bourbons can't keep them out of the general election."

The next day, George called a list of county chairmen, the Negro chairman of Republicans for Roosevelt, and Senator Archie Parr. He then drove to Lyons's Grocery.

After George Nalle and Louis Lyons exchanged exuberant greetings, Lyons took Nalle to a small room in the back and, despite the early hour, opened two beers. The men clicked bottles; then Lyons sat back and listened while Nalle explained that both Ma and Governor Roosevelt needed his votes. Nalle was not particularly surprised when Lyons replied, with little enthusiasm, that he would have to talk to his organization.

Nalle was not coy: He said that Ferguson was willing to pay Lyons two dollars a vote plus poll tax expenses. With that, they agreed to meet in three days at Nalle's house on Rio Grande Street. Lyons said he would like to bring Dr. Everett Givens with him.

Before anyone said a word at that evening's "weekly meeting," each of the men went through the small ritual of biting off the end of the big cigars that Perry had handed them. Almost in unison, they put the cigars to a large flame and took long draws before expelling streams of smoke. In the midst of these pleasantries, and while Ferris was serving pre-war doubles, Perry abruptly said,

"It's about goddamned time. Colonel, you got to ask Mister Nalle to help old Charlie find a lawyer."

Turning to Mr. Fuller, Perry said, "Will, it's worth it to you to pay Louis and Everett their poll tax expense, if the Colonel can't get them Fergusons to pay and get a lawyer, too. Our deal has got to be 'no lawyer, no votes.'"

Without dropping a beat, Rhambo's head turned back to Louis, "Colonel, this might be old Charlie's last chance."

Then to Everett Givens, "Dr. Givens, have you got your votes ready?"

The big man laughed a hearty "Yes man! Let's get old Ma and Pa some votes!"

Two crows in the sprawling live oak tree flapped and cawed; and Perry gleefully shouted, "Y'all hush now while these gentlemen talk."

To Mr. Will Fuller he said with a wink, "Them crows started talking a lot more since the screech owl got his satisfaction from the Stewart trial and flew off."

With the exception of a brief flash of a smile, Mr. Fuller's dour expression did not change.

Louis Lyons and Everett Givens went to Mr. George's house at the appointed time and gave him their terms. Nalle told them that he would cover their poll tax expenses whatever happened, but he said he would have to talk to Governor Ferguson about the lawyer. He asked them to come back the next day.

When they arrived, Mr. Nalle introduced them to Governor Jim Ferguson himself. Louis was immediately struck by a wicked twinkle in Ferguson's blue eyes. After a few minutes, Louis felt like he shared some old, deep secret with the man—just the two of them. 'And we just met,' Louis marveled.

"Mister Nalle tells me y'all are organized so good you can get us a thousand votes, is that right?"

"Yes sir," Givens replied.

"You want a lawyer, I understand. I can help. In fact, I've already made inquiries. But I need two things from you. One is your absolute promise that if I get this lawyer, you'll get Ma those thousand votes. I tell you, if the votes don't show, I'll jerk that lawyer, and your friend is as good as fried. What do you say?"

"We have the votes, Governor; and they'll be there," Everett Givens said in a deep, quiet voice.

"The other thing I need is your absolute secrecy, and I think you understand why. If any of this gets out, I'll know it's your doing. I'll not only pull the lawyer; I'll make you wish you never heard of old Pa Ferguson. You understand?"

"Yes sir," in unison.

"Okay, we understand each other. Now tell me about your friend and what he's done."

Louis began, "Well, sir, his name be Charlie Johnson..."

George Nalle interrupted, "Sure, Dad, you remember. This Charlie Johnson shot a white boy from Corsicana—Albert Allison's son. Mob damned near lynched Johnson; might have taken the courthouse if Allison himself hadn't stopped them."

"I remember," Ferguson said. "I've known about this Allison for years. He's a Navarro County landlord who screws his tenants every way he can. Big supporter of Lynch Davidson when he ran against us in '24. Him and Fat Boy Sterling's man, Bill Tarver, are big buddies."

Ferguson stood abruptly and began ushering Louis and Givens out of the room. "Y'all have Johnson ready to talk to his new lawyers. Don't worry, boys. Your friend has found himself a new protector. That boy shot the son of the right landlord."

Perry Rhambo's entire large frame shook with delight. Mr. Will Fuller forced a smiled. Then Perry, who was seventy if a day, managed to balance on the narrow porch railing offering toasts to the live oak tree, to "Governor Ma," to the sacred memory of his brother, to Carl Stewart's jury, and to the families of the present company. After each toast, Ferris refilled the glasses. Soon the four men were dancing barefoot in the grass arm-in-arm.

While Perry and his friends were celebrating, Will Hart waited for his partners to join him at the Austin Club, which was much busier than usual. 'The Fergusons are truly in,' Will thought, 'and the parole fee largesse is about to flow.' Anticipating Inauguration Day, families of robbers and murderers had started bringing $3,000 fees to Austin's young lawyer sharps and courthouse cronies, many of whom were in the club that night celebrating. 'And Jim Ferguson hasn't even started directing clients to them, yet.'

For more than sixty years, since the wild frontier days, the Hart family had been Austin's focal point for civility and order. Were it not for them and a few others, the new breed of lawyer-twisters—protecting larcenies by exploiting vulnerabilities in the law—would have swamped Austin's legal profession.

However, the Depression had weakened the Harts and their kind. Long-time clients were too broke to pay fees; no new clients walked through the door; and, due to the election outcome, sympathetic friends in the state agencies were in no position to engage their services.

When John Patterson and Will's older bother, James, joined Will's table, Patterson noted the atmosphere in the club and mentioned that he would soon have to make his ritual call on the Fergusons to assure them of the loyalty of the Travis County Democrats in the upcoming general election. He figured that since Governor Sterling had endorsed the Republican, the Fergusons would be especially appreciative. John did not say that Ferguson's appreciation could mean that Ferguson might direct families seeking paroles to them. Patterson did say that he dreaded Ferguson's gloating over their firm's well-known position on Ferguson's parole fee practices. Will Hart could not react; neither could James. Nor could John Patterson or Will Hart react to the one-page financial summary that James gave them.

'Our silence speaks for itself,' thought Will. 'We will have to bend.'

Two days later, John Patterson stepped into Will's office and said a little breathlessly that Jim Ferguson had called out of the blue and was coming to see them. Patterson had not yet made his dreaded courtesy call; so he was delighted.

Within the hour, the firm's secretary-receptionist led the former (*de jure*) and future (*de facto*) governor to the conference room. John and Will greeted him civilly, if not warmly. They apologized for the absence of the senior partner, who was out of town.

After a brief exchange of pleasantries, Ferguson got to the point.

"Miriam and I have come too far to have our governorship stolen by misguided traitors. That's why I'm buying insurance." Ferguson smiled wryly and looked squarely at Patterson. "I'm turning out the organized nigger vote. As you know, John, East Austin is organized; and you can't stop them from voting in the general election."

Hart saw Patterson move to protest; but Ferguson reached across the table and gripped Patterson's arm, "East Austin's leaders can deliver 1,000 valuable votes," Jim said. "They have the poll tax receipts; and they have a hell of an organization. But you know this. Well, they want something; and I think you can help."

Patterson started shaking his head, "Governor, I know they want the primary vote next time; but there is nothing we can do. The County Committee will never agree, even if I get down on my knees and beg. I'm sorry."

"That ain't it," snapped Ferguson. "They want a lawyer, a good lawyer, to represent a boy who's got a trial coming up in a few weeks."

Will asked, "What'd he do?"

"They say it's murder, Will," Ferguson's voice was agitated. "The name is Charlie Johnson. They say he killed Albert Allison's boy last summer. If you don't know Allison, he's a Navarro County landlord, big Sterling man—been making speeches against Ma and me for years. Lately he's on some kind of crusade to stop cotton growing, hoping that the price would go up. Crazy bastard would starve all the tenants and not give a damn."

The increased reddening in Ferguson's face led Will to suspect that a thousand Negro votes were not the reason for Ferguson's personal interest in the Johnson matter. Then the governor almost blustered, "I would be remiss to the people of Texas if I did not insist that you help Johnson."

Silence. Ferguson's hands folded on the table. Will felt Ferguson's blue eyes drilling into his own. He could sense his partner's mind racing.

Finally, Patterson said, "Governor, our firm's long-standing policy is not to work *pro bono*. Our legal associates have already paid their dues. Surely, Johnson is a case for young men to get their feet wet, or for lawyers looking for a cause."

"Y'all listen to me good. I didn't come here to get advice about *pro bono*. I want you to take this nigger's case. For one thing, having you listed as defense attorneys signals to the court and everybody else that this case is to be taken with white man seriousness. For another, I want competent representation that'll get the nigger freed. That Bill Yelderman makes a big deal about nigger-rights, and he may get good write-ups in Yankee newspapers and communist magazines. But he don't know shit about winning in a Texas court. He'll just piss everybody off, and get the boy hung. Him and Waterston got one hung last week. And, of course, you'll be compensated, if you want. I mean if you aren't too high-faluting to do parole work for me and Ma, you'll be compensated a lot more'n your ordinary fees. I guarantee you."

Will's throat tightened. He had been given a forceful reminder why James and he so disliked this crude son of a bitch. But Will saw that John's jaw was set in fury, so he decided to speak for the firm.

After a small cough Will said quietly, "Thank you, Governor Ferguson. We will discuss your offer with our senior partner."

Will had tried to disguise his disgust; but Ferguson cocked his head and caught Will's eye, indicating that he was reading Will perfectly. Then Ferguson stood, reached for his hat, and started for the door.

"Call me day after tomorrow at 10 AM," he ordered.

After Ferguson left, the partners said nothing for a long minute, and then John Patterson banged his fist on the conference table. Seconds of more silence, he stood and walked to the window.

"Will, if we do this, it will have to be you. You're the top criminal defense lawyer in these parts."

Will could only say, "Warren Moore might have something to say to you on that point, John. James'll be back tomorrow. Let's see what he says.

"In the meantime," Will added, "I'll do some digging with Henry Brooks to find out what I can."

In the meeting with James and John the next afternoon, Will did not mince words. Based on his conversation with Brooks, Will was not so sure that he was the best possible lawyer for the case. He told his partners that he had never represented a Negro accused of murder and wasn't at all sure how to deal with a court determined to send Johnson to the hangman. Worse, this Charlie Johnson had signed a confession that sounded pretty cut and dried. He said that Brooks thought that the Allison boy and his friends had provoked Johnson, but not enough to justify murder, and "sure as hell not enough to justify a darky murdering a white boy."

Will paused a moment; he wanted to make sure of his words. "Brooks said that not only did the boy's father stop the lynching—you remember that, James—he called on Warren Moore and Bill Yelderman to see if they would represent the killer. In fact, Brooks thinks that the reason the boy doesn't have representation now is because Judge Wheeler committed to the father not to appoint the usual *pro bono*. It's hard to know what to make of it."

John Patterson lowered his head and rubbed his eyes. "I remember this Allison. He was an Alternate at the Chicago Convention. He made quite a hit with the Platform Committee, much to the horror of the cotton brokers. I remember one night in the Drake bar; he and Bill Tarver agreed with that old Judge Teagarden from San Antone when he preached about letting the darkies into the party."

James Hart let out, "Humph. Wonder what Mr. Allison thinks now."

"Yes. I wonder what old Warren thought when Allison visited with him. Obviously he didn't take the case."

The senior partner laughed, "Warren? Hell no. He thinks the darkies have no right to trials."

"But," Patterson said, "He is as good at criminal defense as Will, and some say when it comes to self-defense there's nobody better. If I heard you right, Will, Henry might have been hinting at a self-defense provocation."

Will, picking up on the hint, said, "It looks like I better talk to Warren. I think I better do it this evening."

His brother agreed and said, "Warren and I have been friends a long time, Will. I imagine he's in the same fix financially as we are, and I also imagine he'd not be averse to parole fees. He and Leah have an expensive way of life."

The three partners agreed to meet again the next morning.

Warren Moore invited Will to take advantage of the warm autumn evening with him and his wife on their summer porch, where they routinely took their pre-dinner gin and tonics. Both men wore their white linen summer suits, and Mrs. Moore was in a frilly, light blue dress. As the Moore's Negro butler served the drinks, Will quietly surveyed the large back yard and gardens surrounded by live oaks and magnolias.

'This is the way of life Warren Moore will defend at all costs,' Will thought. 'Like my brother Jim and me, he is un-Reconstructed.'

"I felt sorry for Mr. Allison," Warren said. Looking at his wife, he added, "Didn't I?"

"Oh, yes," replied the agreeable hostess. "Warren genuinely grieved for the poor man."

"I know it sounds odd for a man of his sophistication, but he seemed not to have understood our system. He was under a delusion that the darky killer was entitled to white man's justice, and he wanted to make sure his boy's killer got what he was entitled to. He said something about the last chapter of his boy's life being a credit to justice."

"Well," Will replied, "the boy's father isn't the only one who wants the killer defended, Warren. We had a visit from Jim Ferguson."

Looking at Mrs. Moore, he went on, "I know I can count on your discretion."

At the mention of Ferguson, Will saw the older man's face turn to stone, then, as Will talked, soften a little.

"I remember thinking that I might be able to make a case for the darky," Warren said after Will had finished. Will caught Warren quickly glancing at his wife, who seemed to nod, as if saying, "Yes dear, go ahead."

"Allison never got back to me, you know. I thought maybe he had dropped the idea. But he said he would cover my fees; so despite all my misgivings, I confess that I was intrigued by the challenge."

"You think we could put up a credible defense?"

"The nigger's a dead man, Will. We both know that; but, yes, from what I understand, we could fashion a credible defense."

Will noticed that the Moore's butler, standing within earshot, showed no reaction to the "word."

"You will join me then?"

With Mrs. Moore nodding ever so slightly, Warren asked, "Do you really trust the Fergusons to make good?"

"Well, Jim's a funny duck. I guess you'd say he's honestly corrupt. He even brags about it. But he is reputed to be a man of his word. I have to call him tomorrow. The trial is November fourteenth; so we have much work to do, including getting ourselves appointed."

"And getting Wheeler to move the trial date," said Warren Moore, as he stuck out his hand to seal the partnership.

The next morning, John Patterson, Jim Hart, and Warren Moore were in Will Hart's office when Will called Ferguson.

"Hot damn! That's great news," enthused the former governor. Then, without waiting for a reaction, "Now I been thinking, Will—and I don't mean to inter-fere—but, as I recall, your nephew is due to take the DA's job in January. And he's employed by your firm, along with Hardy Hollers, who is due to be Jim, Jr.'s assistant. If the trial date is moved to next year, they could recuse themselves from prosecuting on the grounds of conflict of interest since their firm is defending. That'll force the county to go to the law school to get a prosecutor, and that'll go someway to even the odds on this deal."

"No wonder he wins these elections," Will said to his partners with his hand cupped over the phone, "he's always two steps ahead."

Will thanked Ferguson and said they were happy to have his ideas.

When Will related Ferguson's ploy, the senior Hart cursed and spat out, "I guess Jim and Hardy would be in an awkward position, that's true. And if some-body has to recuse, it can't be the firm."

Patterson frowned worriedly. "Ferguson is taking an extraordinary interest in this case, gentlemen—far more interest than is necessary for a thousand darky votes. And he doesn't give a hoot about the Negro. No, I reckon old Jim is hell-bent on getting back at Allison for those anti-Ferguson speeches he made."

Will looked at Warren Moore, who was nodding.

'I wonder if Ferguson would be as intent if he knew about Allison's visit with Warren,' Will thought. 'Probably. Probably he thinks that good lawyers will impugn those boys with young Allison that night, and thus, by inference, impugn Allison's boy. Ferguson's hatred is deep and boundless, dangerously deep and boundless.'

Lately, despite his lawyer worries, Charlie Johnson had been sleeping deeper and feeling fresher. The insurance and lottery businesses were doing well. The cooler nights were clearing the stuffiness from Rhambo's office at the funeral par-lor, and Charlie was at peace with his fate.

Thursday morning, October twenty-seventh, Charlie and Everett Rhambo arrived at the office at eight and, by mid-morning, completed the policy forms for next week's drawing. As they were about to take a coffee break, Louis Lyons's loud laugh came from the porch steps. Within a minute he and Reverend Adam Black walked into the office. Both men were in high spirits. Through a large smile, Louis said that Perry wanted to see Charlie right away; and they were there to take him.

On the drive to Perry's farm, if anyone had news for Charlie, he kept it to himself. Louis talked about his latest policy earnings, about his daughter's children, about Blind Lemon Jefferson's sweet blues at Perry's the night before, about Mr. Roosevelt, and about Ma Ferguson. The reverend made the amiable noises of an appreciative listener. Despite the men's upbeat manner, Charlie racked his brain to recall a mistake or problem that might have provoked Perry to summon him like this. When they arrived at the farm, Mr. Will Fuller and Dr. Everett Givens were seated on the sun porch. At this point, the only reason that Charlie could figure was important enough for this gathering would have to do with a lawyer; and, of course, he was right.

Perry and Mr. Fuller already had drinks. Lyons agreed to join them; Reverend Black and Charlie asked Ferris for coffee. Perry then motioned for the men to be seated. He remained standing and assumed a serious posture, like he was making a speech to a large audience.

"Gentlemen," he said too loudly, "I appreciate you coming out here at such short notice; but I wanted to be the first to tell you that the plan we worked out for old Charlie is alive and kicking. At eight o'clock this morning, Mr. George Nalle, representing the past and future Governor Ma Ferguson, notified Louis here that Charlie has his lawyer."

Charlie felt a sort of relief and made the appropriate expression of gratitude. But he tried not to be entirely enthused; not yet. Reverend Black praised the Lord, but he did not try to lead a prayer. Mr. Fuller broke into the widest, happiest, most relaxed smile on the porch. Perry held up his hand, and the men returned their attention to him.

"Colonel, did I say *a* lawyer?" Lyons was nodding and shaking with a large grin. "Excuse me, gentlemen, I meant *two* lawyers, two white lawyers and not just any two white lawyers, Charlie. Tell him, Colonel."

Charlie was not sure whether to be overwhelmed more by the news or by Louis's excitement. By now, the colonel was sweating and breathless, "Charlie, they is Mr. William Hart and Mr. Warren Moore, the two best criminal lawyers in Texas. Mr. Hart's the partner of Mr. John Patterson, the Democrat Chairman."

As Everett Givens exhaled in awe, Charlie nodded dully, as it was frankly too much for him to absorb.

Perry continued, "Now, gentlemen, before we get to the next step, let's see how well we done so far. First, we had to get old Charlie working with my nephew Everett in the jail. Sure enough, they work together good and get the businesses back on its feet. That means old Will Fuller here sticks around to see if we can make the plan work. Then, somehow, between the Reverend's praying and my money, we get old Charlie bailed from jail. Then Ma beat the governor, but not so bad she don't need our help next week. In fact, old Pa want that help so bad he line up Mr. Patterson's best lawyers for Charlie."

"Anybody still think I'm crazy?" Perry giggled as he sipped his pre-war. "Brother Givens, the next step is up to you and the colonel. One thousand votes."

Givens said, "Sure is, Perry. We'll do it easily."

"Well, you better, or Charlie's hung for sure; and you and the colonel won't be worth a shit in East Austin. Hee, Hee. Let's see now; yes, there's one more thing—it's a little present for Brother Fuller and more good news for Charlie, right Colonel?"

Perry's mild threat might have dampened Lyons's mood a bit; but he had no trouble sounding enthusiastic, "Well, when Mr. Hart and Mr. Moore take the job, because the trial is only three weeks away, they see they don't have no time to do right by Charlie. So they pick up the phone and tell the judge; and right then and there he change the date to next March. You hear, Charlie? Next March! And the judge tell them he'll get the other judge to make your bail good to next March, too. How do you like that?"

"Oh my," Johnson tried to find words, "I thought I'd be hung by now and look here, next March." Overwhelmed, he shook his head and muttered, "Glory, glory."

"Amen," sounded Reverend Black's deep, rich voice; and Mr. Fuller nodded his appreciation for the three-month gift of Charlie's expertise.

"Well," said Perry, "we've done pretty good until now, even though Charlie's getting a mite nervous. But it ain't done until Charlie walks. So, two things—the vote, as we've said, and Charlie doing a top-notch job with those lawyers."

Charlie felt the pressure of the other men's eyes on him. For an instant, he wanted that tree stump.

"And to get started, Charlie, they want to see you at two o'clock this afternoon."

Charlie found the door to Mr. Warren Moore's office in the Littlefield Building at about quarter to two, but he waited in the hall the full fifteen minutes before knocking and entering. The lady behind the desk gave him a brief look and pointed to a chair. During the half-hour he sat in that chair, not daring to move, the lady talked warmly to several telephone callers, busied herself with papers, typed a small form, but did not once look in Charlie's direction. Finally, an office door opened; and a tall man with white flowing hair and wearing a white linen suit came out, "You Charlie Johnson?" Charlie nodded, and the man motioned with his head to the office "Come on in here."

Another man, probably forty-five or so, tall and thin, sat at a rectangular table. He motioned for Johnson to sit opposite him as the white-haired man closed the door and took the other chair opposite Johnson.

Abruptly, the younger man said, "Charlie, I'm Mr. Hart and this is Mr. Moore. We've been retained to defend you in your murder trial. To make our appointment official, we need you to sign this paper; and then we want to make a few things clear."

Hart passed over a contract with the pages turned to the signature line indicated by a large "X." Charlie knew that even to make a gesture to read the contract or to presume to ask about it would insult these men, and perhaps even cause them to drop him then and there. He simply signed the document.

"Charlie, you know you're in a bad fix," the tall man began, "You shot and killed the unarmed boy of a very prominent man. That you have managed to stay alive this long is just short of a miracle. But, you seem to have some pretty influential people pulling for you, and that helps. Mr. Moore and I have reviewed your case, and we believe that we might have a chance to save your life. Now, listen to me hard: I said a *chance,* a small one at that. And even to have that chance we have got to have your complete cooperation. That means you must be completely truthful with us; and when we ask you to do something, you do it. Do you understand?"

"Yes sir, Mr. Hart." Charlie made every effort to show no emotion, even though his stomach began to churn.

"Okay," the lawyer went on, "fortunately we have the time to do this right. If you don't know, the judge has moved the trial date to March thirteenth; so between now and then we are going to be talking to you about what happened that night; and we will be talking to black and white folks who know you and can attest to your character. Right now, we need two things from you. One is to spend as much time with Mr. Moore as he needs in order to go over what happened that night and to get a grip on that confession you signed. The other is that you give us the names of people who will speak for you."

On October twenty-eighth, Henry Brooks called Albert Allison with the news: "Jim Hart's uncle Will Hart has taken Johnson's case. He'll be assisted by Warren Moore."

"Warren Moore?" Albert sounded surprised.

"You visited with Mr. Moore on this matter last summer, didn't you, Mr. Allison? Well, Will Hart's a persuasive man. They'll make a formidable team."

"To what do we owe Johnson's good fortune?" Albert asked.

"Well, I'm not real sure. Jim Hart, Jr., and I have been discussing the problem of Negro legal representation ever since you talked to us. You saw the Stewart trial. Nobody can say Stewart had poor representation. Now, just as you wanted, Mr. Allison, the same will be the case for Johnson. He's a lucky man."

"Also," Brooks continued, "Judge Wheeler has granted their petition to delay the trial. The new date is March thirteenth. We didn't object because we figured you would want them to have sufficient time to prepare."

Albert was a little stunned. Hart, Patterson, and Hart was Austin's most prestigious law firm. John Patterson had been enormously influential during the Wilson administration, and he still carried considerable weight. 'Their fees must be onerous,' Allison thought, 'way too onerous for Johnson. Did Brooks mean to imply that he and Jim Hart were so concerned about Negro representation that they prevailed on William Hart and Warren Moore to take the case *pro bono*? That would be most curious, given Young Hart's conduct in the Stewart trial and Mr. Moore's attitude toward Negro justice.'

Whatever the reasons, Albert was relieved that he could finally tell Mabel that everything was in order. Charles Johnson had capable lawyers who would insist that Johnson be tried, convicted, and executed according to the highest standards of justice. Five more months of patience was a small price to pay.

24

Preparing for Trial

Within two weeks of the lawyers taking his case, Charlie had met with Mr. Hart several times to provide a list of character witnesses, largely recommended by Louis Lyons, Reverend Black, Dr. Givens, and even Mr. Will Fuller. Charlie was flattered, almost embarrassed, by the hundreds of people who wanted to testify; even the whites he put on the list, including the assistant school superintendent, agreed. But he harbored no illusions about his sudden popularity. He knew Perry Rhambo was behind this effort; and he knew that the colonel and Dr. Givens would have a chat with each person before they would let them talk to Mr. Hart.

'East Austin was better mobilized for me,' thought Charlie, 'than it had been for the November election.'

Despite the curious circumstances, Albert Allison was at first relieved that Hart, Patterson, and Hart had taken Charles Johnson's case. But just before Christmas, Bill Tarver called with news that George Nalle had joked to friends about Jim Ferguson prevailing on Will Hart to defend Johnson. Apparently, East Austin's political bosses had wanted Ferguson to help Johnson in exchange for East Austin's vote in November. But when Ferguson found out that Albert Allison's son was the victim, he had become passionate about helping Johnson.

"Everybody knows how vindictive the Fergusons are," Bill said. "What's more, Nalle apparently thinks that because Jim Hart, the new DA, is an employee of Hart, Patterson, and Hart, he will have to remove himself from prosecuting Johnson."

Both Allison and Tarver had been around politics enough not to get too excited about rumors like this one. It was always best to wait for developments before reacting. To end the telephone call, Bill said that he expected to be fired the day after Miriam was inaugurated in mid-January. He said that he had put out feelers for a job in the new Roosevelt administration. Albert did not tell Bill that Henry Wallace—due to become Roosevelt's Secretary of Agriculture—had written asking him to help the new administration with cotton policy.

Will Hart began interviewing Charlie Johnson's character witnesses after Christmas. Mr. Will Fuller had made his new funeral parlor available—where witnesses would feel less intimidated than in Hart's office—and for a month Hart sat in an office dominated by a stuffed screech owl and saw one person after another. If they felt less intimidated by the surroundings, they were obviously in awe. Hart sensed that he was getting the unvarnished truth to his questions. Some witnesses attested to Johnson's skill with a clarinet when he played at Perry Rhambo's hotel bar. These Hart would leave off the witness list. A few mentioned that Johnson sold something called "policy." At first, Hart thought they meant insurance; but after a little questioning, he realized they might be talking about an illegal lottery. These Hart would also leave off the witness list. Many of the witnesses wanted to complain about white rowdies terrorizing East Austin before the incident. These Hart included on the list.

From the outset, Hart had accepted Warren Moore's argument: they should try to establish that the road incident and the boys' actions understandably caused Johnson to believe that his life was threatened. Therefore, they would argue, he fired his gun in justified self-defense. They would also argue that Johnson intended only to frighten his assailants, not to harm them.

'Well,' Will had thought at the time, 'we won't keep Charlie from being strapped into Texas's new electric chair, but at least we have a hypothesis to make a serious case. And at this stage, despite the bluster, a serious case is all that Jim Ferguson can reasonably expect.'

At their initial strategy session, Hart and Moore reviewed the historical background for the liberal scope of Texas self-defense law: in order to bring acceptable law to a lawless land, early lawmakers had accommodated the sentiments of frontier Texans about self-defense and property protection. That meant that a person who reasonably believed his life or property to be threatened could preemptively kill to defend either. Warren concluded that the questions in this case were first, whether Johnson believed the boys were threatening his life; and, second, if he did, whether it was reasonable for him to believe it.

Warren did not need to state the obvious problem—Texas's "self-defense" applied exclusively to white-on-white or white-on-black killings. Black-on-white murder was customarily denied the self-defense argument because it would arm blacks with dangerous grounds to react violently to the discipline sometimes necessary to maintain racial harmony. In other words, Will reflected, their hypothesis entailed a major breach of hallowed Southern custom—custom in which both lawyers were thoroughly imbued, and on which neither man would tread with enthusiasm. Knowing what they were being called on to do clearly troubled Warren.

With Warren concentrating on Johnson, and Will on the witnesses—that is, the boys in the car, the law enforcement officials, and Johnson's character witnesses—the lawyers soon realized that the boys' version of the incident and Johnson's version differed on a critical point: the direction young Allison's car faced—north or south—after crossing in front of Johnson's Model T and skidding into the ditch on the west side of Chicon Street. The boys said south; Johnson, north.

The boys claimed that after they thwarted Johnson's apparent attack on them in the first instance, they pushed the car southward from the ditch to the corner at seventh and Chicon; at which time, Johnson drove at them again and this time fired.

According to Johnson, he had stopped in the first instance and approached the boys' car, which was facing north, to be "solicitous" (as Warren put it). After being assaulted by curses and rocks, he returned to his car and slowly drove off. Before he went far, the boys' car overtook him and sped to the corner of seventh and Chicon Street, an intersection Johnson needed to cross to go home. But as he approached, the boys threw rocks; so he turned left at the intersection to avoid them. In a matter of seconds, he heard what sounded like a bullet careen off his car. At that point he felt that in order to save his life he had to use his own gun.

If young Allison's car faced north after skidding into the ditch, the boys would not have been able to push it south on Chicon and likely would have had to start the car and drive it to the intersection of Seventh and Chicon, as Johnson claimed. That meant that the boys were the likely aggressors; and, therefore, the self-defense argument had merit. If the car faced south, Johnson was more likely the aggressor; and the self-defense argument collapsed.

While reviewing notes over Four Roses and cigars during an evening in January in Will Hart's home library, the difference in the witness testimonies together with the consequences became clear to the lawyers.

Hart muttered to Moore, "Damn. This is hopeless."

After a moment Moore said, "Yep. It's tough. Two white boys, maybe all four, testifying against one darky."

'Yep,' thought Will, 'another custom.' Southern judges and Southern juries always took the word of a white over a black. And, as Bill Yelderman had found out in the Carl Stewart trial, lawyers who tried to challenge the racial composition of the juries or to impeach white testimony in these cases usually made matters worse.

Will's mahogany-paneled library was dark at the lightest of times, but that night a sort of wintry gloom worthy of a Bronte setting descended onto the room. After Will had refilled both men's tumblers, he returned to his stuffed high-back chair opposite Warren. He turned his face to the fire at which Warren was staring. The flames shooting from red-hot oak logs seemed to be accompanied by crackling voices pleading: 'What are you doing? What in hell are you doing?'

Will and Warren were lawyers of custom, of the common law, of the law that evolved through centuries of tribal experience, of the law that emerged from the gut of the people. And when custom provided inadequate precedent, Will and Warren were lawyers of the "people's will," necessarily qualified on meaning of "the people," of course. Despite Warren's growing conviction that their case had merit, they both knew that Texas custom and the people's will would hang their client. In the process, they began to realize, their reputations would suffer and that the defeat just might cause Ferguson to renege on the parole money.

"Suppose," Warren quietly, hesitantly offered, "suppose we try to look at the situation as if Charlie were white. What do you think, Will?"

Hart pondered for a minute. "Well, in that case, we would try to impeach the boys' version by cross-examination and by introducing witnesses to contradict them. Then, we would validate our client's version and introduce witnesses to verify his character."

"Do we have the witnesses, Will?"

"We certainly have the character witnesses. The only witnesses to the incident were Johnson and the boys—except that Mexican who, according to Sheriff White, fingered Johnson. But he's disappeared."

"I've talked to a lot of darkies complaining about white boys raising hell in East Austin last summer," Hart added.

Moore said quiet voice, no longer hesitant, "Will, I have a strong opinion that the man's version approximates the truth."

The "man," Moore said that the "man" was telling the truth. Hart wondered if Moore knew that he had used the word.

"Warren, old buddy," Hart said, "Johnson's a smooth one. We better be careful not to be taken in."

Yet…Hart recalled the first time they had met Johnson back in October: when Warren had summoned Johnson to the office, when Johnson had stood with such dignity, approaching the lawyers in that straightforward manner, standing erect, making eye contact, Will had almost extended his hand. In that instant, Will knew he was not as certain about blacks as he had been an instant before. 'Warren must have had moments like that during his sessions with Johnson,' thought Hart.

Bill Tarver's foreboding about the prosecution became reality in early February when Judge Wheeler telephoned Albert Allison with the news that both District Attorney Jim Hart and his assistant had removed themselves from the case. The judge said that both had been employees of Hart, Patterson, and Hart at the time the firm was engaged to represent Johnson; and they were concerned about a conflict of interest. The judge added that the only official remaining to prosecute the case was the county attorney, a young man named Brian Blalock. He had never prosecuted a case, but he had told the judge he was confident he would "ensure justice."

Without hesitating, the judge went to the point of his call: If Albert wished, the judge could appoint a special prosecutor. In fact, the judge would give priority consideration to anyone Albert recommended.

Albert wasted little time. To him, there was but one man to do the job. Bill Tarver was a former prosecutor. He was not working. And he was a prominent former officeholder, whose prestige would offset the prestige brought to the trial by Will Hart and Warren Moore. Two days after the judge's call, Albert drove to Austin, strode into the Tarver living room, and propositioned his old friend.

Tarver tried to protest. He pointed out that he had not practiced law at all since he had become insurance commissioner four years earlier; that he had not conducted a trial since he was Navarro county attorney ten years back; and that he had never prosecuted a capital case.

"Moreover," Bill laughed, "If the rumors are right and Ferguson really is helping Johnson, having old Bill Tarver in the courtroom would be like waving a red flag at a mean old bull. We were worried about the usual kangaroo court, and now it looks like the animal is jumping the other way."

Allison slapped his thigh, "That's just what I mean, Bill."

Allison argued that the trial was an opportunity to gig Ferguson. If the governor paroled Johnson, neither he nor Tarver could do much about it; but Albert doubted even the Fergusons would parole a Negro murderer destined for the electric chair. Moreover, Allison had no doubt that a fair-minded jury would convict and execute Johnson, no matter how much help he had.

But Allison was concerned that the young prosecutor would go overboard to get a conviction—like he had seen Jim Hart do in the Stewart trial.

At this point, Albert realized, he had cornered Bill, who succumbed graciously. The two men went immediately to the courthouse, where the judge swore Bill in and gave him an office.

Once committed, Bill Tarver went straight to work. After Allison departed for Corsicana the next morning, Tarver called on County Attorney Brian Blalock, who, officially, Tarver would assist. Undoubtedly, Blalock had been looking forward to being featured in a high profile trial against the best criminal defense lawyers in central Texas; and he did not try to hide his disappointment. Nevertheless, despite the young man's occasional abruptness, he and Tarver were able to agree on a strategy. Tarver would be responsible for the prosecution argument, including witnesses and opening remarks. Blalock would be responsible for countering the defense argument, including cross-examination of defense witnesses. Since Tarver was an accomplished public speaker, he would make the opening and closing statements.

In February, just a month before the trial, during one of the preparation meetings with Will Hart, Warren Moore abruptly declared, "If the son-of-bitch were white, I'd put him on the stand."

Hart knew that when Moore first started working with Johnson, the last thing he had expected was a client who could be a credible witness in his own defense. He had expected the evasiveness, contradiction, and obfuscation he believed was characteristic of the race. He had expected to spend fruitless hours trying to ascertain enough of the truth to construct a workable defense. But time after time, without changing one detail, Johnson had reeled off the same sequence of events that occurred on the night of the killing: from dropping Annie Davis at her house on Chestnut Street to pulling the trigger of his bone-handled Colt .45. Moore said that Johnson could relate this story clearly, coherently, and credibly in sufficient detail to impress any jury. And Johnson would not be deterred or shaken from his version, not even by a skillful cross-examiner employing all the tricks.

"Will," Moore said insistently, "this man was terrified of the summer marauders. At the moment he fired that pistol, he was convinced those boys were going to kill him; and he did what he had to do to survive."

'This "man,"' thought Hart. 'Warren has said it again—this "man" did what he had to do.'

Like his colleague, Will had to struggle with inescapable beliefs woven tightly into the fabric of his family. Unlike Warren Moore, the Harts did not view Negroes as the enemy. Negroes, they believed, were children, permanent children to be guided and nurtured and confined to "their place." The virtuous and well bred of both races understood both this fact and the consequent separation necessary for white "adults" and black "children" to thrive. From a Hart perspective, trouble occurred only when the scum of one or the other race crossed the boundaries in contemptuous disregard of place. And while it was preferable that this scum be controlled and disciplined by its own kind, sometimes the law had to step in.

'Scum,' thought Hart after many nights pondering how he and Warren should deal with the racial dilemma. White scum crossed the line. Black scum was not involved.

In exploring this thought one evening with his brother, Hart realized how starkly Southern convention categorized Negroes. Whites like the Harts wanted to believe that a significant part of the Negro community thrived in their devotion to their subordinate roles in the white world. Aunt Bessies and Uncle Willies filled Southern romantic fantasy, rearing the white young, guiding the white ladies, and sharing wisdom with the white bosses. Newspapers regularly printed multi-column obituaries when a family's domestic servant of long standing passed away, telling how the entire white family attended services at the Ebenezer Baptist Church and relating a few anecdotes revealing the good nature and faithfulness of the departed. This archetypical "good nigger" was as necessary to the Southern story as the "pure Southern white woman" and the "chivalrous Southern gentleman." "Good niggers" were never lynched and seldom seriously punished, at least for minor transgressions; but if a Negro lost his "good" status—for instance, for inappropriately addressing a white woman—he was deemed to harbor the passions characteristic of the untamed race. Then, for even the most insignificant transgression, he was shown no mercy—in or out of the courts.

Hart was soon outlining to Warren Moore how they could argue that Johnson was a "good nigger," a model in the narrative of Southern harmony. If they succeeded, Hart argued, the Southern system of justice must grant Johnson the same serious consideration it grants its white participants. Moreover, Johnson's state of mind the night of the killing—the "good nigger's" terrified state of mind that convinced him that the boys wanted to kill him—was created by night-riding scum who violated the code, upset Southern harmony, and deserved the scorn of Southern justice.

Bill Tarver, on the other hand, had become convinced that the facts of the case so clearly pointed to first-degree murder that to convince the jury, he would only have to present them without embellishment. First, he would establish that the boy had died by gunshot. Then, he would establish that Johnson fired the

gun and that he intended to do so. Finally, he would establish that Johnson had
not been threatened by the car incident sufficiently to justify murder. His main
witnesses, the arresting officers and the boys in the car, would strongly corrobo-
rate his argument.

Albert had asked Bill to try to avoid requiring Sonny Mayes or Bob Cobb to
come down from Dallas. Bill had assured Albert that he could easily make the
case with Derden Wofford and Harry Granberry.

The first time Derden Wofford came to Tarver's office, he arrived unshaven,
in his Magnolia mechanic's shirt and denim trousers, both streaked with grease
and sweat. He needed a haircut, and he was chewing tobacco. 'Why in heaven's
name were young Albert and Harry Granberry hanging around this fellow?' was
Tarver's first reaction. His next reaction was to make the most of what he had.

"How's the arm, Derden?"

Derden responded that the bullet wound in his left arm had healed by the end
of July. But he had returned to hard pitching too soon after the shooting and had
wrenched something in his right shoulder. Yet, he was confident the arm would
be okay for the season. He hoped to be at his best when the scouts started hanging around Austin in a couple of months. Tarver said that he understood completely. There *are* times when we simply have to be at our best, like when we
appear in court. And with that, Tarver got Wofford to agree to wear a suit and tie
in court and to wait until his testimony was over before he had a chaw.

Wofford told Tarver essentially the same story that Harry Granberry had told
Tarver the day before—that is, in effect, Johnson had initiated the aggression—and that corroboration lent both of them credibility with a jury. Moreover, Tarver was sure the Negro's version in his signed confession would be
viewed as self-serving. And, a Texas jury would be inclined to accept the word of
a white over a black. In this case, he had the word of two whites.

Still, Tarver had an uneasy feeling. It occurred to him that he had not taken
the usual precaution to challenge either Harry Granberry or Derden Wofford on
the crucial elements of their stories. For an instant he fretted that perhaps his trial
instincts were dull; that maybe he had missed inconsistencies that could be
exploited by the defense; and, as he continued to think about it, that he had no
idea how his witnesses would fare under tough cross-examination. Nor, Tarver
realized, had he prepared them for surprises.

'Well,' Tarver assured himself, 'Hart and Moore would have to make a show.
They might be able to pick at details and even make the boys look a little foolish,
but the esteemed counselors would not overcome the fact that Charles Johnson
had carried a loaded pistol with which he murdered an unarmed white boy.'

Two weeks before the trial was scheduled to begin, Judge Charles Wheeler was in the Austin Club having a quiet drink with Tass Waterston, who was seeking to mend fences following his and Bill Yelderman's insulting behavior toward the court in the Carl Stewart trial.

A young city council candidate named Tom Miller and former State Senator Alvin Wirtz were conspicuously dining with Charles Marsh, owner of the Austin newspapers. After a while, Wheeler noticed Miller and Wirtz get up from Mr. Marsh's table and head in his direction. When they got to his table, they were in high spirits. The next day they were traveling to Washington for the Roosevelt Inauguration on March fourth. Miller made a lot of noise about Austin getting its share of the new largess to be pumped into America by Roosevelt's people. Wirtz said he was aiming for an appointment in the Department of Interior and thought he had a chance. Evidently, the judge figured, Mr. Marsh would be a strong supporter for both causes. He was a close friend of the president-elect.

When the two politicians invited themselves to sit, Wheeler was at first relieved. His conversation with Waterston was heavy going, more so because Waterston was a teetotaler. After Miller shared a couple of new jokes, Wirtz mentioned that the Scottsboro trials were causing the Roosevelt people to become disgusted with Alabama, no matter how loyal it was to the Democratic Party. He had heard on good authority that the new powers-that-be were carefully watching the retrial ordered by the United States Supreme Court and scheduled for later in March. "If the Alabama jury kills those boys," Wirtz had said, "no way will Alabama see a dime from the New Yorkers when they take over the federal government."

Wheeler had been following this Scottsboro matter carefully. In March 1931 two white women of questionable repute accused nine Negro hoboes of raping them while they were traveling in a railroad boxcar near a small town in Alabama called Scottsboro. To avert a mass lynching, the local authorities had arranged a swift trial; and within a few weeks, a jury sentenced all the boys to death. Wheeler recalled the editorials at the time praising Scottsboro authorities for settling the matter under the rule of law. At least it was progress, they had argued. Because of the publicity given the case, the Communist Party of New York saw the opportunity for a cause; and eventually, with the help of the NAACP, they got the boys' appeal before the United States Supreme Court. In November the court ruled that the boys had had inadequate representation. The Alabama authorities then ordered a new trial for March twenty-seventh, just two weeks after Charles Johnson's trial.

When Wirtz had mentioned the Scottsboro matter, Miller's smile faded. With his eyes bearing in on Wheeler, the hefty man began to lean forward in such a way that he took up much of the table. He seemed to fill the room.

"We could have a case like this, couldn't we, Judge?

Without waiting for Wheeler's response, Wirtz got to the point. While in Washington, he and Miller would be in discussions with important Roosevelt people crucial to Austin's future. They did not want to be hampered by the burden of a Scottsboro. In the Roosevelt era, Wirtz went on, Austin stood a better chance of generous consideration if the city were perceived as a citadel of progressivism. If Charles Johnson was given the death penalty, those New Yorkers would believe he was hanged because of the influence of the murdered boy's father. Justified or not, they would associate the Johnson trial with Scottsboro; and Austin would pay a huge price.

Wheeler had been more than a little taken aback. Tass Waterston made a move to rise, but Wheeler grabbed his forearm and motioned him to stay. Wheeler distinctly remembered nodding noncommittally for a full thirty seconds.

"No need to worry fellows," he had then responded, "Johnson'll get a fair trial, all right. He's already got Will Hart and Warren Moore to defend him, and Jim Hart and Hardy Hollers can't prosecute him. Those boys in Washington won't find an instance of 'legal lynching' in this town, right Tass?"

Nodding in Waterston's direction, the judge had continued, "Hell, Tass and old Bill Yelderman were the defense attorneys for the last darky we tried in a capital case. The boy was convicted, but he had a hell of defense."

25

The Prosecution

Austin Statesman, Saturday, March 11, 1933, page 5, column 7:

NEGRO'S KILLING TRIAL ON MONDAY

"Charles Johnson, 60-year-old negro, charged with murder in the pistol death here last July 8 of Albert Allison, 18, son of A. A. Allison, well known Corsicana businessman, was scheduled to go on trial before Judge C. A. Wheeler.

"Young Allison was shot to death by a negro on Chicon Street near its East Eighth street intersection. Officers arrested Johnson the following day.

"With young Allison at the time of his death were four companions, Derden Wofford, Austin athlete; John C. Mayes of Corsicana; Harry Granberry of Austin, and Robert Cobb of Dallas. Wofford was wounded in the arm.

"A special venire of 100 men has been ordered to report as prospective jurors in the case.

"County Atty. Bryan Blalock is handling the prosecution since Dist. Atty. James P. Hart and his assistant, Hardy Hollers, are disqualified. The two state's attorneys are members of the law firm of Hart Patterson & Hart, representing Johnson.

"W. A. Tarver, former state life insurance commissioner, is assisting Blalock as special prosecutor at the request of A. A. Allison, Sr., father of the slain youth. Tarver is a former resident of Corsicana and a friend of the Allison family. Mr. Allison was a leader in the cotton holiday program for Texas last year."

Judge Charles Wheeler relaxed in his chambers, enjoying his traditional morning cigar and mug of coffee and contemplating this troubling case. Ordinarily in cases like this, he would automatically guide the jury to a death sentence. But ever since the father had visited him in July, he realized that there would be nothing automatic about this trial. And lately he had been receiving signals from Austin's political and civic leaders to go easy on Johnson.

When Hart, Patterson, and Hart, the most politically powerful law firm in Austin, and Warren Moore, the most able defense lawyer in Central Texas, became Johnson's attorneys, the judge at first thought that Allison had made good on his strange quest to secure Johnson competent representation. Then around Christmas, at the Austin Club, he overheard George Nalle bragging that Jim Ferguson was involved.

Wheeler had hated to hear that, but he could not discount it. For Will Hart to take a case like this, politics probably did lurk in the background.

'Why wouldn't Hart, Patterson, and Hart have refused the case on the grounds that Jim and Hardy would prosecute it? Would Will or Warren have taken this case *pro bono?* Maybe one of them, but not both. No, fees were involved, substantial fees, or some other *quid pro quo.* And, no, they are not from Allison. Where would Johnson or his supporters get that kind of money? What *quid pro quo?*

For a moment, the judge reflected on nothing but the stream of cigar smoke rising through the open window. He figured he would never know all the answers; but, recalling Tom and Senator Wirtz's remarks at the Austin Club, he knew that this trial had stirred up unusual interest in unusual circles.

'This little city of Austin has no commercial premise,' the judge pondered. 'That's why, unlike other Texas cities, its leadership consists of lawyers, state employees, politicians, lobbyists, university professors, and hucksters like that Miller fellow. Business-led cities like Dallas or Houston approach their problems systematically and work in a businesslike manner toward resolutions. In Austin, problems are politicized: that is, they are parsed into issues; issues are pitted in conflict; and conflict is the conduit though which politicians amass personal power. For the politician, results are the least desirable goal—results do away with problems. If there are no problems, there are no issues, no conflict, and no political power. Dallas and Houston look nowhere but to themselves to finance their great civic enterprises. Austin has become adept in having its city built on the backs of taxpayers, and it is eager to employ this skill by exploiting the unprecedented economic power due to come out of Washington. But this means Austin will have to be viewed as progressively acceptable and that means the city will have to be viewed as racially progressive. Jim Crow will not be eradicated overnight, but Austin cannot afford a red flag like a legal lynching.

The judge sipped the last of his coffee and drew on the short butt of his dwindling cigar. 'I reckon Charles Marsh is part of this program,' Wheeler thought. 'A man with his ambition is not going to allow his own strong anti-Negro attitude to stand in the way of Austin's progress. Marsh's newspapers will provide uncharacteristically balanced coverage of this trial, and they will likely protect a cooperative judge.'

Unconsciously, Wheeler nodded as he snuffed out the remains of his cigar and rose to enter the courtroom to preside over jury selection.

Bill Tarver recognized a few names on the list of jury candidates—Walter Bowman, the wealthy landowner, Jim Williams, the former County Tax Collector, and Tom Gregory, the furniture dealer. If they represented the kind of citizens summoned, Tarver's job that morning would be easier than he had anticipated, especially in light of comments Albert had made to him earlier.

"You know these juries, Bill," Albert had sputtered. "The prosecution looks for bigoted ignoramuses, and then manipulates their fears, prejudices, and resentments to obtain quick convictions of Negroes."

While Tarver did not concur with recent descriptions of southern juries in northern papers ("bewhiskered, slovenly, tobacco-driveling, squinty-eyed, bigoted, and mean"), Tarver understood Albert's point. He reassured his friend that their effort to ensure a proper process would not be undermined by a rogue jury. Johnson was going to hang and decent men would do it. To be certain of such decency, Tarver had prevailed on Brian Blalock to put him in control of jury selection.

Before proceedings had begun, Tarver had stood, facing the courtroom, and watched the prospective jurors creep into the intimidating, unfamiliar surroundings. Some wore suits and ties; others overalls. The ranch hands kept their Stetsons on; the mechanics were in their uniforms. Those not smoking were chewing. Some faces were bewhiskered; many carried deep lines chiseled by the sun, and most bore the solemnity that seemed to characterize the times. And why not? Only two weeks before, they had stood nervously in lines outside their banks to retrieve their meager funds. Ten days before, every Austin bank had shut its doors; and just the week before the new President had declared a national bank holiday to prevent a run on the banks.

Because Will Hart and Warren Moore were looking for the same juror profile as Tarver, the selection process was amenable and fast. In addition to W. C. White, the unemployed druggist, the attorneys agreed on Hal Armstrong, a farmer who operated a gin and had a son the age of Albert, Jr.; Tom Gregory, a furniture dealer, whose son, also Albert, Jr.'s, age, worked in the family business; Fritz Priem, probably a bootlegger, but who carried himself as a respectable farmer; Eric Anderson and William Thiele, farmers who appeared to be struggling; William J. Bell, in coat and tie, a draftsman with the Highway Department; burly E. L. Crowe, who worked on county road construction crews; J. S. Whilhite, who owned a small company that made peanut brittle; James R. Williams, formerly the Travis County Tax Collector, recognized in *Who's Who in Texas;* and finally, the venerable Walter D. Bowman, a wealthy landlord and one of Austin's leading citizens.

Before Judge Wheeler swore in the panel, he made a little speech about jury duty being one of the great platforms of our sacred freedom, that the jurors belonged to the small group of ordinary men privileged to be part of our great system of justice that guaranteed Texan life and property. But in the judge's visage and tone, Bill Tarver saw the judge empathetically imply: 'Yes, gentlemen, you must do this; even as your world collapses, you must do your duty.'

That night, President Roosevelt's comforting, optimistic voice thanked America and wished everyone well. Judge Charles Wheeler, still smoking his bedtime cigar, turned off the radio and walked onto his porch to catch a breeze. The President exuded competence. He was convinced that he could handle the banking crisis, but time would tell.

When he heard the telephone jangle, he stubbed out his cigar and walked inside.

"Judge Wheeler? This here is Jim Ferguson. I don't think we ever met, but I've heard many complimentary things about you from your friends in the Littlefield Building."

"Why thank you, Governor." Wheeler's throat tightened. He realized that Jim Ferguson would not call at this time of night without a reason, and the only apparent reason is something to do with this Johnson trial.

"What can I do for you, sir?"

"Well, thank you for asking, Judge. I noticed in the paper that you appointed Bill Tarver as 'special prosecutor' in this nigger killing trial. Now, Judge, I don't in any way question your authority or your wisdom in this matter; but I would be remiss if I didn't bring certain facts to your attention."

The judge interjected, "Mr. Allison asked me to appoint Tarver after Jim Hart bowed out. Tarver seemed to me to have the credentials, Governor."

"That's what the *Statesman* said. I just wanted you to know that Miriam has been shocked at the condition Tarver left the Insurance Department in. I don't have many facts at this stage, but I can tell you the man spent so much time going after old Ma and Pa Ferguson he left the people of Texas in a sorry insurance mess. Now, I'm sure if you knew this to begin with you'd not have tainted your courtroom with such a scoundrel. But you got him now—that is, unless you decide to kick him out—but if that ain't possible, I just figured you'd want to know. Anybody who knows anything about the case tells me that the nigger

didn't do anything any self-respecting white man wouldn't do in the same circumstances. But that's not my concern. Ma and me just want Texas courts to
serve the people."

"Thank you, Governor," the judge replied, trying to camouflage his anger.

"Well, I guess I've done my duty, Judge. I hope to have the pleasure to meet
you sometime."

Whether the judge was outraged more by Ferguson's affront or by his crudeness, he did not know. A few minutes later, when he could reflect, Wheeler told
himself that given Ferguson's incorrigible reputation he should not be surprised.
Moreover, he could see Ferguson's point. When Mr. Allison requested Bill
Tarver, wittingly or not, he was inviting Ferguson's ire.

'Not only is this trial being scrutinized by Washington,' Wheeler thought,
'now the Fergusons are interested. But does Ferguson really care about a Negro
accused of murder? Was that call really about Tarver? What is Ferguson's dog in
this hunt?'

Judge Wheeler had much to ponder. 'What about Bill Tarver?' Frankly,
Wheeler had given little thought to Tarver since he had sworn him in. Wheeler
discounted Ferguson's accusations of impropriety at the Insurance Commission.
'But,' he admitted, 'Ferguson had a point about Tarver's irritating "progressivism," or whatever the man liked to call his race-mixing beliefs.'

Years ago, during the War, Wheeler and Tarver had both attended a Bar association seminar at which Tarver's mentor, Judge L. B. Cobb, argued against
Oliver Wendell Holmes' proposition that the Constitution is not a logical construction, but a blueprint that adapts to man's different needs as he progresses.

Wheeler had argued that Holmes seemed to be a better fit for the needs of the
South than Judge Cobb's rigid rule of reason, which absurdly had to regard
blacks as equals and, therefore, entitled to equal treatment. Tarver had defended
the judge's position.

'I still think that way,' thought Wheeler. 'Judges are not logic machines; we
are community leaders vested with the responsibility for protecting our way of
life. Our justice must first serve the community good as we understand it, not
high flown, rigid dictates of principle.'

Wheeler realized that his meandering thoughts stemmed from his growing
concern about the threat to Austin's communal good.

'If the new president's liberal friends would solve our problem,' Wheeler
thought, 'then we must not upset them. So if Roosevelt wants lenient treatment
of Negroes, he will have it, at least for a time.'

Thus resolved, Judge Charles Wheeler turned in for the night, ready to be a new kind of judge for a different kind of trial.

Austin American, Tuesday morning, March 14, 1933, page 5, column 4:

ALLISON SLAYING TRIAL IS STARTED
Negro Trial for Death of Corsicana Lad Here

Testimony in the case of Charles E. Johnson, 61-year-old negro schoolteacher, charged with the fatal shooting of Albert A. Allison, Jr., 18, of Corsicana, near Seventh and Chicon streets, last July 8, will begin before a jury in the 53rd district court at 10 AM Tuesday.

With surprising swiftness the jury in the case was completed Monday afternoon and was sworn in at 6:08 PM. Dist. Judge Charles A. Wheeler, in swearing in the jury, told them it was the quickest time that a jury in a capitol offense had been qualified here.

"Mr. Allison sat in the courtroom during the day and conferred with special prosecutor William A. Tarver during the selection of the jury. He passed on most of the jurors as they came up for acceptance or rejection. Nearby sat S. E. Kerr of Dallas, brother-in-law of Mr. Allison and an uncle of the slain youth.

The state through its questioning of veniremen indicated it will ask the death penalty. The defense announced it will file an application for a suspended sentence in Johnson's behalf.

The defense will plead self-defense in the case and will contend that Johnson had been attacked before the fatal shooting occurred, it was indicated from questions asked the veniremen as to whether they had any objection on the plea of self-defense.

The president's "fireside chat" had also lifted Bill Tarver's spirits; and, he sensed, not just his. The atmosphere in the courtroom was decidedly brighter. The blue sky and the first spring bluebonnets peeking through the cacti helped, but it was the president's sunniness that folks seemed to bring with them to court that day.

After Judge Wheeler called the court to order and made a few opening remarks, Tarver stood and walked to the jury box. Affecting *gravitas*, he opened by saying that the case before the jury was not complicated. He said that no one disputed that on the night of July 8, 1932, at the intersection of Seventh Avenue and Chicon Streets, Austin, Texas, Charles Johnson fired his pistol into the body of eighteen-year old Albert Allison. He then asserted that the state would prove beyond a reasonable doubt that the accused did so willfully and with malice aforethought. The defense, Tarver contended, would argue that the defendant's willful act was self-defense. But the jury would clearly see that Charles Johnson was not defending himself when he used his bone-handled Colt .45 pistol against an unarmed youth after a minor traffic altercation. Tarver told the jury that, aggravated by the traffic mishap, Charles Johnson deliberately took that gun in hand, deliberately drove his car at the victim's car, deliberately aimed that gun, and deliberately fired that gun at his helpless victim.

"Gentlemen," he concluded, "that is first-degree murder and warrants no compensation less than Charles Johnson's life."

Tarver then called his first witness—Mr. Albert Allison.

Tarver's first aim was to impress on the jury just who it was Charles Johnson killed. He had Albert describe his own attendance at the Democratic National Convention while his son and a friend were celebrating the Fourth of July at Galveston. Then Tarver asked about the telephone call from R. C. Granberry, about Albert's arrival at Brackenridge, and about his visit to Cook's funeral parlor to view his son's body. Only Mabel's sniffles were audible in the hushed courtroom. Tarver thought he saw jurors Hal Armstrong and Tom Gregory frown in empathy as they imagined a dead boy resembling their own sons lying on a concrete slab.

Before Tarver excused the father, he had a deputy bring out the boy's clothes. As Tarver started to ask Albert to identify them, Will Hart jumped to his feet to object that the clothes had been taken to Dallas and out of the court's custody; and therefore they could not satisfy the criteria for admissible evidence. Tarver peered at the judge, who gave him a sideways glance over his glasses, and sustained the objection. Tarver was taken aback. But the signal was clear: this would not be a trial that would allow questionable evidence to accumulate with impunity. And, Tarver realized, the judge was signaling a great deal more: To get a conviction, Tarver would have to conduct a first-class prosecution. This he was not sure he was prepared to do. After Tarver thanked Albert for his cooperation, the defense said it had no questions. Albert returned to his seat behind the prosecution table and took Mabel's hand.

Next, Tarver had Dr. Caroline Crowell, the duty doctor at Breckenridge hospital, describe in detail young Allison's condition when the boys arrived. Again, the defense had no questions. Then, Tarver called former Texas Ranger Earl McWilliams, once again a Bexar County deputy sheriff. Like Tarver, McWilliams had been a casualty of the election: The day after Ma Ferguson was inaugurated, she had fired the entire Ranger force for helping Sterling in the vote fraud investigations. Tarver had McWilliams describe Johnson's arrest, the rock marks on Johnson's Model T, and the bone-handled Colt .45 pistol found in Johnson's bedside table drawer. McWilliams then testified that he was present when

Johnson dictated, reviewed, and signed his confession. Tarver thanked the former Ranger and said that Texas owed him a debt of gratitude for service not always appreciated by certain high officials. At this, Albert let out an artificial cough. Noticing Albert's lifted eyebrows, Tarver recalled Albert's comments about McWilliams during the Stewart trial.

This time, Will Hart stood from his chair next to the defendant and walked slowly to the witness stand. After endorsing the special prosecutor's closing remark, he asked McWilliams to describe the circumstances surrounding Johnson's confession.

"Well, sir," McWilliams said, "the reason Captain Hamer asked me to work on this case is because, if I say so myself, I'm an expert on talking to darkies about their crimes. I just know how to ask them the right questions. After we found the gun, I said something like 'you fired that pistol last night didn't you, Charlie?' Before we knew it, he told us the whole story, which he repeated for the Sheriff."

Tarver noticed Hart's theatrical frown as he locked on McWilliams eyes, "Did you or any other officer tell him that he was incriminating himself? That he ought to have a lawyer with him before he said anything?"

"Wasn't necessary. He just talked, and we listened."

"There were five of you, every one of you armed and ready. Did you or any other officer manhandle the defendant or threaten him in any way?"

"No sir. Nothing like that."

Looking at the jury, Hart asked "Did you say 'you stupid nigger you killed a white boy, the son of a big shot. Your life ain't worth nothing now, but you just might make it to the county jail if you tell us everything now?'"

McWilliams grinned sheepishly and shrugged, also looking at the jury, "Well, we did inform the boy of what he done. He said something like he didn't think he hit nobody and that's why he didn't report it."

"Thank you, Mr. McWilliams."

Tarver had no redirect questions; but he grasped the fact that Hart had made sure the jury saw five, big, armed, uniformed officers taking one small Negro into custody. Tarver knew that the jurors were aware that the police were capable of coercing a confession from a suspect, especially a Negro. Also, Tarver figured that Hart did not just want the jurors to have qualms about Johnson's confession; Hart wanted to get on record the latest defense lawyer's fad protest about police procedures for extracting confessions. Even though Tarver had his back to Albert, he imagined his friend's eyes burning holes in him.

Neither Deputy Sheriff Jack Newman nor Harry Granberry could be in court until that afternoon, so Tarver called Derden Wofford to the stand.

When Derden heard his name called, he reached to the knot in his tie to make sure it was right. He walked purposefully to the stand, put his hand on the Bible, and pronounced a forceful, "So help me God." Then, following Mr. Tarver's questions, he related the story as he had told it to Mr. Tarver two weeks before. He stated that on leaving House Park field, he sat in the front seat middle and John "Sonny" Mayes sat by the window. Bob Cobb and Harry Granberry sat in the back seat. Allison drove. He said they headed from House Park to the capitol building, "then out Eleventh Street east to Red River, down Red River to Seventh, east on seventh to Chicon, up Chicon to Eighth Street to the street's dead end, where we turned around and came back west on Eighth Street to Chicon."

"What happened next?" Mr. Tarver asked.

"We turned south on Chicon; but as we turned, a Model T Ford came by and ran us into the ditch."

"What'd you do then?"

"Me and some of the other boys jumped out of the car and started chunking rocks at the Model T. Then we started inspecting the Chevrolet for damage."

"Did Albert Allison get out?

"Naw, sir. He stayed in the car and tried to get it restarted."

Wofford then testified that Allison could not get the car restarted and that it was too dark to assess damage. The boys then pushed the car out of the ditch, and down the inclined road to get it started. They then drove to the streetlight at the corner of Seventh and Chicon Streets on which the power substation was situated.

"What happened then?"

"I looked up and saw a Model T roadster and recognized it as the same car we'd had trouble with a few minutes before. I saw a gun pointed at us; then I saw the gun shoot fire, and felt a sting in my arm."

"What did you do next?"

"I jumped out of the car; and me and the other boys threw rocks at the Model T; and then I ripped off my baseball shirt to see if I was hurt bad."

After determining that he had suffered a flesh wound, Derden testified, he and the other boys returned to the car where they found Allison slumped over the wheel. When they could not revive Allison, they took him to Brackenridge Hospital.

"Thank you, Mr. Wofford. I have no further questions, your honor."

Derden could not help but smile when he saw in Mr. Tarver's eyes both relief and approval.

Then the tall, thin lawyer sitting next to Charlie Johnson unraveled from his chair and slid slowly toward the witness stand. Looking more dangerous than a stomped-on rattler, the lawyer's eyes went straight into Derden's.

"Derden, how long have you lived in Austin?"

"Almost four years, sir."

"Why did y'all choose that section of Austin to ride around in? Didn't you know that section is largely populated with Negroes?"

The lawyer did not have a knowing smile, not like the fellows at Derden's work who joked about "nigger hootchie-kootchie." The message in his stern visage was unmistakable to Derden, as well as to the jury.

"I don't know why we went there. When Allison said he'd take me for a ride, he said his brakes weren't working real good. He wanted to be where they weren't no cars. Allison was driving; he chose the streets we went on."

"Your testimony is that young Allison chose the route that took y'all into the Negro section?"

"Yes sir."

"Even though Allison was new to town and didn't know the streets or the sections of town?"

"Yes sir."

"But you do know the sections of Austin, don't you Derden? You know where the Negro section is, don't you?"

"Yes sir. But I wasn't paying attention. We was on Chicon Street before I realized where we was."

"Derden, you know there are places to buy beer in that section, at that time of night, don't you?"

Mr. Tarver objected on the grounds that the witness's knowledge was irrelevant. Judge Wheeler overruled, and Derden heard Mrs. Allison gasp.

What Bill Tarver had just heard was surreal. Will Hart had implied that Albert and Mabel's dead son had not only deliberately broken the color taboo, but had done so for the purpose of violating the law. Maybe he did both; but that was hardly relevant to the salient fact that Charles Johnson had deliberately killed the boy. "Why besmirch the boy's memory? Why dirty the Allison name?" Tarver asked himself.

Although the thought had occurred to Tarver that a fair trial for Johnson might entail implicating young Allison, he had quickly dismissed it. Considering Albert, Sr.'s, standing and the nature of the case, he assumed that the defense would be constrained not to embarrass Albert or his family.

'And Albert and Mabel are so proud,' Tarver thought, 'so conscious of their reputation for rectitude. They will be permanently wounded.'

After Judge Wheeler overruled Mr. Tarver's objection, Mr. Hart repeated his question, "You know there are places in East Austin to buy beer, don't you?"

Derden affected the contemptuous sneer that had accompanied so many fast-balls. But he was the batter now. This pitcher was an ace, but Derden was determined to hit his way out of the witness box.

"Reckon I do, like everybody else. Reckon I know there are places in west Austin to buy beer, too." The courtroom tittered slightly. 'Ball one,' thought Derden.

Hart, unperturbed: "Didn't you make a statement to Ted Klaus and other officers that you were out there to buy beer?"

"No, sir. I did not."

"Did you make any statement to Detective Klaus or any other officer?"

"Well, I did talk to Mr. Klaus about what happened to Allison and all that; but I didn't say nothing about beer." 'Ball two,' Derden looked at Mr. Tarver, but he was writing something.

"Well, young man," Hart asked, "isn't it true that you had been over in East Austin numerous times prior to this occurrence and had trouble with those darkies over there?"

Wofford's face went from sneer to querulous. His ambiguous answer was not lost upon the court, "Not that I know of." 'Ball three,' Wofford smirked.

"Not that you know of." Hart was disdainful now, "Not that you know if you've been riding around East Austin many times? Or not that you know if you had trouble with the darkies?"

"Sure. I've been through East Austin a few times, but I never had no trouble with nobody over there." 'Ball four,' Derden smiled with the corners of his mouth turned down.

'Strike three,' thought Bill Tarver.

He looked at Brian Blalock. Blalock appeared not to comprehend that Wofford had developed a possible credibility problem. For one thing, Ted Klaus was a respected police official whose testimony for the defense would contradict Derden. Blalock would have a tough job with the detective's cross-examination.

More importantly, the defense strategy began to unfold for Tarver. Derden was part of a group of boys who had been making trouble in East Austin early last summer. When Allison and his friends came to House Park, Derden had intimated that they could have some fun raising cane in East Austin—beer and hootchie-kootchie. Since the boys were up to no good, the jury would believe that they were rowdy enough to provoke Johnson into justified violence.

Will Hart had no further questions; Tarver had no questions on re-direct. Judge Wheeler excused Wofford, who walked from the courtroom acknowledging no one.

Harry Granberry had arrived during the Wofford testimony. Tarver realized that by calling Granberry next he could give the defense an opportunity to plant the seeds of their defense deeper, but he needed young Granberry to shore up Wofford's damaged testimony.

After the eighteen-year old redhead recited the sequence of events from when Albert and Sonny Mayes had arrived at the Granberry house, Tarver asked, "Did you sign a statement about the shooting before a police officer, Harry?"

"No sir."

"Did you submit a signed statement to the grand jury?"

"No sir."

"How about at the hospital? Did you make a signed statement to anyone there?"

"No sir. Not at the hospital, neither."

"Did y'all drive over to East Austin with rocks in the car, Harry?"

"No sir, we had no rocks in the car. The rocks we threw we just picked up from the road."

"Did y'all take liquor in the car with you to East Austin?"

"No sir."

"Is that why y'all went over to East Austin that night, Harry? To find intoxicating liquor or beer?"

"No sir, we weren't looking for no intoxicating liquor."

"Thank you, Harry. I have no more questions."

Years of overexposure to the sun had embedded Will Hart's middle-aged face with wrinkles that made his smiles blessedly happy and his scowls frightening. When Hart started for the witness stand, Tarver could see from Harry's expression that the face was having an affect.

"What were you boys doing in East Austin if you weren't there to get beer, Harry?"

"Just driving, sir. Albert was driving and didn't know the streets and got in this dead end. So he was about to drive out of that area."

Tarver winced. By slightly elaborating beyond the answer the lawyer required, Harry unwittingly gave Hart an entree to challenge the boy's version of events.

"Harry, remind the court about what happened after the car turned into Eighth Street"

"Well, sir. We came to a dead end, turned around and headed west to Chicon."

"Go on, Harry."

"Well, we turned left onto Chicon Street just in front of the T Model Ford that was heading in the same direction."

"Then the car passed your Chevrolet on the left and ran you into the ditch." Hart interjected, "Is that your testimony?"

"Why, yes sir."

"Then you boys pushed the car out of the ditch and down the incline to the corner of seventh and Chicon. Isn't that what you testified?"

"Yes sir."

"The car wouldn't start. So y'all pushed it. When you got to the corner by the substation, had the car started?"

"I don't think so. Naw, sir."

"But after the shooting, the car started right up. Y'all just started the car and drove to Brackenridge."

"Yes sir."

"Well, it's clear that the car started after the shooting. No doubt one of you boys drove it to Brackenridge."

"Yes sir. It was Sonny Mayes."

"Now, this car starts almost by magic after the shooting; but it won't start before the shooting. Harry, didn't the car start right up when you were in that ditch?"

"Naw, sir, we pushed it out."

"Harry, instead of turning left onto Chicon, didn't young Allison turn the car right? Didn't he come out of Eighth Street too fast, swerve into the left hand lane of Chicon Street, on a collision course with the Model T which was oncoming, and to avoid a collision, didn't the deceased swerve into the ditch on the west side of the street—facing north?"

"Naw, sir. We turned left; ended up in the ditch headed south."

"Harry, when you were in that ditch, didn't you boys see the driver of the Model T Ford stop his car down the street, get out and walk toward y'all to see if you were hurt? Didn't y'all answer his concern with rocks and shouts of abuse?"

"Well, we threw rocks after we was run into the ditch; but I recollect the Ford was driving away from us."

"Didn't somebody say something to the driver?

"I don't recollect."

"You mean you just quietly chunked rocks and didn't try to communicate with the driver."

"Well, maybe somebody said something."

"What do you remember the words were, Harry? I don't need to remind you that you put your hand on the Holy Bible and swore to tell the whole truth."

Harry's cheeks blushed, his gaze dropped, then he blurted, "Derden Wofford yelled at him, 'you black son-of-a-bitch, go on. We don't want any trouble with you.'"

A gasp rippled through the courtroom. One of the women in the balcony audibly murmured "Lawsy, Lawd."

"Your honor," Will Hart said in a raised voice that expressed dismay and regret, "my apologies to the ladies present for any offense. I did not expect the response to be so graphic."

Hart let the remark sink in, then proceeded, "I appreciate that it's hard to say some of these things, Harry. But you did the right thing. Now I want you to be just as forthright about what really happened that night. Let's review what you have said," Hart was looking at the jury, "you said you turned left about ten yards in front of the Model T, that the Model T passed you on the left and forced you in the ditch. That's when y'all jumped out of the Chevrolet and threw rocks at the Model T as it drove away. Now, just when did Derden Wofford shout those ugly words at the driver of the Model T? When he was chunking rocks at a car already down the road?"

"I think it was when the nig...T Model passed us; I can't remember exactly."

"Harry, isn't it true that I was correct about y'all turning right onto Chicon and running into that ditch facing north? Isn't it true that *after* y'all threw rocks and cussed at the driver who had stopped his car to help y'all, Albert started the Chevrolet in that ditch, drove out of it, turned the car around and headed south on Chicon?"

"I don't think so sir."

"Harry," Hart continued with his largely rhetorical interrogation, "isn't it true that y'all did the passing that night, that you sped down Chicon, caught up with the Model T and passed it on your right? Didn't y'all holler and shout things at the driver as you rode by?"

Tarver could see Hart destroying the boy's testimony right before his eyes. Before Harry could respond, Tarver objected. "Your honor, the defense is hardly giving the witness time to respond."

Hart replied that Granberry was a hostile witness obviously getting twisted in his story. He would leave the witness plenty of time to answer when he had finished his questions. The judge overruled Tarver. The special prosecutor threw a look at the judge in an attempt to convey that he was getting suspicious.

Hart plowed on, "Isn't it true, Harry, that when you stopped at the corner of Seventh and Chicon, the Model T followed you to the intersection and turned right on Seventh? That y'all once again chunked rocks and even shouted more things as the Model T drove away from that corner?"

When Harry did not respond, Hart said with a slight edge, "Well? Did any of you say anything as the Model T came to that intersection?"

"When I saw the car heading for us, I said something like 'Here comes that car again.'"

"Is that all you said, Harry?"

"Why, yes, sir."

"Didn't you or one of the boys shout, 'Here comes that nigger again. Let's kill him.'"

"Naw, sir," Harry said emphatically, "Not me and not anybody else said anything like that."

"Well, Harry, you know what happened after you or one of your friends called the driver of the Model T names and rocked him after he drove off down Seventh, don't you? You know the car stopped, turned around, and headed back to where you were, don't you?"

Before Harry could respond, Hart looked at the jury in an exasperated tone and said, "This witness can't give the court a straight answer. I have no more questions, your honor."

This time Tarver did conduct redirect questioning. He had the young man reaffirm his and Derden's version of the sequence of events and repeat that their reason for being in East Austin had nothing to do with "marauding the darkies" or buying beer. Tarver, however, knew that Harry's reaffirmations were hesitant and not convincing.

After the judge dismissed Harry Granberry, Tarver called ex-Deputy Sheriff Jack Newman. Another political casualty, Newman had been fired when the new Sheriff had been sworn in. Newman testified that he, ex-Ranger Earl McWilliams, Deputy Constable Jack Cowey, and Deputy Sheriffs Homer Thornberry and Paul Blair went to Johnson's home the morning after the murder. They found the Model T in a shed next to the house. It had several chalky marks. Newman said Johnson denied having any trouble the night before, but admitted owning the car. When asked about a pistol, Johnson pointed to a washstand in his bedroom by his bed. Newman said that Deputy Paul Blair retrieved a .45 cal-iber pistol from the washstand drawer and an empty .45 shell from the top of the stand. The pistol had bullets in all its chambers, but smelled as if it had been fired recently. Tarver showed Newman a bone-handled .45 revolver, and Newman said it was the same pistol Blair had retrieved on July ninth.

Deputy Sheriff Paul Blair followed Newman to the stand and corroborated Newman's testimony.

As with former Ranger McWilliams, Will Hart cross-examined both deputies regarding the conditions under which Johnson made his confession. Again, Hart intimated that when five, large, well-armed officers surrounded a small Negro while shouting accusations, any confession they received was tantamount to being coerced.

Blair was Tarver's final witness. After Blair stepped down, Tarver turned to the judge and announced, "Your honor, the prosecution rests."

Judge Wheeler warned the jury not to discuss the case and ordered a recess until 9 AM the next morning Wednesday, March fifteenth.

26

The Defense

Conversation at dinner centered on the trial, of course. For Mabel's sake, Albert tried to change the subject; but his guests could talk of nothing but the trial. Tarver repeatedly assured Mabel, Albert, and the Kerrs, who were plainly upset, that, despite the quality of the cross-examinations and the surprising rulings of Judge Wheeler, Charles Johnson would be convicted and given the maximum penalty. Nothing the boys did, Tarver asserted, could mitigate the fact that Johnson deliberately pointed that pistol at Albert and fired.

"Employing a pistol against a few rocks is not self-defense; it is murder!" he exclaimed.

All Albert could do was nod politely, Mabel likewise. Neither wanted further elaboration.

At the close of the trial that day, Albert had noticed how calm Johnson was when the deputy led him from the courtroom in handcuffs, as if he had no cause to be troubled. Instead, Albert was troubled. That day, for the first time, he and Mabel had seen squarely what they had always feared: Son, in some measure, had brought this calamity upon himself—he was up to no good in East Austin. He had violated Prohibition, and it appears he and his friends had acted badly toward Johnson.

During the course of the day's proceedings, Albert and Mabel had become aware that Son was on trial as well as Johnson. If Son was being judged, his parents were being judged. Johnson would have to die for his part in this tragedy, but the Allisons would have to live forever with the private horror of the judgment against them.

At the end of the evening, Tarver told Albert that despite the strength of the State's case, Tarver wanted to ensure Johnson's conviction. He said the defense had driven wedges in the boys' stories; they were not serious enough to affect the outcome, but enough to give the defense a plausible argument. To buttress the boys' testimonies, he wanted Albert to ask Bob Cobb and Sonny Mayes to testify during the redirect argument on Thursday.

Albert said that he had hoped not to involve them; but, yes, he would make the calls.

At the Austin Club, Warren Moore told Will Hart that he reckoned they had had a good first day. Hart replied that he was still worried. The two boys, he opined, had held up sufficiently during his cross-examination to force the defense to ask the jury to do what a Southern jury never does: That is, accept a Negro's version of events over a white's. In this case, there are two whites—maybe four, if the prosecution introduced the other two boys during redirect.

To put the court and the jury on notice that they were aggressively seeking to have their client freed, Hart and Moore agreed that they would open by petitioning to have the charges dismissed on the grounds of self-defense. They had no expectation of succeeding; but by doing so, they hoped they could make the jury realize that it had more to consider than the black-white aspects of the case. Next, they would put considerable emphasis on the marauding and vandalism in East Austin prior to the killing. Not only would they establish a factor in Johnson's state of mind, they would make the jury see that due to the behavior of white Austin's sons—behavior about which some people snickered, and others merely tut-tutted—East Austin had become a tragedy waiting to happen. Charles Johnson and young Allison were just hapless victims of inevitability, or so Warren Moore would vigorously argue.

Wednesday, March fifteenth, 9 AM. Will Hart noticed immediately that the courtroom audience and atmosphere were different from the day before. So many colored people were in the courtroom that they filled the last five rows and the balcony. 'Yes,' thought Hart, 'today East Austin bares its wounds.'

After Judge Wheeler denied Warren Moore's petition for dismissal, Hart's colleague walked to the jury box. "The defense will show," he said, "that sixty-year-old Charles Johnson—driving home from Bible study in his own community—had every reason to believe that his life was threatened.

"Who wouldn't fear for his life when showered with rocks? What man wouldn't be shocked and terrified when spewed with verbal venom in response to his kindness after a near accident? Who wouldn't protect his own life by firing at a threatening adversary when that was the only reasonable response left open to him?"

Moore concluded that once the veniremen understood the events as they actually happened that night, they would have no alternative but to find schoolteacher Charles Johnson innocent on the grounds of self-defense.

Moore first called City Detective Ted Klaus, the duty detective on the night of July eighth. He testified that immediately after being notified of the killing by hospital staff, he had gone to Brackenridge Hospital. He said he questioned each of young Allison's companions, including Derden Wofford; and that he smelled no liquor on the boys' breaths. Wofford, however, told him that the boys went to East Austin that night "to get a few bottles of beer."

Brian Blalock on cross-examination asked Klaus if he might have misunderstood Wofford. "Couldn't Wofford have said 'to get some air' instead of 'to get some beer'?"

"I don't believe he said 'air,'" replied Klaus.

Will Hart noticed Judge Wheeler try to affect a stern countenance at the courtroom titters.

Next the police department fingerprint expert and photographer testified that he took photographs of Johnson's car the morning after the shooting. He said that the Model T had small dents in it, that a portion of the windshield was broken, and that fingerprints in the car matched Johnson's.

For the remainder of the morning, Moore called more than twenty residents of East Austin in addition to several police officials before the court to bear witness to the frequent assaults by white youths during the two months prior to the killing. The prosecution initially objected on grounds of irrelevance; but after the judge's repeated rebuffs, Brian Blalock and Bill Tarver kept quiet.

The last of these witnesses, Mrs. M. A. B. Fuller, who identified herself as president of the Women's National Baptist Convention, said that numerous of her fellow East Austin residents had complained to her of assaults by white boys. She said that she, in turn, had asked the chief of police "to take steps to prevent any more of them and thereby prevent any trouble."

Chief Thorp testified briefly that during the two months prior to the shooting, he had received many complaints about white boys attacking residents in East Austin, including the complaint from Mrs. Fuller.

Moore studiously avoided asking the chief to describe the steps taken to stop the harassment. He did not want to put the chief on trial for not acting on the complaints.

In response to Brian Blalock's follow-up questioning, Chief Thorpe confirmed that he had received no complaint from Charles Johnson.

Next, Police Captain Sam Griffin testified that during that time he too had received complaints "about white boys going into the eastern section of the city and attacking Negroes with rocks, green peaches, green plums, watermelon rinds, banana stalks, and other things." Moore did not challenge the Captain to describe how he had responded to these complaints.

Captain Griffin also confessed to Blalock on cross-examination that Charles Johnson was not one of the complainants.

By the end of the session, Hart felt that Moore had done his job. The courtroom sat in silence. The white spectators could not escape the shame. The balcony and the five back rows let their anger briefly show in small ways, but their indignation that day was showcased in subdued dignity.

Charles Marsh had instructed Raymond Brooks to report both sides of the trial, no matter whose feelings were bruised. Still, Brooks was sure that his description of this day's proceedings would be edited out for being too sympathetic to the Negroes. He was shocked along with the rest of Austin when he saw the story in print, especially the prominence given to the following paragraphs:

> *Testimony developed Wednesday through defense witnesses centered on two points—that negroes in East Austin were frequently struck with banana stalks and other weapons by white boys riding in automobiles—and that Johnson by reputation is a good and law-abiding citizen. Otherwise the testimony was routine.*

> ### Senate Porter Testifies

> *All women were invited to retire as Gus Goss, senate porter, told the jury of an obscene remark directed to him and his wife one night last June by a person in an automobile which passed them as they were going home from prayer meeting. Goss had previously stated he "was called bad words," and defense attorneys wanted to get the exact words to the jury.*

> *Various negroes took the stand to testify they had been struck on the head or shoulders by white boys in an automobile on several nights last May or June. These included Otho Warren, 1608 New York avenue, who was taken in an ambulance after he had been knocked unconscious when struck by "something that left no scar;" Hulon Hunter, employee of the Texas cafeteria; Jodie Bunts, cook at the Texas cafeteria; Harlan Searcy, cleaner and presser; and Goss.*

> ### Mission Meeting Rocked

> *Evaline Gregg, 54-year-old negro cook, testified that a mission meeting at Chestnut and East 14th one night was forced to disperse after a rock had been thrown into the church. Mary Marshall, also attending the mission meeting, said she saw five white*

boys drive by the mission building in an automobile and, through a window of the well-lighted church, saw one of the boys throw a rock into the building.

Brooks saw clearly that Hart and Moore were putting the white marauders on trial versus the city's "good niggers." When defense counsel Warren Moore asked the judge to invite the ladies to leave, he was reminding the jury that Southerners have standards that no decent person, black or white, dare contravene. No decent person, black or white, uses bad language in mixed company (even in formal testimony) or directs abusive language against members of the other race. Those who do, black or white, warrant only contempt; and they deserve no consideration from the conventions and laws that give the South its special way of life.

During Will Hart's long interviews with Charlie Johnson, Hart learned that, except for trips out of town, Johnson seldom had reason to leave the confines of East Austin. For this reason, Will Hart could introduce to the court no white employer to whom Johnson was a loyal retainer, or white doyens harboring fond memories of Uncle Charlie telling them Uncle Remus-like fables when they were little girls. But Hart did have highly regarded residents of East Austin who would testify that Johnson was one of them, and a few whites who could attest to Johnson's good reputation. More importantly, the defense had Johnson himself, who had the demeanor of a "good nigger," even though he was unusually self-contained and was in no way obsequious to whites. Johnson managed to display great dignity without seeming "uppity."

Out of the dozens of East Austin residents who wanted to attest to Johnson's character, Hart introduced six whom one or more of the jurors would know as a "good nigger."

Following their testimony, Mrs. George Felter, the white Superintendent of Travis County's colored schools, testified that during her administration Johnson had taught for one year at Hornsby-Dunlap, a community in western Travis County. She said he was "of good reputation."

R. F. Jones, a seventy-five-year-old white farmer from Hornsby-Dunlap, said he had known Johnson for twenty years, "when the Negro was a school teacher out there." Jones drew a few chuckles when he informed the court that he did not know if Johnson had a reputation as peaceable, law abiding citizen. "I ain't never heard it discussed," he said.

White farmers Charles Buck and his son Henry, both of Del Valle, just east of Austin, said they had known Johnson for years and attested to his "good reputation."

As each witness completed his or her testimony, Hart held his breath. Blalock declined cross-examination one after another. The young prosecutor seemed to be allowing the defense a free hand in defining the character of the murderer.

In fact, Hart had guessed correctly that the prosecutors would be too complacent to do all their homework. They knew nothing about Johnson, and this was good news for the defense. The court would not learn that, while Johnson did teach school a few years, he really sold insurance; and that insurance selling might have been a cover for running numbers. Former Sheriff Coley White could have told them this. Also, the court would not learn that Johnson spent most nights not at Bible study but at Perry Rhambo's hotel and other hootchie-kootchie joints, drinking moonshine and applying a fair clarinet to the raucous jazz the darkies played. Finally, the court would not hear Annie Davis and Estelle Watson testify that Johnson had fathered their daughters. Had the defense done its homework, Hart would not be able to get away with painting Johnson as a "good nigger." Had Blalock's cross-examination dealt with these matters, he could have so blurred Hart's picture, that, given the starkness of archetypes in the southern narrative, the blur would have been enough to make Johnson "bad"—"bad," and therefore guilty—"bad" and therefore hanged.

Because the prosecution had proved to be unprepared to press a serious cross-examination, and because Hart and Moore knew that Johnson would be a credible witness, over lunch that day they decided to put Johnson on the stand. So when the last character witness was excused, Warren Moore dramatically called the accused. But before Johnson could testify, Judge Wheeler noted the time (just before 5 PM) and ordered a recess until 9 AM the next morning.

Bill Tarver knew that the jury would have a hard time convicting a black saint; and he understood that Blalock had allowed Hart to beatify the defendant.

Later, over drinks at the Tarver home, he mentioned to the younger county attorney that it was one thing to rely on the jury's loyalty to the family of a white victim, it was another for them to develop sympathy for a man like Johnson. As prosecutors, he said, their job was to help the jury see Johnson in the sort of light that would back up a first-degree murder conviction.

Blalock nodded.

Tarver added that the defense lawyers must have felt they were losing, because they were taking the unusual step of having a defendant testify. That would give Blalock the opportunity to nail the defendant himself. Bill then began to outline the points that he had been developing in his mind for Blaylock's cross-examination: that Johnson was not in an agitated state of mind from the occurrences in

East Austin prior to the killing, that Johnson could not have felt threatened enough by a few rocks to react murderously, that he knew what he was doing when he took the gun and deliberately fired, that he never much liked whites, and that he fired because he had the opportunity to vent his hate on helpless youths whom he knew would have no chance to defend themselves.

But Tarver never got to make his points. Before he could say three words, Blalock excused himself; and, after thanking Esther for her hospitality, he bade Bill good evening. Esther commented that the young man had seemed a little testy.

An hour after the court recessed, Reverend Adam Black came to Charlie's cell with a clean brown suit, a white shirt, and a blue tie.

"Mr. Warren say he want you to look clean and respectable for the stand tomorrow, Charlie."

"Why, bless you, sir. How can I ever thank you? Everybody so good to me."

"Big day, tomorrow. Yes sir, big day. We're having a special prayer meeting for you Brother. The Lord'll be protecting you."

"You know, Reverend, what I hate most about getting up there? I have to look straight at that boy's poor mama and daddy. They're good people. I hear Mrs. Allison's daddy were a judge who was fair to coloreds; and Mr. Allison, he save me from the mob that day and offered to give you the money for my bail."

"Lord, Charlie, these white folks sometime make no sense. That Mister Allison is hell-bent on you hanging. I can tell by the way he always be talking to the prosecutor."

"He loved that boy," said Charlie sadly.

"We be praying for the boy and his folks, Brother."

"Amen."

When Johnson walked into the packed courtroom, he saw a sea of hopeful faces and wanted to run for his tree stump. His friends and neighbors were counting him to vindicate them to the white world, and he was not at all confident he could do it. When the judge asked him to come to the stand, he placed his right hand on the Holy Bible and swore to tell the truth. As he looked away from the bailiff, he caught sight of the Allisons seated on the first row—four eyes with a steady gaze, no hate, no hostility, just firm determination. Charlie shuddered involuntarily; he would have preferred hate. Mr. Warren Moore walked toward him and looked at him in a friendly but stern manner.

"Charlie," Moore began, "you have heard the testimony in this court during the past three days, have you not?"

"Yes, sir."

"Were you the driver of the Model T Ford that drove by those white boys in the open-top Chevrolet the night of July eighth last year?"

"Yes, sir, I was the driver."

"Did you fire a pistol through the window of that Model T Ford?"

"Yes, sir."

"What did you fire that pistol at, Charlie?"

"At the open-top car, sir," Johnson replied softly. He felt the mother's eyes on him. They were determined to kill him.

"Did you see boys inside that car?"

"Yes sir. There was two. There was three more outside the car, I think."

"Did you fire that pistol at one of those boys in that car?"

"No, sir, just the car. I just wanted to scare them off. I don't want to hurt nobody."

"Now, Charlie, I want you to tell the court, in your own words, just what happened that night to make you want to scare those boys by firing your pistol."

Charlie had rehearsed this part with Mr. Moore many times. He testified that after Bible study at the Rising Star Baptist Church, located at Twentieth and Salina Streets, he took Annie Davis to her home on East Fourteenth Street and then proceeded to his own house, located at 205 Salina, just off Second Street. At approximately 11 PM, he was proceeding south on Chicon Street at a place just south of Tenth Street when a car heading north swerved erratically in front of him and veered into a ditch on the west side of Chicon.

"Now, Charlie, for the record, you heard two of these boys swear under oath that they turned left out of East Eighth Street heading south. Are you certain their car was heading north?"

"Yes sir. Their car was going north. It was pointed north when it be in the ditch."

"I just wanted the court to be clear that the Chevrolet was headed north, not south. Now go ahead and tell the court what happened after the boys' car went into the ditch."

Charlie stated that he drove around the car and stopped about thirty yards away, got out of his Model T, and walked to the boys. He could see by the moonlight that four or five white boys were walking around the car. He called to them, asking if everything was all right. The boys, in turn, started to throw rocks at him and to curse him. One of the rocks struck him on the head, drawing blood and making him dizzy, so he returned to his car and proceeded south on Chicon.

Mr. Moore interrupted. "Now, Charlie, let's get this clear. Did you shout at the boys or just talk in a normal voice?"

"I kind of hollered, Mr. Moore."

"And just what did you holler, Charlie."

"Something like 'Are y'all all right?'"

Mr. Moore then stated rhetorically, "In other words, you were being solicitous, stopping to render aid to someone in trouble."

"Yes sir."

"And you got rocks and cursing in return. Go on and tell us what happened next, Charlie."

Charlie then repeated the statement in his confession. He said that as he approached Seventh and Chicon he heard one of the boys shout, "There he is again, let's get him." Then, just after he turned the corner, he heard a crack and a ping then several more.

"So I turned my car around and drove close to the boy's car and fired my pistol."

"Thank you, Charlie. Now please tell the court why you turned that car around. Why didn't you just keep on driving?"

"I was afraid they was going to follow me and kill me, Mr. Moore."

"Please tell the court why, Charlie."

"Well, first, there was lot of trouble in East Austin last summer. Lots of folks was hurt by white boys riding around in cars. We was afraid they'd get worse. Then, Mr. Nathan Rhambo was carried out and murdered. When I heard the crack against my car, I was scared they would do me in, too."

"Did you personally have any trouble with these boys before?"

"No, sir."

"Then why did you think they would want to hurt you?"

Charlie could not help looking at the Allisons, "God as my witness, I didn't know they was just boys out on the town, maybe being mean just to show off to each other. If I did, I would've just drove off. I thought they was the fellows that was coming into East Austin to hurt and kill us, like they did to Mr. Rhambo."

Charlie noticed that Mr. Allison's face lit up, as if something just occurred to him. Mr. Allison leaned forward and started talking to Mr. Tarver, who had just walked into the courtroom. Charlie wondered if he had made a mistake in mentioning Rhambo. But Mr. Moore seemed not to notice.

Mr. Moore continued, "How many shots did you fire at that car, Charlie?"

"Just one, sir. I didn't want to hurt nobody. Then I keep on driving until I get to my home."

"Were you aware that you hit anyone?"

"Naw, sir. I didn't think I hit nobody and didn't know it until the next morning."

"What did you do after got home, Charlie?"

"Well, sir, I went to bed."

"What did you do with your pistol?"

"I took it inside the house with me, took out the empty shell from the chamber and reloaded the pistol, just in case they come for me like Mr. Rhambo."

Charlie bit his lip in self-chastisement. Rhambo's name slipped out before he could stop it. But again, Mr. Moore seemed not to notice.

"Have you owned that pistol long, Charlie?"

"Why, I've had it for the past fifteen or twenty years."

"Have you always carried it in your car, Charlie?"

"Naw, sir, not all the time. I carry it in the car and other places with me for a short time before that night."

"Thank you, Charlie. You are to be congratulated for being so forthright about a night that obviously pains you deeply. Mr. Blalock, your witness."

Bill Tarver had been late because he had spent most of the morning with Sonny Mayes, who at Albert's request had arrived from Corsicana to testify. Robert Cobb's father had prevailed on Albert to leave his boy out of it. Tarver had missed most of Johnson's testimony, but he did hear Johnson's reference to Rhambo. He agreed with Albert's observation that there was a possible connection between the pistol and Rhambo, and that it might reveal a different side to Johnson. Before Brian Blalock took the floor, Bill Tarver urged him to follow up the Rhambo line of inquiry. After a little discussion back and forth, Blalock grabbed the list of questions Tarver had hastily scribbled on a notepad and stuffed them into his vest pocket.

After a few minutes, Tarver realized that Blalock was sticking to the line of inquiry he had originally discussed with Tarver: that is, to show that the incidents last summer could not have put Johnson in an excitable state of mind, that in fact Johnson had no special concern for the alleged attacks that summer.

The young county attorney acidly forced Johnson to admit that he himself had reported to the police none of the incidents which were supposed to have upset him.

Then Blalock demanded, "State whether you phoned any peace officers to report the occurrence after you got home on the night of July ninth."

Judge Wheeler sustained the defense objection to correct the date. "Okay," Blalock corrected, "the night of July eighth, did you make any effort to report the incident?"

"Naw, sir."

"Why didn't you report the incident, Charlie?" Blalock asked.

"I didn't know anyone had been hit," Johnson replied.

Just what Blalock was trying to demonstrate was unclear even to Tarver. Blalock did not challenge Johnson's claim to have been hit by rocks—enough to dent his car, enough to make his head bleed, and certainly enough justification to report the incident to the police. Surely Blalock had not overlooked this point. Maybe he did not want to invite Johnson to embarrass the police by saying that he didn't think it would do any good. Whatever his reason, Tarver observed, Blalock missed an opportunity to punch a couple of holes in Johnson's credibility. Nor did Blalock establish where Johnson carried the pistol, nor the means by which he got it in his hand. Moreover, Blalock did not try to show that Johnson's taking the pistol in his hand was a deliberate act, that firing it was a deliberate act to do harm. Nor did he try to ascertain exactly why a schoolteacher like Johnson needed protection, or why he was threatened by the Rhambo murder. In fact, he employed none of Tarver's questions on the Rhambo point. Tarver realized that the young man assumed that since Johnson was as good as hanged, the prosecution's argument warranted only that Johnson did nothing to report the incidents.

When Blalock finished, the judge excused Johnson; Warren Moore declared that the defense rested; and the judge announced a recess for lunch. When the trial resumed, Tarver introduced rebuttal witnesses, Sonny Mayes, Annie Davis, former Sheriff Coley White, and police officer Guy Smith.

Mayes described the incident much as Derden Wofford and Harry Granberry had. Annie Davis testified that she had gone with Johnson to Bible study and that he had driven her home. She said she had seen no gun in Johnson's car or on his person. Moreover, she testified, Johnson had said nothing to indicate he was nervous about the incidents with white boys that summer. Next, Coley White testified that he had interviewed Johnson at the courthouse the morning he was arrested. He said he examined a bump on Johnson's head that Johnson said was caused by a rock, but saw no evidence of bleeding. Officer Smith testified that in his examination of Allison's Chevrolet that he found a .45 caliber bullet on the floorboard of the dead boy's Chevrolet. Without objection, Tarver introduced the bullet into evidence.

The defense had no further questions; the prosecution rested; and the judge called for final arguments.

27

The Verdict

As the time approached for the state's summation, Tarver began to feel at a disadvantage. The difference in the versions of the incident was crucial. If the jurors accepted the boys' version, they would likely see Johnson as the aggressor; an aggressive Negro would be doomed. If the jury accepted Johnson's version, they would likely see the boys as provocateurs; Johnson's self-defense claim would have merit. To accomplish the latter, Hart and Moore had masterfully undermined the boys' credibility while validating Johnson's. Moreover, Tarver began to realize that the prosecution was not going to be buttressed by Southern court tradition.

For his summation, Tarver decided that he had to divert the juror's attention from Johnson's state-of-mind and the shameful actions of Austin's youth, and bring them back to the stark facts of the incident. So he addressed the jury with a matter-of-fact, low-key demeanor. He emphasized that each of the three boys in the car testified that young Allison had turned the Chevrolet left off East Eighth Street onto Chicon, and that the Model T driven by Johnson passed the boys on the left and forced the Chevrolet into the ditch. "The defendant," Tarver pointed out, "had a different story, and that story, they claim, justified his killing an unarmed boy."

"Now," Tarver continued, "The defense will claim that rocks and curse words are a threat to one's life sufficient to use a firearm in response. That's nonsense. The defense will claim that troubles in East Austin created a state of mind in the defendant that made him justifiably anxious for his safety because of a few rocks and curse words. But if these incidents disturbed Johnson, he certainly made no complaint prior to July eighth. Moreover, Johnson was vague about the reason he carried that pistol in his car that night. He said he had been driving with it a short time, a couple of weeks prior to July eighth. In other words, he had been carrying the pistol since the time of a certain Nathan Rhambo's murder—which he said had scared him. Please note that Johnson had not felt threatened enough by the white boys to carry that pistol during the two months in which they are alleged to have caused trouble in East Austin. Finally, you heard Annie Davis testify that she saw no pistol when she was driving with Johnson. The pistol wasn't on a seat; it wasn't on the floor. Wherever that pistol was in the car, in order for Johnson to put it in his hand, he would have had to reach for it deliberately.

"The word is 'deliberate,'" Tarver said slowly, "and a man in an excitable state of mind does not deliberate. He just acts."

"No, gentlemen of the jury, Charlie Johnson did not act in self-defense when he deliberately sought the pistol, when he likely unlatched the lid to his glove compartment, when he consciously gripped the pistol, when he deliberately turned his car, when he deliberately drove at the Chevrolet, when he purposefully aimed the pistol, when he deliberately wrapped his finger around the trigger, and when he consciously squeezed the trigger sending a bullet into and through the young body of Albert Allison and into the left arm of Derden Wofford."

Tarver paused as he stood in front of the panel with his arm extended, his fist and finger in a pistol configuration, aiming at the courtroom.

Next Tarver informed the jury that everyone in the courtroom knew what happened that night. Then, pointing at Johnson, Tarver declared, "He knows what happened; and he knows that Derden Wofford, Harry Granberry, and John Mayes are telling the truth."

"Charlie Johnson," Tarver went on, "knows that he was angered when the boys turned left from Eighth Street in front of him as he drove south on Chicon Street. Maybe he had to brake a little to avoid a collision. Charlie knows that in his anger, he sped up and passed the boys so close that he forced them into the ditch. He knows that after they tried to fend off his aggression with rocks and shouts, he was even more infuriated. Charlie Johnson knows that's when he decided to really hurt the boys."

Tarver looked into the impassive faces of the jurors. He had no idea whether they followed him. But he was confident they would accept the boys' version of events; and, if so, they would almost certainly hang Johnson.

In conclusion, Tarver argued that Johnson deliberated and then sought a weapon that could only cause injury or death; therefore, he deliberately intended to cause injury or death.

"And on this point Texas law is clear: When Johnson fired that weapon into the car, it makes no difference whether he intended to harm young Albert Allison personally. In Charlie Johnson's signed confession, which you have in evidence before you, he said, 'I shot at the one driving the car.' He shot…at…the…one…driving…the…car—Johnson's own words. And he wants you to believe that he took a gun, pointed it at someone, and fired, thinking it would not hurt them? That the bullet would not follow the path to which it was pointed, pierce that body and suck the life from it? The fact is, gentlemen, Charlie Johnson did intend to harm that driver, whether he knew him or not...and, gentlemen, he succeeded. That is murder in the first degree, and the punishment for first-degree murder can only be the death penalty. Now do your duty and render the verdict."

Before Tarver could take his seat, Albert Allison stood and grasped his hand, saying nothing, but nodding vigorously in approval.

Warren Moore began by restating that Johnson acted in self-defense and was thus entitled to go free. First, he argued, the jury should try to put itself into the shoes of the people of East Austin last summer.

"You heard the witnesses; you saw their distress. Why, every white person in this room was shamed. Is it any wonder, then, that Charles Johnson would be agitated when those boys threw rocks at him and cursed him? Johnson, with everybody else over there, lived in fear of wild white boys careening around late at night in a part of town in which they had no business. He, like all those people who testified, lived in fear of that scum that violently attacked innocent, good, colored folks minding their own business in their own place. Charles Johnson lived in fear of the fact that just two weeks before one of their leading citizens had been taken out and murdered. He said he was afraid those boys were going to kill him, too; and can you blame him? Now, it's important for y'all to understand that in Texas a man doesn't have to be under an actual threat to defend himself; and he is not obliged to walk away from a threat in order to avoid killing a perceived assailant. If someone behaves toward you in such a way as to make you reasonably think that he is going to take your life, you have a right, preemptively, to take his life in self-defense. And that right applies to any man, of any race."

After letting the self-defense point sink in, Moore continued, "Finally, let us consider this man himself. For one thing, no reasonable man in this room would claim that Charles Johnson is a menace to society. In fact, Charlie is the very kind of colored man that white people always hold in high regard. He is quiet and cooperative. He teaches school and goes to church. He's not a rabble-rouser. He doesn't look for trouble. He doesn't get drunk. He doesn't ogle our ladies. He carries no grudge against white folks. I can tell you that after all he's been through, after being slandered and rocked and arrested and jailed, he still has no grudge against white folks. If he walked out of here a free man, as justice dictates he must, he would simply go back to his new career selling insurance and maybe teaching, if the school district will have him back.

"Every one of you knows that I am right. You also know that you would not be sitting here today if Charlie were white. That's because once the authorities realized that the dead boy and his friends had threatened Charlie to the point that he thought they were about to kill him, the authorities would not even have arraigned him.

"Now, gentlemen, since Johnson was not white enough to be given that consideration, since perhaps the victim's father was too powerful and influential for Johnson to be given that consideration, Johnson does sit in that chair; and you the jurors are left with the responsibility of freeing him. You must uphold the law and find Charles Johnson 'not guilty' by reason of self-defense."

Warren Moore sat down. Hart heard approving grunts and ruffles from the back of the room. The Judge then adjourned the court until the next morning at 11 AM, when he would read his charge to the jury. He informed the attorneys that copies of the charges would be available at 8 AM. Their comments would be due by 10 AM.

Will Hart saw Mr. Allison grab Brian Blalock by the arm, obviously congratulating him.

At the bar in the Stephen F. Austin that evening, both Bill Tarver and Stanley Kerr assured themselves and Albert that Warren Moore's argument simply did not succeed. Also, despite Judge Wheeler's bending over backward for the defense, they were sure that the judge's instructions to the jury would clearly guide the panel to a verdict of first-degree murder.

Like the night before, Albert wanted the evening's conversation to be on anything but the trial; unlike the previous evening, the men allowed the conversation to go on to other matters. During the half hour or so before the ladies joined them for dinner, Albert and Bill talked with some anticipation about the New Deal and the roles they might play. Albert said that just the previous week Senator Tom Connally had asked him to go to Washington to advise on cotton policy in the new Agriculture Adjustment Administration. If Mabel agreed, he thought he might just give it a try. Bill was looking forward to working in the Department of Justice's Criminal Division. Stanley said that he was grateful to be able to return to his job in the Dallas headquarters of the Lone Star Gas Company. 'Good,' thought, Albert. 'It's nice to feel upbeat about something.'

At the Austin Club, Will Hart and Warren Moore were also upbeat; in fact, Warren was allowing himself to think that they might be on the verge of making history. Will would not allow himself to go that far. Too much hinged on Judge Wheeler's charge to the jury, he told Warren.

A number of people dropped by the table to comment on the newspaper accounts of the trial. Some were polite; some were guardedly hostile; but some, like Alvin Wirtz, were positive, even congratulatory.

Wirtz said, "I just wanted you to know how much everybody in Austin appreciates what y'all are doing. We have a lot of work to do to make amends for what Derden Wofford and his friends did to East Austin last summer."

Since Wirtz had just returned from the Inauguration, he was full of optimistic tales about the coming New Deal.

"The trial publicity is sure to help us get the dam financing," Wirtz said before he moved to another table.

As the former state senator walked away, Will Hart raised his eyebrows and looked at Warren Moore, who returned a slightly puzzled look. Like everyone else in Austin, they were well aware that Austin badly needed a dam network along the Colorado River to provide flood control and a source of electricity. Alvin Wirtz had been working for years to secure federal assistance for the project, and they were pleased that Wirtz was pleased. But they saw no connection between the trial and Wirtz's dams.

As soon as Judge Charles Wheeler had finished dinner, he returned to his chambers to prepare his instructions, which needed to be ready before 6 AM for his secretary. Fortunately, he had prepared charges for many murder trials over the years and was able to borrow relevant paragraphs for standard charges from those previous trials. He wanted to concentrate on the instructions peculiar to this trial. And this trial demanded a great deal of thought.

Indeed, ever since his encounter with that young Councilman Miller and Senator Wirtz two weeks before, he had been thinking about this moment. And, recalling Jim Ferguson's telephone call a couple of nights before, the judge wistfully mused that in a community of competing needs, justice could be complicated.

'Damn,' he thought, 'I wish I could say, "Gentlemen of the jury, I know you think you have a duty to hang this murdering darky; but more than your duty to the law, more than your duty to order, more than your duty to your race and to our sacred way of life, you have a duty to your community. Look at your lives, gentlemen. Look around you, at the hundreds of men loitering at the labor exchange, at the little children looking through bulging eyes while their daddies and mommas sell their furniture and costume jewelry to try to make it through another day. Well, you can help; you can help Mr. Miller and Mr. Wirtz get the necessary money from President Roosevelt to build Congressman Buchanan's dam and put those daddies to work. You can help by not upsetting the president and his New York advisors by appearing to sentence Charles Johnson unjustly. And don't think that those New Yorkers won't holler that you hanged old Charlie Johnson because of the daddy's influence. And when they holler, the money for those dams will go someplace else; and our Austin daddies will still be out of work; and those children'll still be standing at the windows with puffed bellies and bulging eyes. So what's a small compromise with justice compared to those little children's big eyes, gentlemen. Let Charlie go, maybe manslaughter, if it will make you feel better, but don't hang him."

'Somehow,' Judge Wheeler thought, 'my instructions will have to get this message across.'

Friday, March sixteenth, 11 AM., Judge Wheeler called the court to order. Before him, Charles Johnson sat between Will Hart and Warren Moore. Albert Allison and his wife sat in their usual first row seats just behind Bill Tarver and Brian Blalock. Next to the Allisons were Mr. and Mrs. Stanley Kerr.

Not one of the lawyers looked happy.

As the Judge had stipulated the day before, the lawyers had come to his chambers at 8 AM to obtain copies of the Judge's instructions to the jury. For the next hour, both teams prepared requests for exceptions and amendments, which they had submitted to the Judge at 10 AM, as required. With the exception of one small amendment requested by the prosecution, the Judge refused every submission. He could see that both sides were concerned that his instructions were weighted against them.

During the trial, the Judge had seen the attention of the twelve men in the panel box drift from time to time; but that morning they were riveted. As the Judge read the nine-page charge sheet, he could see that many points were lost on the jurors. But he could also detect that the men had started to realize they were not serving on an ordinary jury in an ordinary case.

Juror Jim Williams could understand why Will Hart and Warren Moore treated the darky almost with the deference due a white man; they had a duty to try to win. But the fact that the prosecution also treated Johnson with such deference mystified Williams. Hart and Moore had performed brilliantly, no doubt about it. Bill Tarver made a lot of sense, too. Yet, Williams had expected a little fire and brimstone from Tarver. Williams didn't hold strong opinions on Negroes, but those opinions he did hold supported the death penalty as an object lesson to any Negro thinking he could kill white boys and get away with it. He just needed Tarver to say that it was right to vote that way. But Mr. Tarver said nothing of the kind. In fact, he spoke of Charles Johnson as if he were prosecuting a white defendant.

The Judge's instructions were no help, either. He, too, spoke of the defendant almost as if he were white. Williams heard the Judge describe the various degrees of murder, the legal meanings of "malice," "self-defense," "murder in the first degree," and "manslaughter." He heard the judge weigh the law against the testimony of the witnesses. But Williams detected no encouragement to find Johnson guilty of first-degree murder.

After Judge Wheeler finished speaking, he ordered a recess pending the jury's decision. Williams and his fellow jurors followed the deputy out of the courtroom down the hall to a room with a large table and a number of chairs.

Charlie Johnson was alone in his cell. Adam Black had just left after praying for the grace of God and Jesus to be with the jury. The preacher was so passionate that two other inmates in adjacent cells shouted "Amen's" and "Yes Lord's." Despite Mr. Hart's encouraging words to Charlie just before the deputy escorted Charlie back to his cell, he was sure he would need Reverend Black's divine intervention. He had not detected nuances in Judge Wheeler's instructions that might favor him. In fact, he sensed that his lawyers were mad at the judge. And he had heard the judge tell the jury to impose the death penalty if they found him "guilty of murder with malice aforethought."

Frankly, Charlie was no longer sure why he killed the boy. 'I was mad some. I was scared some. But did I mean to hurt one of those boys? Maybe deep down inside I did. All I remember is that I just headed for that Chevrolet and whipped out that Colt .45, which was just in my hand—I have never been able to figure out how. I remember that I pointed it at the car, pulled the trigger, and drove off. Did I hate those boys? Maybe…maybe I was full of hate after they hurt me—I sure hate being called "nigger." Do I hate white folks? Maybe…maybe ever since those nightriders killed daddy. But, no, that was a long time ago, and since then I seen good in whites, too. But even that "good" don't mean I likes them much neither. I sure don't hate that Mr. Allison. I really feel sorry for that man…and the boy's poor mama, too.'

11 AM, Saturday, March eighteenth. The jury was about to announce the verdict, and the courtroom was packed, especially the gallery and back rows. Albert Allison was gripping Mabel's hand. He looked at Johnson, nicely dressed, sitting erect between William Hart and Warren Moore, who were uncharacteristically fidgety.

After calling the court to order, Judge Wheeler asked Foreman Bowman if the jury had reached a verdict. When the foreman affirmed that it had done so, the judge asked to see it. Bowman passed a paper to the bailiff, who in turn passed the paper to Judge Wheeler. The judge looked at the paper without expression and passed it to the bailiff, who passed it to Bowman. The judge asked the Foreman to read the verdict.

Albert felt as if he had been slammed in the stomach. But he was not shocked. After hearing Judge Wheeler's instructions the day before and after listening to Bill Tarver's cool analysis the night before, he and Mabel and the Kerrs had expected the worst. Still, when Mr. Bowman made the verdict official, Albert was again struck hard by the realization of his own guilt. He and Mabel had tried to be good parents and good citizens, but they had just been judged to be failures. Albert instinctively turned his head in Charles Johnson's direction. Despite the happy sounds coming from the rear of the courtroom, the Negro did not demonstrate outward signs of celebration. After brief words with his lawyers, Johnson turned toward the courtroom; and Albert caught his eye. He forced himself to stand erect, facing Johnson man to man. Albert knew he shared something more with this man than this tragedy that would forever connect them. He was not sure what it was; but ever since Albert had encountered Johnson in jail, he had recognized something in him that was common to both.

After Albert watched Johnson disappear through the door, he went to the front to thank the prosecutors. Brian Blalock shrugged his shoulders, grabbed a stack of papers, smiled a good-bye to Albert, and walked briskly away. Bill Tarver frowned, fumbled with papers, and also shrugged, but grimly. He was clearly embarrassed.

Albert made reassuring remarks and thanked Bill for doing his best. Before Albert could say something he would later regret, he told Bill, perhaps a little abruptly, that the Kerrs, he, and Mabel had to get on the road. Bill nodded. He did not say that he was sorry, nor did Albert want him to do so. The two men wished each other good luck in their new jobs and made mutual assurances that they would see each other soon.

Stanley Kerr extended his arm to Mabel and proceeded to the door of the courtroom with Albert behind. Albert heard him say, "Mabel, don't take this verdict personally. It smells of politics. The way that judge set up the jury smells of politics. That's all I have to say."

Albert had to agree.

'Three years! Oh sweet Jesus, I'm saved; oh my God, I am saved.' Charles Johnson wanted to dance and shout; but he managed to keep his dignity. The muffled cries of joy from the back of the court spoke for him, too. Even though Mr. Moore looked displeased, he and Mr. Hart shook hands; and Mr. Hart said to Charlie, "Be thankful for this day, Charlie. We'll be by the jail to see you in a few days."

Instinctively, Charlie turned in the father's direction and saw the man looking straight at him. In Mr. Allison's face, Charlie saw a proud man, deeply hurt, but no meanness or hate. Mrs. Allison was still sitting, motionless, her head down. From Mr. Allison, Charlie's gaze went to the gallery where his friends were smiling and waving. Then the deputy tugged at him and led him out of the courtroom.

An hour later, as Albert was checking out of the Stephen F. Austin hotel, a porter approached him. "Mister Allison?"

"Yes," Albert replied. "Our bags are by the door, and our car is the Buick just outside."

"Yes sir. I'll get them. But I have to tell you, there's a colored man over there that wants to talk with you. His name is Perry Rhambo."

Just outside the door Albert could see a well-dressed, elderly colored man look at him, tip his hat, and smile thinly. Albert gave the porter a quarter and told Mabel to wait for him in the lounge. He walked through the door and introduced himself.

Rhambo softly spoke, "Mr. Allison, nothing nobody from East Austin can say'll make your sorrow go away. We want you to know that we know what you done for old Charlie. This money here is yours. Charlie don't need it no more."

Rhambo gave Albert an envelope stuffed with cash.

"We been praying for Charlie all week. Tomorrow Charlie's friends be praying for y'all," Rhambo said quietly.

In an instant of disbelief, followed by momentary gratitude, Albert realized that he had not thought about the bail money in weeks. Something about the

Negro's bearing prevented Albert from asking how he got the money. He almost extended his hand as he thanked the Negro for his sentiments.

Rhambo turned and walked to a large new Buick across the street, where a uniformed chauffeur jumped from the front seat. In the instant Rhambo entered the opened back door, Albert thought he saw a couple of large black birds on the back seat. Albert shook the untoward image from his head and put the envelope in his pocket. 'How would he explain to Mabel what he himself did not fully grasp? Well, I won't. Mabel isn't interested in business details, anyhow.'

Saturday afternoon, March 18, 1933, *Austin Statesman*, p. 7, column 5:

Three Years Given Negro in Killing

"*Charles E. Johnson, 60-year-old negro schoolteacher Saturday faced a three-year penitentiary term for shooting Albert A. Allison, Jr., 18, to death here last July 8.*

"*A 53d district court jury Friday about 6 P.M. returned the guilty verdict against Johnson after four hours of deliberation.*

"*Young Allison, son of Mr. and Mrs. A. A. Allison of Corsicana and member of a prominent Navarro county family, was shot to death while riding with four other companions in East Austin. The negro pleaded self-defense, claiming that the youths threw rocks at him and cursed him after a near-collision between his car and theirs at 11th and Chicon streets.*

As soon as Will Hart pulled into the parking lot of the Austin Country Club, John Patterson walked briskly to his car.

"Well, Will, y'all did it. I can hardly believe it."

"Thank you, John. I didn't think we had a chance until I thought about what the Judge was doing. Old Warren still thinks we lost. He's at the office right now preparing an appeal for a new trial."

"Hell, Will. Tell him to lay off. Louis Lyons or Perry Rhambo or one of those darkies badly wants him out of jail. There are parole fees coming our way from them. I'll bet on it."

Hart responded, "Nothing'll stop Warren from doing what he has to do; but there's a snowball's chance he'll get that trial."

Albert and Mabel Allison had hardly spoken since driving from the Stephen F. Austin. In fact, during the past couple of days they had developed a tacit understanding that they must keep conversation about the trial to a minimum. As far as they were concerned, the jury had condemned Son's behavior as much as Charles Johnson's. By extension, they believed, they were judged, too. And the shame would not just be theirs to bear. Unless the Allisons took measures to stop discussion of this judgment, the shame would burden their children and even their children's children. No, for the sake of the children, for the sake of the extended family, Mabel and Albert must never talk about this matter, and the family must be admonished never to discuss Son again.

As the Allisons drove through Waco, at a nearby farm Tucker and Ellie Childs watched in dull resignation as their sweet baby Alicia went to the Lord. The little thing paid just thirty days hardship to this world before Jesus sent the blessed fever to bring her home. They had the two dollars for a churchyard burial with nice words from the preacher, but Tucker would have to work a second gas station job to pay the doctor. This year's crop, they promised one another and the children, this year's crop would set them free. But if it failed, this time they would abandon their windswept Texas prairie for the California promised land.

During the week following the trial, Judge Charles Wheeler could not get a queasy feeling out of his gut—a feeling that he had somehow been violated. In his arguments with himself, he was able rationally to argue that in the Johnson trial he had acted for the community good; but a voice kept whispering that he had compromised justice, and that was a greater evil. Yet, he thought, Warren Moore seemed to have no such qualms. His defense was masterful, and the verdict was a great achievement. But Warren was manic. He had called the judge at least five times to cover one detail or another for his appeal. He genuinely believed that Johnson killed young Allison in self-defense. 'No, more accurately,' thought the judge, 'Warren had come to believe the arguments he himself had contrived.' In one call, he challenged Wheeler in his smooth, gentlemanly way on conditions pertaining to the appropriate punishments for murder without malice. In another, Warren wondered why the judge had not questioned the efficacy of Johnson's confession. 'Moore's a determined man,' thought the judge, 'but under no circumstances will I entertain his petition for a mistrial; and I will not accede to any grounds for an appeal.'

'At least,' the judge told himself, 'Charles Johnson is in Huntsville state prison for a three-year stay. At least he will pay that much.'

28

Explanations

After Jury Foreman Walter Bowman read the verdict, Raymond Brooks rushed to the nearest telephone and called the paper. He submitted his story, then went to the courthouse steps to try to get reactions. The Allison boy's parents were so distraught he thought better of bothering them. And he could not find the prosecutors. Will Hart just smiled and shook his head, and said he had no comments.

Then, Brooks spotted Walter Bowman and his wife walking down the steps. Bowman looked pleased.

"How does it feel to be the jury foreman in a such an historic case, Mr. Bowman?" Brooks asked.

"Fine," Bowman replied. "We did our duty. I am very proud of the men I served with."

Brooks knew he had little time for small talk, so he got right to the point. "What would you say was the key factor in your consideration in letting Johnson off?"

Bowman gave Brooks a knowing look. "Weren't you dining with Charles Marsh at the Austin Club the other evening?"

Brooks nodded, "Yes sir."

Wednesday evening, over dinner, Charles Marsh, Brooks, and the city editor had been planning the paper's strategy for getting the people of Austin to align with the Roosevelt Administration's new programs. The editor had recognized Bowman, who was dining with his wife at a nearby table, and mentioned to Mr. Marsh that Bowman was on the jury of the Johnson trial. Marsh and Bowman were old friends, so after a few minutes Mr. Marsh excused himself and went to the Bowmans' table and exchanged pleasantries.

"Well," Mr. Bowman said, "your boss's comments that night had a lot to do with it. You can ask him. But I'll tell you this: He made me realize why high-priced lawyers like Will Hart and Warren Moore were defending a darky schoolteacher for murdering the son of a man like Albert Allison—and why the district attorney and his assistant had backed out of prosecuting the boy."

At that moment, Jim Williams, a juror with whom Brooks was acquainted, walked up and shook Bowman's hand as if in congratulations.

Bowman grinned and said, "Mr. Brooks, this man is the real reason Johnson got justice. You need to talk to him. Please excuse Mrs. Bowman and me. We have much to catch up after being tied up here these past few days."

Brooks nodded and thanked the Bowmans for their time, then asked Williams if he would like a cup of coffee.

Brooks's experience interviewing men who had just served on a jury was mixed. Sometimes they gave straightforward answers. He recalled that the jury foreman in the Stewart trial—an old curmudgeon, well-known in Austin, named Tom Brodie—saying flat out that he knew the boy was guilty from the beginning and that he would not have been swayed by the controversial confession, one way or the other. But most of the time, jurors were reluctant to express publicly what they had been forced to express in secret. Jim Williams had earned a solid reputation as the Travis County Tax Collector before he retired, and Brooks knew that he was a first-class source of information.

That morning Williams was not reluctant. He had the time, and he wanted to talk. Williams said that he and his fellow jurors first assumed that they were there simply to rubber-stamp a death sentence for Johnson. And they would have been happy to do so. But by the end of the trial they were confused about what the judge expected of them. They were struck by the competence and preparation of Mr. Hart and Mr. Moore, by Bill Tarver's rustiness, by Brian Blalock's obvious lack of preparation, by Derden Wofford's surliness and less than honest testimony, by the colored witnesses describing the marauding the previous summer, and by Charlie Johnson's exceptional demeanor.

Williams described how the panelists had entered the jury room a little nervous. They had made small talk; one or two had taken chairs; and then one of the jurors, Fred Priem, had muttered aloud "Let's hang the nigger and go home." Another juror had said, "Amen, Brother Priem."

Williams said he thought that these remarks were a little premature and that he noticed that Walter Bowman had frowned.

"I guess that's why I nominated Mr. Bowman to be foreman. He has a lot of stature and good sense. I figured he would make sure that whatever we did would be well thought out. I guess I figured a man like him would not be as confused as I was."

After Mr. Bowman accepted Williams's nomination, he walked immediately to the head of the table and told the other panelists to take their seats. He then had the men take a piece of paper and write whether Johnson was guilty of murder with malice aforethought, guilty of murder without malice aforethought, or not guilty. These had been the options given by the judge.

After Bowman looked at the jurors votes, he said that no one voted "not guilty," but seven of the men had wanted "malice aforethought; that is, the death penalty."

"So we talked matters through in a businesslike way," Williams continued. "Mr. Bowman said that he was convinced the darky had reacted without much thinking, even though he could and should have driven away."

Williams then winked at Brooks and said, "Damned if that Fred Priem didn't say that he figured about the same thing. Hal Armstrong said that the night after the Negro witnesses testified, he and his boy, who is at the university, had had a long talk. Derden Wofford's a big hero to the boys in this town. At least he was. Armstrong's boy said that Derden didn't have a car, so he had been talking kids with cars into taking him to East Austin. Hal figured that Derden was not truthful about everything he said on that stand."

Williams said that other jurors had contributed similar observations. But after an hour or so, three still did not want to give up on the death penalty.

Tom Gregory said that he had a son almost the age of young Allison, and he kept talking about what he would do if this had happened to Tom, Jr.

"Well," said Williams with a chuckle, "Fred Priem took Gregory on. He said that at first he had no doubt that the colored boy should hang. Then, he had seen how Mr. and Mrs. Allison sat in that trial with so much pain and so much dignity—just letting justice take it's course as if Charlie Johnson was as white as them. He said that when he realized how much Derden lied, he reckoned that Johnson deserved some consideration. He finished by saying that he reckoned if Johnson was white, he would probably get three years."

Williams said that was when Mr. Bowman had again asked for ballots. Two remained steadfast for the death penalty.

"I tell you, Ray," Williams said, "even with Derden's obvious lies, those men did not want to believe a colored over the white boys. And I've got to admit: it was hard for me, too."

After a brief pause, Williams said, "That was when Mr. Bowman called on me to speak up. 'What about the Negro, Jim?' he asked. 'What do you make of him?'"

"Well," Brooks said. "From what Mr. Bowman said a while ago, you must have found a way to bring the two holdouts around."

"I guess so, Ray. I just remarked that Johnson's sixty-one years old, has lived here more than twenty years, teaches school, goes to church and has never been in trouble in this County before. Hell, I personally doubt Johnson's ever looked cross-eyed at a white woman. And I made the point that we need boys like Johnson influencing things over in the east side.

"Then Mr. Bowman added, 'Think about that, gentlemen. All of us know about our Uncle Joseys and Aunt Bessies.' And with that Johnson was saved. No one in that room could condemn a Negro who simply could not do evil—though, being a colored, could at times be misguided."

"The old 'good Negro,'" Brooks responded. "Seems like a mighty weak premise for letting off a black who murdered a white son of a prominent man like Allison."

"I guess it does, now that I think about it," replied Williams. "But that's the way it went."

When Brooks returned to his office, he put his interview with Walter Bowman and Jim Williams in story form. That evening he went to Mr. Marsh's office to get the story approved; but before he submitted it, he told Mr. Marsh that he was missing a crucial piece that only Mr. Marsh could provide. "What did you say to Walter Bowman Wednesday night?"

Mr. Marsh looked slightly bemused. Then he leaned back in his chair and smiled. "We're not going to run your story, Ray. It's best this town not have this verdict rubbed in its face. Yet, it's the best possible outcome for Austin, and that is what I tried to get across to Walter Wednesday night. I complimented him on doing his city duty by serving on the jury. And then I told him what a lot of us in business and politics had been saying: that the trial was an opportunity to show the president that Austin is a citadel of justice and that those dams on the Colorado and a lot of other things depend on the President seeing Austin just that way. I confess that I'm a little surprised that Walter would claim that my remarks influenced him. Anyhow, that's it, Ray—one of your stories never to be told. Now go find one you can tell. How about scheduling a follow-up with the Albert Allison?"

Albert and his father had had a few conversations since the trial. Sometimes Judge Cobb in black suit and string tie stared fiercely at his old nemesis. In one dream, the judge offered to fight Arthur over Albert's actions to ensure Johnson a fair trial. In another, the father just stared at Albert incredulously, "What kind of mess have y'all made there, young man? We struggled our entire lives to preserve civilized life. Eventually, despite the Yankees, with hard work and great ferocity, we got our way of life back. Now, *you* have got to fight to keep it. What the hell is goin' on?"

Albert dared not contradict his father. He would wake from these encounters feeling sad, incomplete. On one occasion, he briefly pondered whether he should personally go after Johnson when the Negro left prison. On another, Judge Cobb growled that Johnson's treatment was a classic case of community politics infecting the purity of the judicial imperative. Whether black or white, Johnson's action was not manslaughter, the judge declared. It was murder, the deliberate taking of a life; and it should have been dealt with accordingly. Judge Wheeler said nothing in response. He just turned his back to Judge Cobb.

These dreams, this guilt, those outrageous consequences for trying to do the right thing weighed so heavily on Albert that he had started to stoop a little and had developed a slight hesitancy in expressing his views.

In August 1933, after three futile months in Washington, D.C., trying to work with the New Yorkers on agriculture policy, Albert left the Agricultural Adjustment Administration and returned home. A few weeks later, he made his annual visit to see relatives and friends in Leon County, where his grandparents had originally settled in Texas. He made a few routine stops to shake hands and catch up on news, and then went to his cousin Herbert's house. Albert's ninety-seven-year old Uncle John was convalescing there, and declared that Albert's visit was a wonderful excuse to break out moonshine and cheroots.

After the usual pleasantries and a swig or two from the jar, the shriveled ancient with an outsized goiter and piercing red eyes rasped, "Albert, they tell me the law isn't going to hang your darky. They tell me that he's just been stuck in Huntsville for forty years or something like that. Your daddy must be rolling in his grave, God rest his soul. Light me one of those cheroots, Herbert."

Albert took the jar from Herbert, sipped, and wiped his mouth with the sleeve of his sweaty white shirt. He decided not to correct Uncle John's mistaken information about the length of Johnson's sentence. 'Whoever told the him it was forty years,' Albert mused, 'probably did the family a good deed.' After the warmth of the shine subsided, he looked directly into the old man's glowing eyes.

"Uncle, I know you and Daddy and your kind gave us our country back. All of us, all my generation know this; and we are forever grateful. But your generation simply didn't have the time to bring back civilization in all its respects. You left much of that for our generation; it's up to us to take our South to its fullest glory. I'm convinced that we not only have to give our young people the highest standard of education, we also have to envelope all the people—white and black—in the fullest reach of the law."

He paused and reached again for the jar. Uncle John's eyes seemed to flare, but he said nothing.

After another sip Albert continued, "Uncle, our civilization derives from our customs, that's certain. But, as I see it, if we've learned anything since Reconstruction, it's that our customs thrive best in the bosom of the law. If Son's killer were not tried under that law, then the custom would have been sullied. In Son's name, Mabel and I could not go outside the law, else we smear that way of life for which you and Daddy strove so valiantly."

Uncle John whispered, "I guess you might have something there. I hope so, Boy."

Then his eyes closed.

Epilogue

By the time of Charles Johnson's trial, Texas had made substantial progress in accepting the rule of law over vigilantism. True, legislators still crafted that law badly, officials enforced it unevenly, and judges applied it erratically. True, such would be the case for decades to come. But most Texans had begun to accept the law, and some would stake their lives on it.

Unfortunately, for many years this progress provided African-Americans only marginal relief: white judges, all-white juries, white prosecutors, and incompetent white defense counsel "legally-lynched" countless black defendants. East Austin would not have its first African-American lawyer until Kenneth Lampkin was licensed on April 17, 1939. James H. Hart, Will Hart's brother and partner, served as one of Lampkin's tutors. But for years Lampkin was alone; and lawyers like Bill Yelderman and Tass Waterston, who served as the Travis County Attorney in the late 1930s, were too few. Austin could only comfort itself that at least the law was gaining.

But it was only gaining. Between 1933 and 1936, white mobs in Texas lynched four African-Americans for alleged offenses against white women; and in 1936, Texas Rangers in El Campo had to rescue five African-American men and four African-American women from a large mob that suspected them of killing a young white man.

Charles Johnson was saved by a combination of Allison's high-mindedness and the political games in which Johnson became both a pawn in Jim Ferguson's war on his "bourbon" enemies and a card in the power poker induced by the New Deal. For Charles Johnson to escape death in 1933 for killing Albert Allison, Jr.—indeed, for him to have received only a three-year prison sentence—required a confluence of special circumstances, the absence of any one of which would have doomed him. Moreover, if he had killed Derden Wofford, the sports hero, he almost certainly would have been lynched. If he had killed, instead of the Allison boy, any of the other three boys in the car with Allison and Wofford, he likely would have been tried in September 1932 and, with inadequate representation and no political help, been condemned to death. If Albert Allison had opted for vengeance, even if Johnson were not lynched, he would not have escaped.

For a time after the tragedy, East Austin was free of white troublemakers. But after a few years, new boys ventured into that far-off, "exotic" side of town, where hootchie-kootchie, blues, and jazz thrived well into the fifties. But after the summer of '32, those that acted up would get their trouble from the law.

During the decade following, Austin's youth made their passage into adulthood thousands of miles from the east side. All of Son's companions the night of July eighth would wear the uniform, as would his cousins Robert and Stanley Kerr, Jr., and his two brothers Lodowick and Kenneth. Most would see combat, some would be wounded, but all returned safely. Kenneth, himself a Naval Academy graduate, observed that only a few years after 1932 the Navy would have overlooked Son's nasal deformity and that the Academy class to which he would have belonged provided the core of the Navy's wartime leadership.

Save being the victim of the South's ceaseless racial war, Albert Allison, Jr., never made the mark on the world that he might have. But other figures in his story were participants of such enterprises and, in large and small ways, did make their marks.

Jim and Miriam Ferguson governed from 1933 to 1935 in much the same way they had governed from 1925 to 1927. While they did tone down their highway and textbook graft, Austin's lawyers happily banked lucrative fees as the Fergusons continued their parole and pardon program unabated. After Miriam left office, Jim Ferguson spent his remaining years more as a kingmaker than an office seeker. Even though Miriam sought the governorship unsuccessfully in 1940, W. Lee ("Pappy") O'Daniel and Lyndon Johnson, whom she supported in 1948, proved worthy successors to Ferguson's brand of politics. Subsequently O'Daniel and Johnson would find their own successors. So the Texas political tradition begun by Senator "Honest" Bob Wilson in 1838, and successfully put into practice for the first time by Jim Ferguson in 1914, continues to the public detriment. It will do so for as long as Texans love a liar with a big promise, a big laugh, and no sense of shame.

To protest Miriam Ferguson's election in 1932, Texas Ranger Captain Frank Hamer resigned before she was inaugurated. She subsequently fired the forty-four Rangers who had served under him. Even though Hamer despised the Fergusons, in 1934, he accepted the governor's assignment to track down the infamous Bonnie and Clyde. One hundred and two days later, with the help of Louisiana police, Hamer set the ambush that killed the bandit duo.

Fourteen years later, Captain Hamer escorted U. S. Senate candidate and former Governor Coke Stevenson to Alice, Texas, to secure the infamous Box

Thirteen after the Democratic Primary for the U. S. Senate. There, with Hamer brandishing his side arms, they forced their way past pistolero guards into the bank holding the ballots that Stevenson suspected Archie Parr's nephew, George Parr, had sold to Stevenson's opponent Lyndon Johnson. Johnson countered by having an Austin judge issue a restraining order preventing Stevenson and Hamer from removing the returns. Eventually, the State Democratic Executive Committee certified Johnson the winner over Stevenson by eighty-seven votes.

James P. Hart served as Travis County District Attorney until 1936. In 1938, he was appointed Special District Judge for Travis County; and in 1947 Governor Beauford Jester appointed Hart to the Texas Supreme Court. The following year, Hart was elected to the office. In 1950 he resigned from the Court to serve as the first Chancellor of the University of Texas, a post he held until 1953. In 1954 he entered the Democratic Primary for the United States Senate against the incumbent, Lyndon Johnson.

Tom Miller won his election to the Austin City Council in April 1933. His new fellow councilmen chose him Mayor, a post that he held for most of the next twenty-eight years. Miller's enthusiastic support of Roosevelt and his personal relationships with New Deal officials helped him bring many Federal projects to Austin, as well as some of the Administration's social experiments—for instance, America's first federal housing project. Miller's persistence in securing federal funding for his and Alvin Wirtz's cherished dam projects finally resulted in the construction of the five dams along the Colorado River, including Tom Miller Dam at Lake Austin. He died in 1962, a year after retiring from office.

John M. Patterson continued to practice law with Hart, Patterson, and Hart and remained Chairman of the Travis County Democratic Party until he died in 1950, at age eighty-three.

Carl Stewart was executed in December 1933, the first Travis County convict to die in Texas's new electric chair.

With Ross Sterling's loss to Miriam Ferguson, William A. Tarver's political career was at an end; but he did receive his appointment to the Criminal Division of the Justice Department. In 1940, at age fifty-seven, he died of a sudden heart attack while on a visit to Corsicana. After the war, his children were active in early efforts to integrate Texas.

At the time Deputy Sheriff Homer Thornberry participated in Charles Johnson's arrest, he was working his way through law school. In 1934, he was elected to the State Legislature; and, prior to naval service in World War II, he served as Travis County District Attorney. In 1948, Thornberry replaced Lyndon Johnson in Congress, where he gradually earned a reputation as a southern liberal. In early 1963, President Kennedy appointed Thornberry Federal District Judge; and, in 1965, Thornberry's friend Lyndon Johnson elevated him to the Fifth Circuit Court of Appeals. In 1968, he was on the list for the United States Supreme Court. While in the Fifth Circuit, among his many pioneering civil rights decisions, Thornberry declared the Texas poll tax unconstitutional, a ruling upheld by the Supreme Court. He died in Austin in December 1995, aged eighty-six years.

In 1934, Alvin Wirtz, state senator from Seguin from 1912 to 1930, succeeded in having the Texas legislature establish the Lower Colorado River Authority and had himself appointed General Counsel. Shortly afterward, farmers around Seguin ran him out of town because they believed his dam projects had cheated them out of their land. While living in Austin, he helped Lyndon Johnson with New Deal projects under the National Youth Administration; and he supported Johnson's 1937 race for Congress to succeed James Buchanan. After Johnson went to Washington, he affectionately referred to Wirtz as his "Texas daddy." In 1940, Wirtz became Undersecretary of Interior, but he resigned in 1941 to return to Austin to help Johnson run for United States Senate against W. Lee O'Daniel. In 1948, Wirtz was a key figure in helping Johnson to secure his eighty-seven-vote victory over Coke Stevenson. In 1951, shortly after he died, the Granite Shoals Dam near Marble Falls was re-named the Alvin Wirtz Dam.

Derden Wofford never made it to professional baseball. He worked in Austin service stations until he went into the Army after Pearl Harbor. After the war, he returned to Austin, where he had various sales jobs until he bought a pet shop, which he ran for twenty years.

After his trial, Charles Johnson continued to benefit from the connection between Perry Rhambo, Jim Ferguson, and Hart, Patterson, and Hart.

Between March and October of 1933, Everett Rhambo and Will Fuller paid Johnson numerous visits in Huntsville. On October 12, Governor Miriam Ferguson granted Johnson a ninety-day furlough. On January 11, 1934, the Governor granted Johnson a ninety-day furlough extension. On April 10, she granted him an additional ninety-day extension. By July 1934 the parole fees had become too expensive for Will Fuller. So on July 13, 1934, Johnson returned to Ramsey State Farm.

However, Everett Rhambo proved unable to do the job consistently. Since the new governor-elect, James Allred, had promised that he would grant no pardons or paroles, Fuller had no choice but to finance a full pardon. On January 7, 1935,

Governor Ferguson pardoned Johnson unconditionally. He was amongst the hundreds of prisoners the Fergusons—notoriously—released that month. Until Charles Johnson died in 1943, he faithfully served William Fuller's extensive insurance and "policy" operations.

In 1931 Albert Allison had had good reason to become Texas's leading advocate for the "cotton moratorium." His two thousand acres of rich cotton land on Richland Creek had lost money for five years. In 1930, a fire had destroyed his uninsured General Merchant store in Richland. The years 1932 and 1933 had heaped disappointment upon disappointment on him. Son was rejected by the Naval Academy, and then killed; Miriam Ferguson defeated Ross Sterling; Charles Johnson escaped justice, and Allison blamed himself; and the Agricultural Adjustment Administration, in which he vested so much hope and so much political capital, turned out to be a travesty. He had never advocated plowing under crops, and no one had foreseen the disastrous consequences of leaving fields plowed in hot and windy Texas.

In 1934, Roosevelt's Postmaster General and political mastermind, James Farley, appointed Allison Post Master for Corsicana, a position Allison would have for the rest of his life. In 1935, he organized a serious, but futile campaign to block Jim Ferguson's election as Texas's Democratic National Committeeman.

In 1939, in fulfillment of one of Albert's most ardent dreams, his youngest son Kenneth entered the Naval Academy. While he walked with Ken to the Corsicana train station for his departure for Maryland, an old African-American walking in the opposite direction stepped out of the way of the two white men and tipped his hat.

"Soon things like that must change, Ken," Ken Allison remembered his father saying. "In your lifetime, the Negro will be brought into society; and I expect you to do your share to help."

In his final years, Albert's letters to Senator Tom Connally and Congressman Luther Johnson railed against most of Roosevelt's policies, including agricultural policy. He finally grasped that Roosevelt's planners never intended their agriculture policy to be a one-time market corrective, that all along they intended to force the once proud American farmer to become a beggar at the government trough. His most poignant protests, however, concerned the momentum carrying the United States to war. He wrote of eighteen-year old Private Perry Allison crushed by the train in the Parisian snowstorm, of his eighteen year-old son lifeless from a weapon of war, of old Confederates living bitter lives with scars too deep to heal, of his surviving sons in harm's way—to what end, to what end? "Let our boys have their lives; let the Europeans have their wars," he wrote.

Albert Allison died in April 1943. Mabel said his heart simply collapsed from the weight of the unbearable news of American casualties in North Africa—too many bullet-riddled corpses lying on cold concrete slabs, too many to bear.

Afterword

"...So that our precious blood may not be shed in vain; that even the monsters we defy shall be constrained to honor us though dead." So wrote Claude McKay.

To McKay, the monster's most obvious manifestation, of course, was the lynch mob that raged across early twentieth century America. But behind that manifestation lurks the subtler, more insidious monster in the tribal self that is part of each of us. That is the monster that objectifies the outsider, that night-rides, that degrades through language, and that skews justice to fit culture. To defy the mob monster is an act of public courage, usually, as with Charles Johnson, born of desperation. To defy the monster in our tribal self, however, requires a mighty struggle between who we are and what is right. This struggle arises from personal enlightenment, recognition, and the desire to be human, simply human. Victory demands we be prepared to forego the comfort and approbation of those with whom we share blood and beliefs and to stride into the terrifying, existential unknown. That is what Warren Moore and Will Hunt did. That, in their own, conflicted way, is what Albert and Mabel Allison did.

Acknowledgements

Well, Sandy Nunnelley, we did it. More accurately, you made us do it, for without your ability to reorganize a pile of tangled information into a coherent story, the manuscript would be still be covered by dust. Your faith in the project inspired me to want to produce a product worthy of your effort. It also inspired your reading team—Christine Allison, Zelda Austen, Akwazi Evans, Jayne Gamel, Nell Martin, and Andy and Betty Shuvalov, each of whom thoughtfully edited, reviewed, and critiqued the manuscript. Each made substantive suggestions, most of which were incorporated into the revisions, which were refined and polished by the able staff at iUniverse.

Given the historical period, the main characters have long since passed, but Elizabeth Kerr Newland and Ken Allison spent patient hours reconstructing their childhood recollections of Corsicana. Judge Joe Hart took the time to share memories of his illustrious family. Professor David Edwards of Huston-Tillotson College gave me valuable advice, and Jo Baylor and Teresa Doggett-Taylor introduced me to East Austin, especially to the late Mrs. O. B. Connally and to Akwazi Evans. Mrs. Connally gave me three delightful hours of her time reminiscing about the East Austin of her childhood. I'm sure she is giving Heaven a reason to smile. Akwazi Evans, an accomplished newspaperman and author, rendered a professional, incisive critique. He inspired Sandy and me to persist to get the book published. My old friends Ken Towery and John Knaggs also gave me the benefit of their experiences as published writers.

My daughter, Carolyn Caplan, and my brother, Wick Allison, have worked with me ever since we discovered that, behind that tragedy of July 8, 1932, a story worth telling was waiting to be told. Their encouragement and intense involvement from time to time spurred me to believe, audaciously, that I could write the story. Critically, Wick's professional and thoughtful final edit has made the story coherent and reader friendly.

Finally, I want to thank my wife, Meg, for putting up with my disruptive, sometimes ornery routine in preparing the manuscript. Her daily support, including a fair amount of editing, was crucial; her good humor was critical; her love was vital.

About the Author

Al Allison is a fifth-generation Texan with degrees from Harvard and the University of Texas. After Naval service in Viet Nam, he worked in business and politics in the United States and Europe, where he lived for twenty years before returning to his Texas roots.

978-0-595-33298-4
0-595-33298-6

Printed in the United Kingdom
by Lightning Source UK Ltd.
108227UKS00001B/97-99